IMAGES
of America

FRACKVILLE

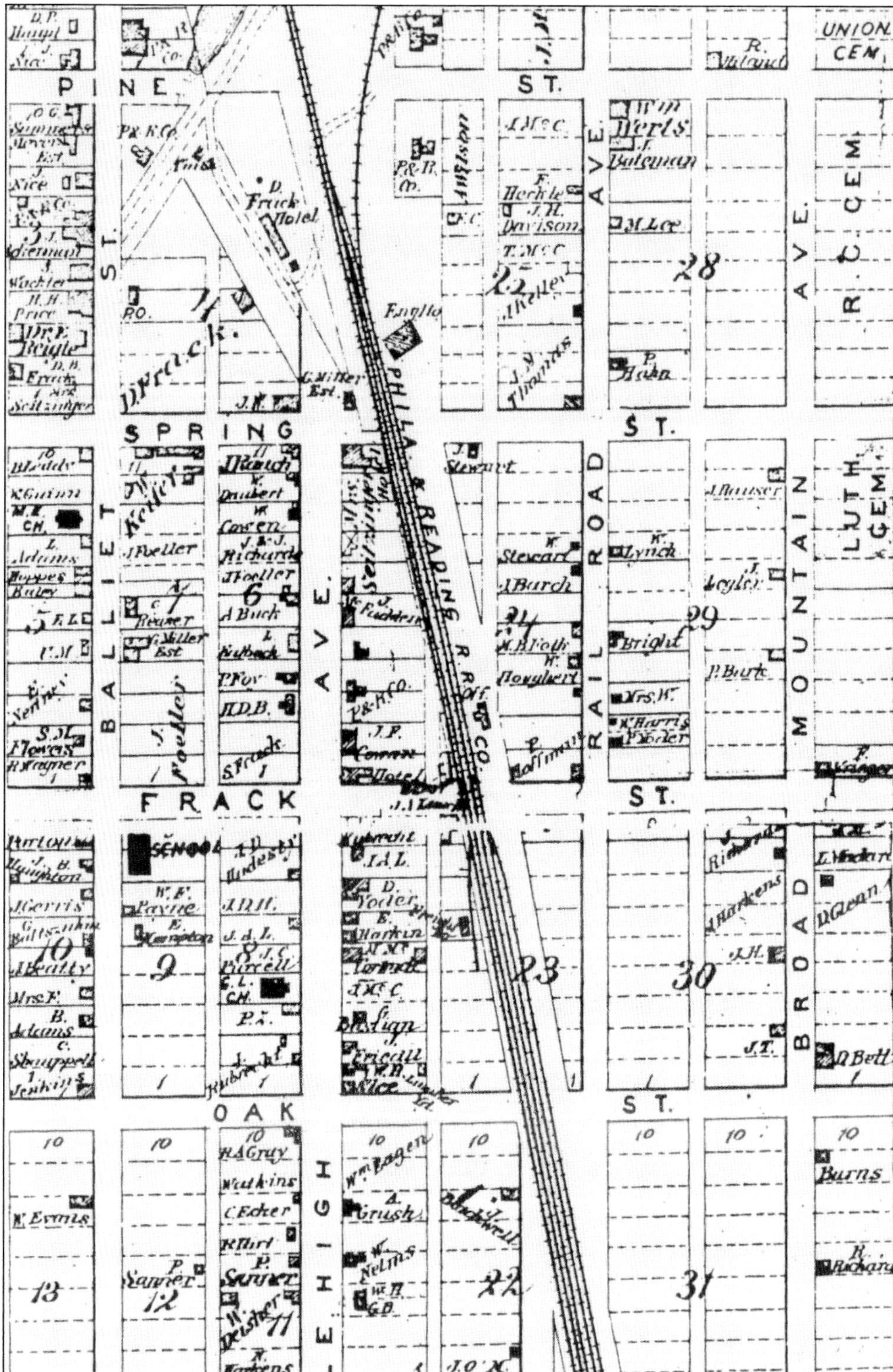

Frackville—1875.

IMAGES
of America

FRACKVILLE

Lorraine Stanton

ARCADIA
PUBLISHING

ISBN 978-0-7385-8741-7

Published by Arcadia Publishing
Charleston, South Carolina

Printed in the United States of America

Library of Congress Catalog Card Number: Data applied

For all general information contact Arcadia Publishing at:
Telephone 843-853-2070
Fax 843-853-0044
E-mail sales@arcadiapublishing.com
For customer service and orders:
Toll-Free 1-888-313-2665

Visit us on the Internet at www.arcadiapublishing.com

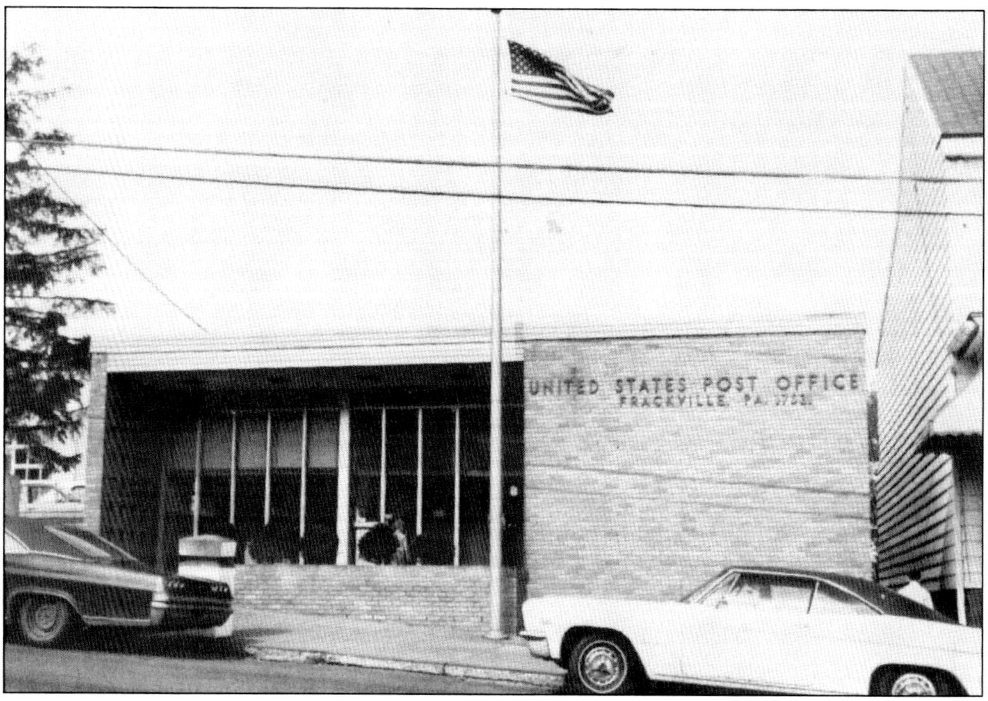

The U.S. Post Office in Frackville was dedicated on April 15, 1961. At the time this picture was taken in 1976, the staff members were: Stanley Bulcavage (postmaster), Carl Pyzowski (supervisor), Stephen Mucha and Harold Schappell (clerks), and Peter Weremedic, Michael Giba, Peter Vinski, Bruce Hinkle, and Michael Rynn (carriers).

Contents

"FRACKVILLE"

Emma Dreher Hoppes — Gertrude M. Tenenholz

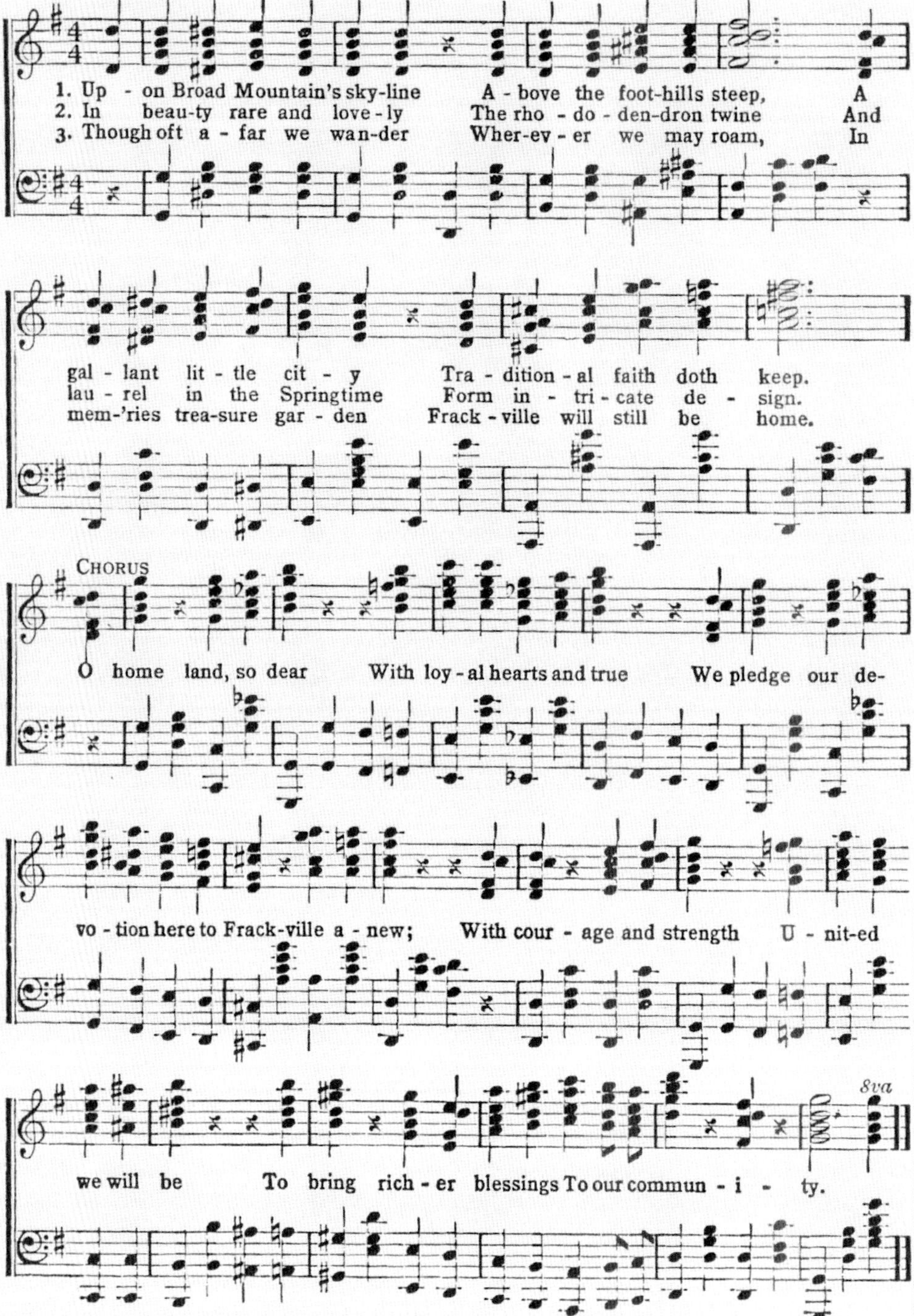

Introduction

This book, *Images of America: Frackville*, shows and tells the borough's history for the centennial years 1876 to 1976. It chronicles the early settlers, the once-thriving businesses (many no longer in existence), the residents often familiar by name only, and finally the Frackville centennial events of 1976. Most pictures are placed chronologically so that the flow of time's progression can be seen and felt.

Since no in-depth history of Frackville has ever been published, this pictorial compilation will serve to enlighten local residents of the rich heritage that abounds in their community. Young and old residents alike will be able to visualize how Frackville changed over the years, noting, in particular, that many of the illustrated buildings have been demolished.

The pictures of early settlers are rare, as few descendants now live in the area. Group pictures are used to highlight members of organizations, bands, and schools, as well as to show churches and buildings long since razed. Each picture's narration offers information about the subject, such as birth and death dates of early settlers. The final chapter presents many pictures of the Frackville Centennial, the largest celebration ever held in our borough. Hundreds of residents will be pleasantly surprised to see their photographs here.

In 1849 Daniel Frack purchased from James C. Stephens a tract of 166 acres of land which is now encompassed in the borough of Frackville. Frack moved his family here in 1852 and converted an existing sawmill into a hotel, which he operated until 1861. The land owned by Frack was divided into town lots and ultimately called Frackville. In 1861 Samuel Haupt purchased 180 acres of land adjoining Frack's and called his property Planeville, but later changed its name to Mountain City.

The controversy over what the entire area should be named continued until a post office was needed for the town. Several legends surround the borough's naming, but the facts detailed here are taken from county courthouse records:

"On November 22, 1875, a group of 190 residents of the area known as Frackville signed a petition to be incorporated into a borough to be named Frackville. This group was led by Daniel Frack, the first resident of this area. This petition was one day short of the required thirty days by law to be advertised before being presented at the January Session of the Grand Jury.

"On January 1, 1876, a group of 147 residents of the area known as Mountain City signed and presented a petition to the court in Pottsville to be incorporated into a borough and to be named Mountain City.

"When the Grand Jury saw both petitions, they and Judges Pershing and Green realized that all residents living in the Frackville-Mountain City area wanted to be incorporated—but a difference developed as to a name.

"In 1875 Pottsville, a borough built on seven mountains, had several businesses and lodges already using the title 'Mountain City' and it would be confusing to name the proposed area, 'Mountain City.' He felt it was the responsibility of the court to name the borough and felt the area was known as Frackville for several years and should be so named."

The Grand Jury report of January 6, 1876, reads as follows: "Resolved: That we recommend to consolidate Frackville and Mountain City, with the continuous territory, into a borough under the name and title of the Borough of Frackville."

All of the pictures included in *Images of America: Frackville* are from my personal files. However, I know of other Frackville residents who have wonderful photographs representative of its changing times, certainly more than enough to fill yet another volume.

Lastly, I'd like to acknowledge Barry and Debi Janov for their help with the picture layout and text editing.

Lorraine Stanton

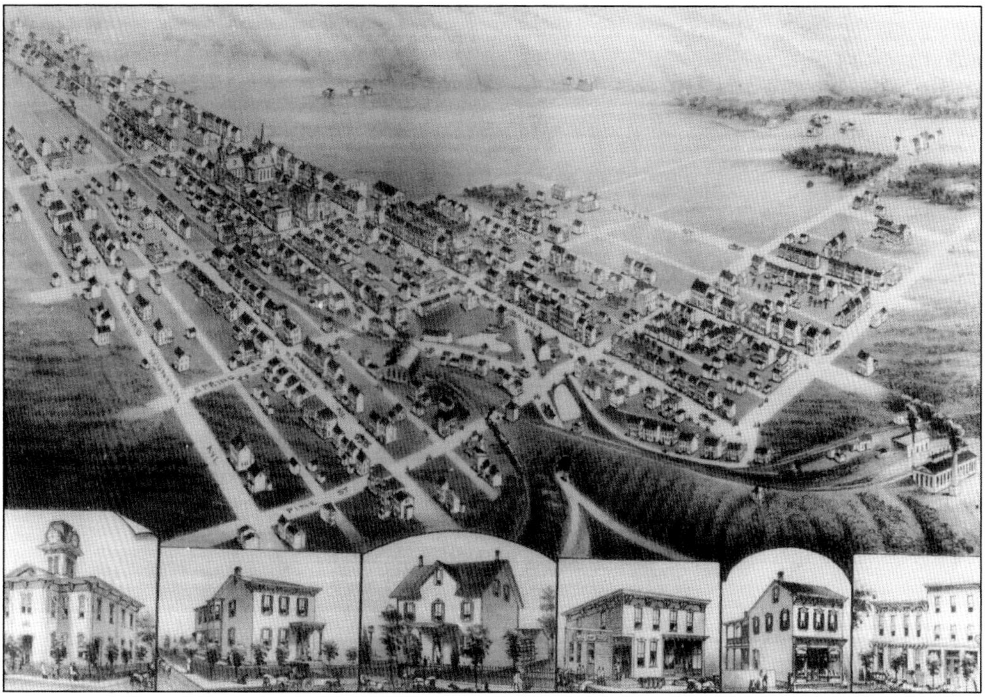

In 1889, the population of Frackville was approximately two thousand people, but the town was rapidly growing and already had some lovely houses. Pictured at the bottom of the image are, from left to right: the Town Clock Building; C.C. Wagner, residence at Arch-Balliet Street; Dr. C.S. Blieler, residence at 114 North Belliot; Depot House, J. Pauly, proprietor (rear of Bohard building); residence and drugstore of Dr. Taggart, 10 North Lehigh Avenue (the first telephone in town was installed in this drugstore); and Union House, Thomas Burke, proprietor, at Lehigh and Frack Street (later became Bohard building). The Mahanoy Plane Engine House can be seen at the right of the picture. The Town Clock Building, the Depot House, and the Union House have all been demolished.

One

The Frack Family

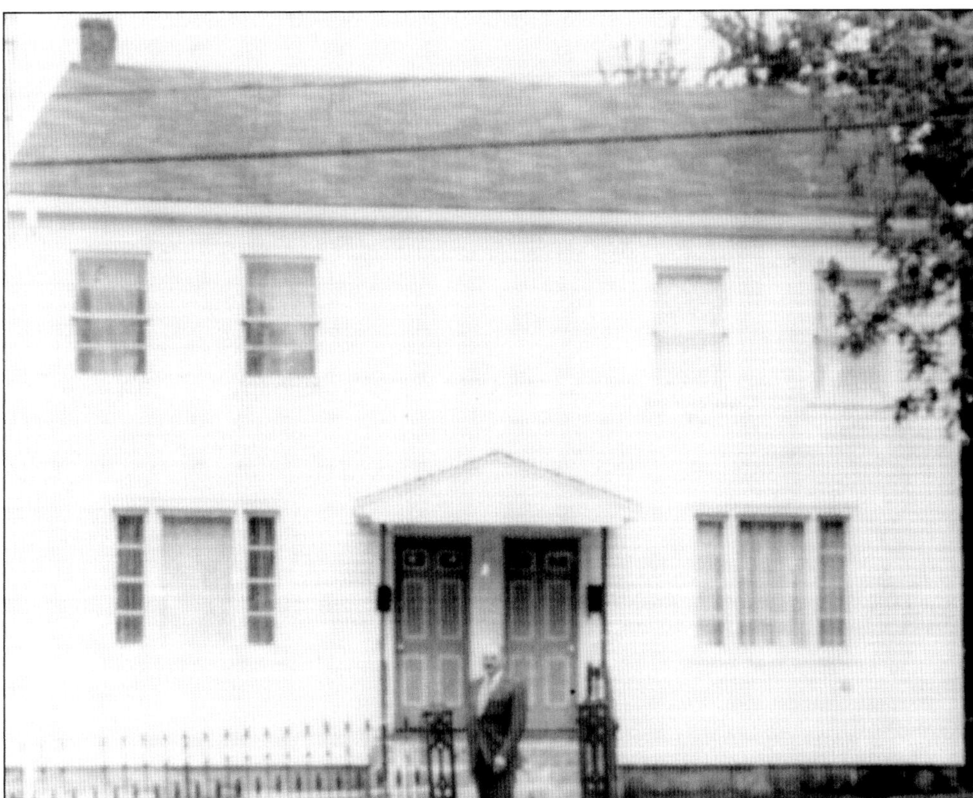

Pictured here at 119–121 North Balliet Street is the home of the founder of Frackville as it looked in 1976, with Jesse Frack Sr. at the gate. Still standing today, the building is now an apartment house.

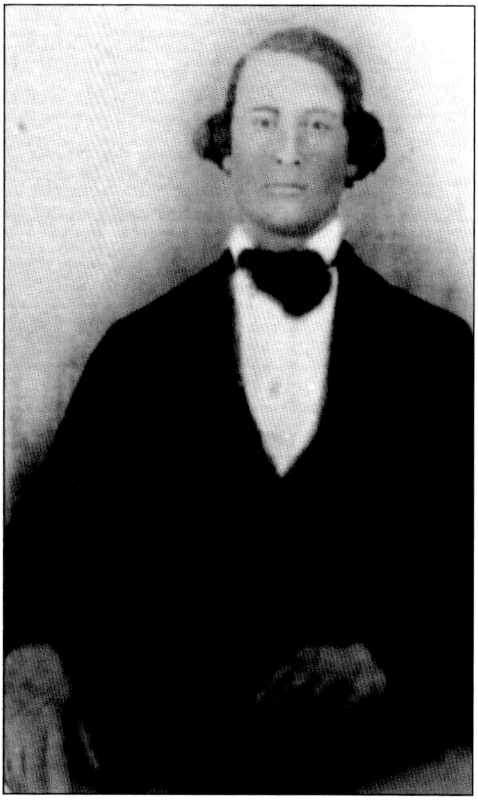

Daniel Frack, the founder of Frackville, was born September 23, 1803, in Northampton County. In 1849 he bought 166 acres of land from James C. Stephens and moved there in 1852. After sectioning the land into lots and naming the town Frackville, Daniel donated many lots in the town for churches, schools, and cemeteries.

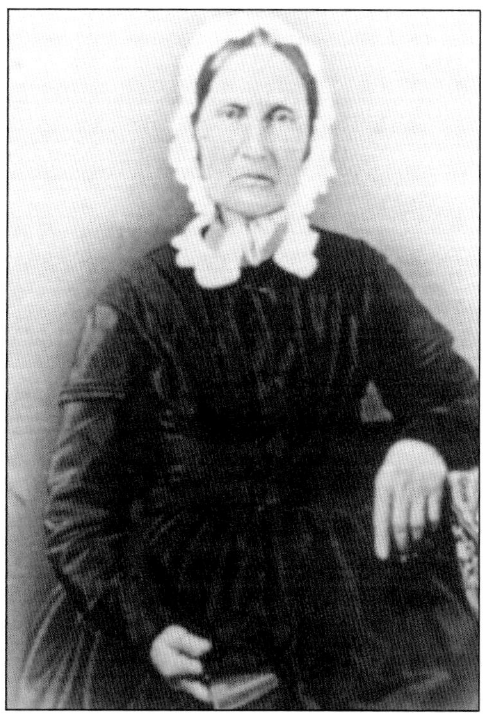

Mary Balliet Frack was born August 2, 1803, in North Whitehall Township, Lehigh County. A genealogy of her family begins with Stephen Balliet, a colonel in the French army. She married Daniel Frack on August 21, 1825, and had three children: Lenora (our first postmistress), Samuel, and Daniel B. Mary died on January 27, 1885, and is buried in the Zion Lutheran Cemetery.

Lenora Frack Meredith was born October 26, 1828, and married John Meredith on April 14, 1849, at the Lutheran parsonage in Pottsville. Widowed at age thirty-five with seven children, she became the postmistress of Frackville and served for nine years, during which time she was paid $1 a month. Lenora died January 4, 1925, and is buried in Orwigsburg.

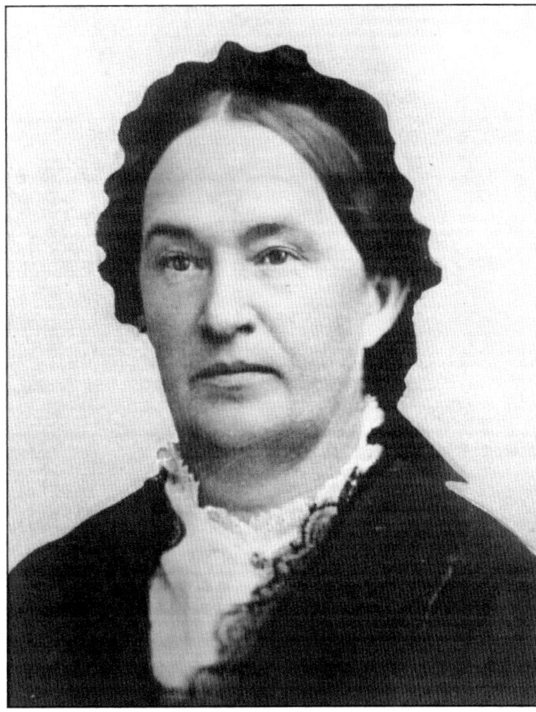

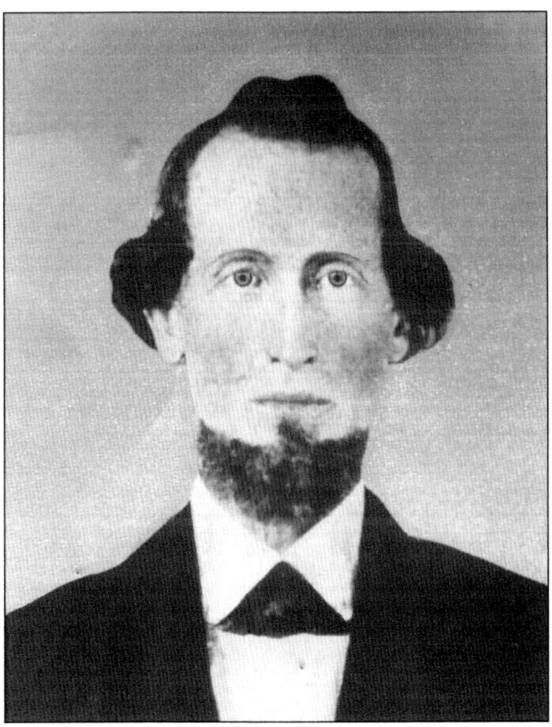

John S. Meredith was born April 7, 1826, and was a recruiting officer at Pottsville and St. Clair during the Mexican War. He was the first volunteer from Frackville to enter the Civil War, as well as the first from Frackville to die in that conflict on March 11, 1863. John is buried in grave 4300 at Old Soldiers Cemetery, Washington, D.C.

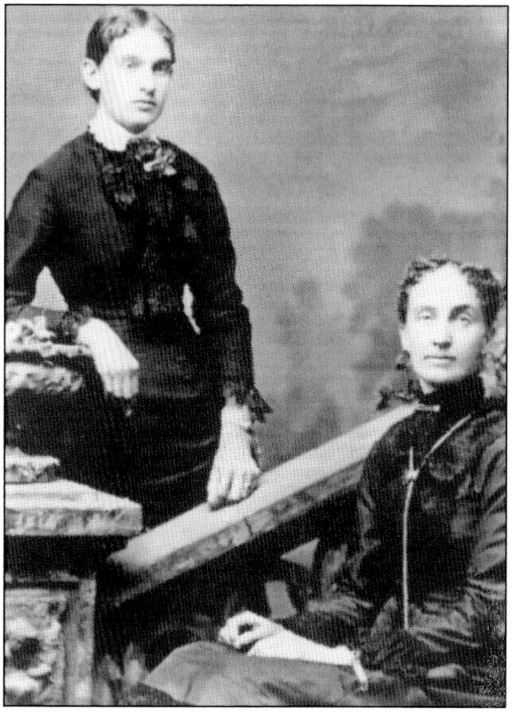

Pictured are Margaretta Carolina Meredith (left, born January 11, 1863) and Mary Elizabeth Meredith (right, born September 13, 1849). Daughters of Lenora Frack and John Meredith, they resided at 111 North Balliet Street.

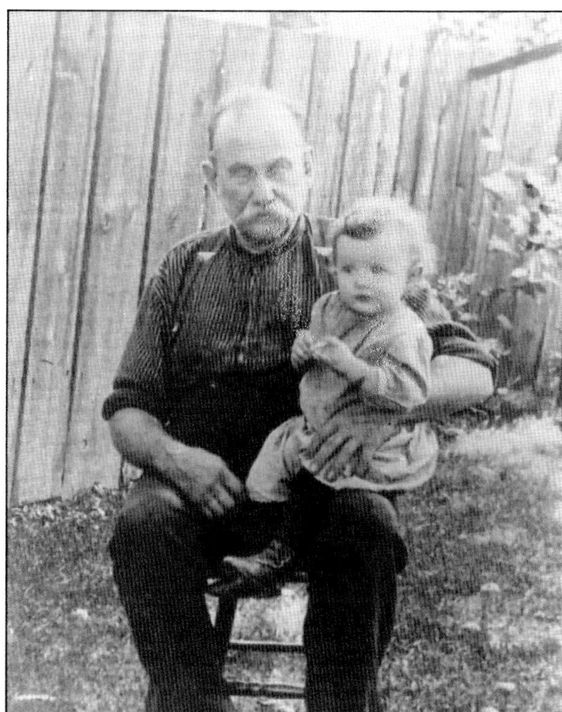

Daniel B. Frack, the son of the founder of Frackville, is shown here holding Nancy Frack. Daniel B. was born in St. Clair on March 13, 1842, and moved to Frackville in 1852. He married Elizabeth Seitzinger and after her death, married her sister, Sarah, with whom he had three sons: Edward, Daniel, and Harry. Mr. Frack died on June 24, 1911.

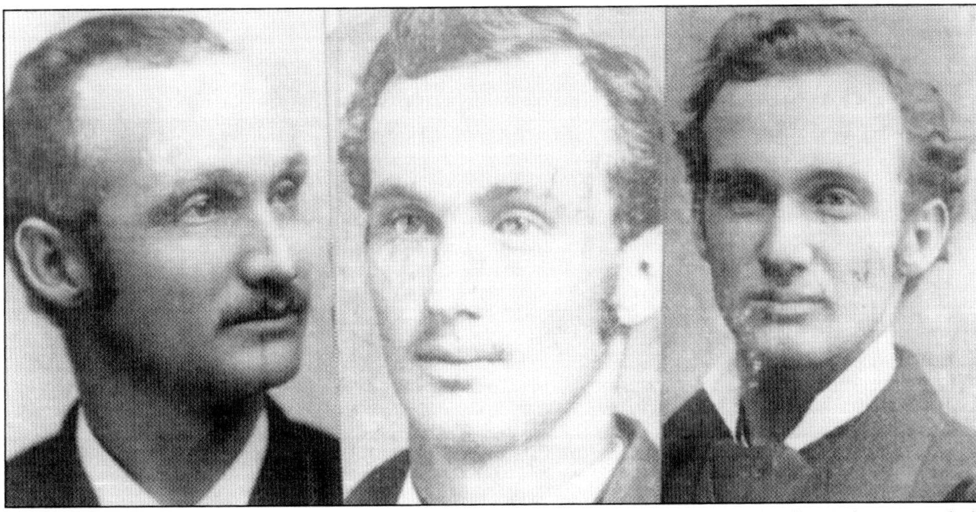

The Meredith brothers started the famed Meredith Cornet Band of Frackville. John Meredith (left) was born on May 14, 1856, married Margaret A. Merkert on October 30, 1890, and died on December 19, 1901. Joseph B. Meredith (center) was born June 28, 1854, and married Mary Ann Curtis on May 6, 1882. James C. Meredith (right) was born August 2, 1852, and was the first child born in Frackville. He married Lena Miller on August 25, 1871, and she died on February 13, 1890.

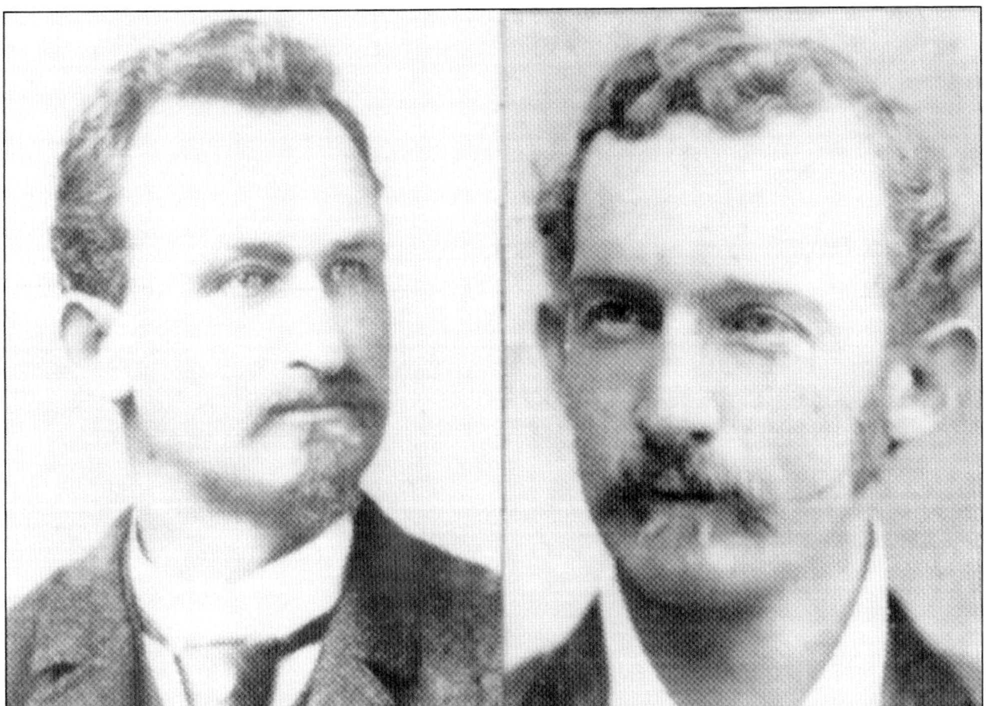

Samuel Frack Meredith was born December 3, 1850, married Emma Flynn on December 22, 1878, and died on November 15, 1896, in Colorado. Asa Balliet Meredith (right) was born September 28, 1860, married Mayme Riley, and lived in New Jersey.

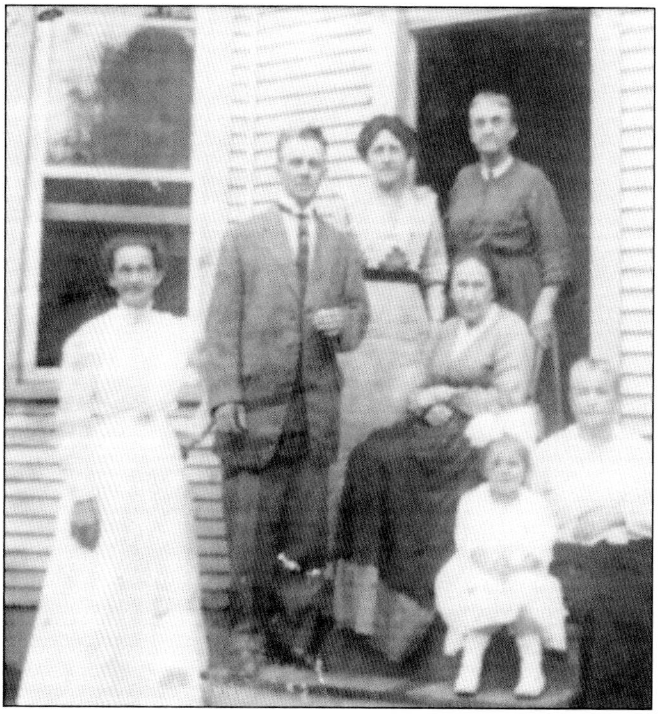

Pictured is the home of Mrs. Lenora F. Meredith at 111 North Balliet Street. Pictured, from left to right, are as follows: (standing) Margaretta M. Houtz, Rutherford Stell, Lenora Meredith Stanton, and Miss Mary Meredith; (sitting) Mrs. Lenora Meredith, Sara Frack, and Shirley Stell (young girl).

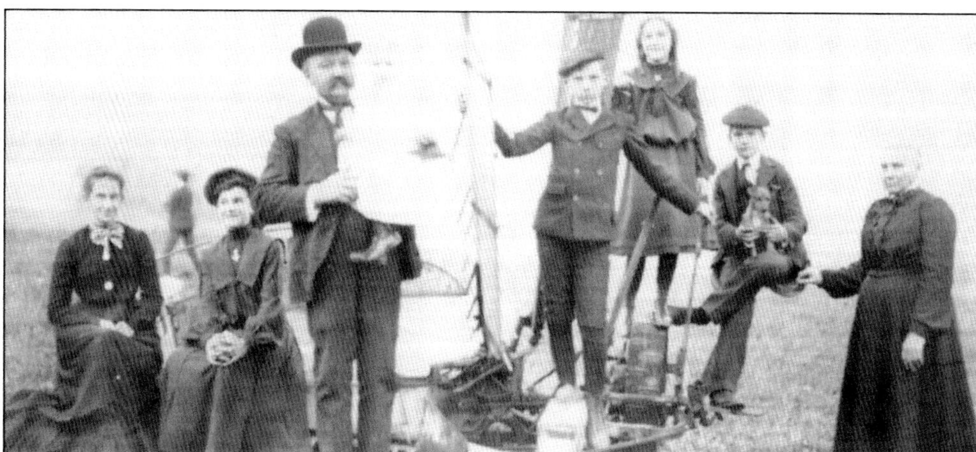

Shown here is the Aaron Houtz family in 1902. Pictured, from left to right, are as follows: Mrs. Margaretta Houtz, Florence (Mrs. Houtz's daughter), Aaron W. Houtz (holding Mildred), Jesse Houtz, Hilda Houtz, Robert Houtz, and Grandmother Salinda Houtz. The boy walking in the background on the left is Harry Houtz.

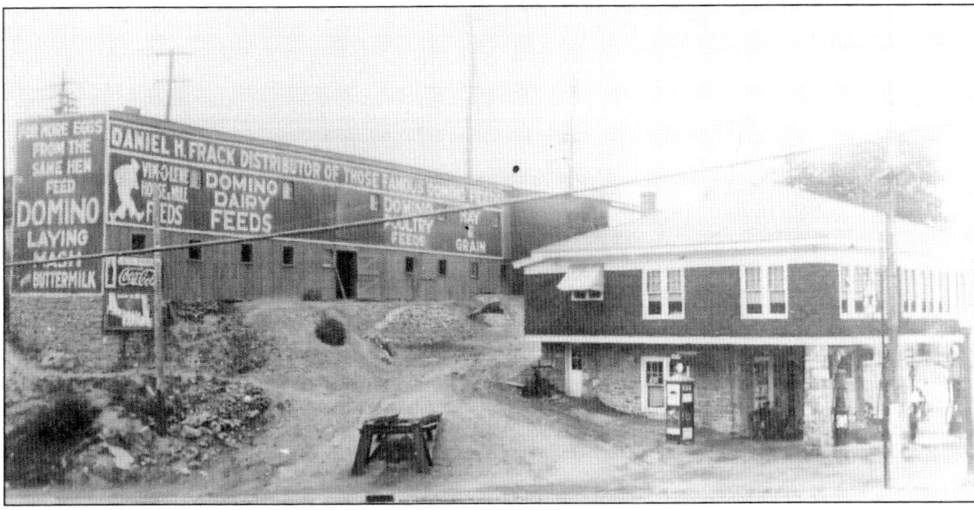

Daniel H. Frack conducted his business at 139 North Lehigh Avenue. An excellent horseman, he had ten to fifteen horses at one time. The second floor of the stables were used as a warehouse for horse feed, and Mr. Frack had the contract to supply feed to the coal companies in our area. The family lived on the second floor of the gas station.

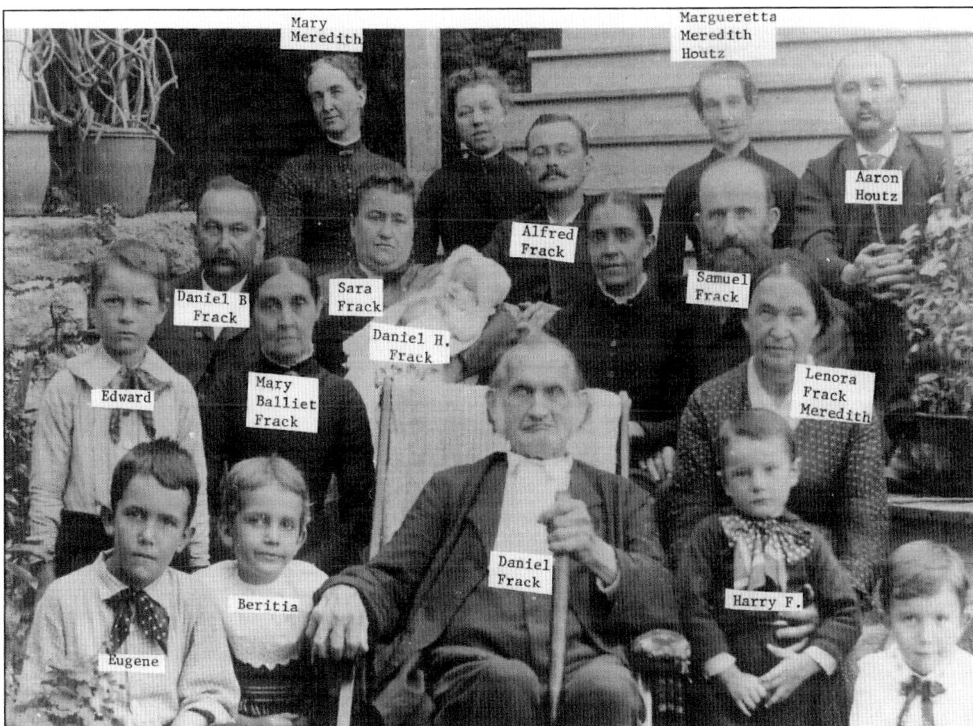

At the time this photograph of the Frack family was taken in 1886, Mr. Frack was eighty-three years old and blind. He died on November 7, 1890, at the age of eighty-seven. Daniel was a very generous man and he donated land to several churches, schools, and cemeteries. Ironically, when he died, a lot had to be purchased for him in a cemetery on land which he had earlier donated.

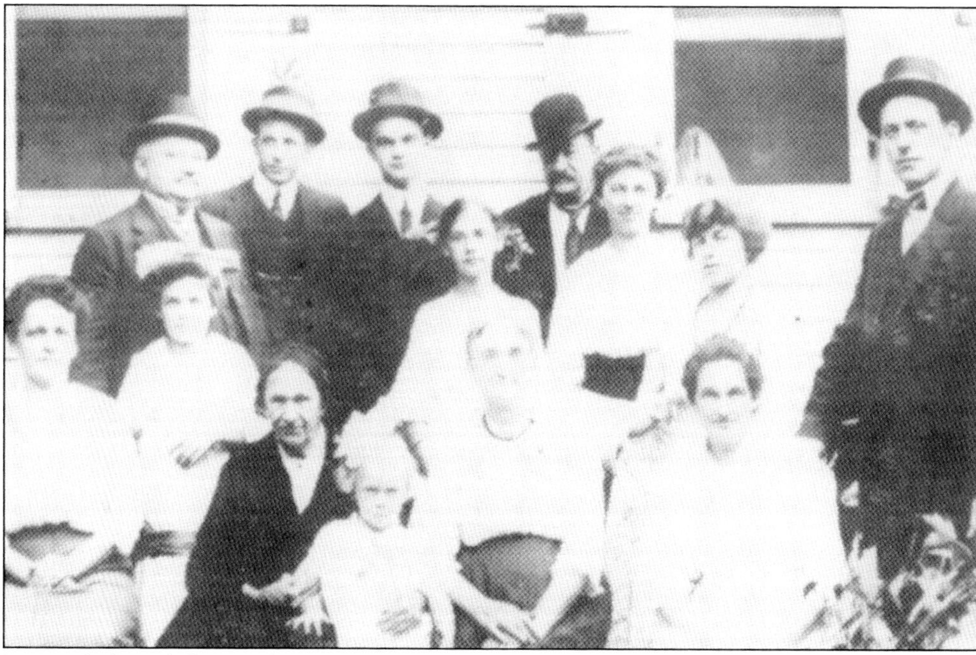

Pictured, from left to right, are as follows: (gentlemen standing) Aaron W. Houtz, Oliver Meredith, Robert Houtz, James Meredith, and Lonzo Meredith; (girls standing) Elizabeth Eltringham, Mildred Houtz Orf, Alvina Meredith, and Dorothy Meredith Eltringham; (ladies sitting) Margaret M. Eltringham, Lenora Frack Meredith, Mary Frack, and Margaretta Houtz.

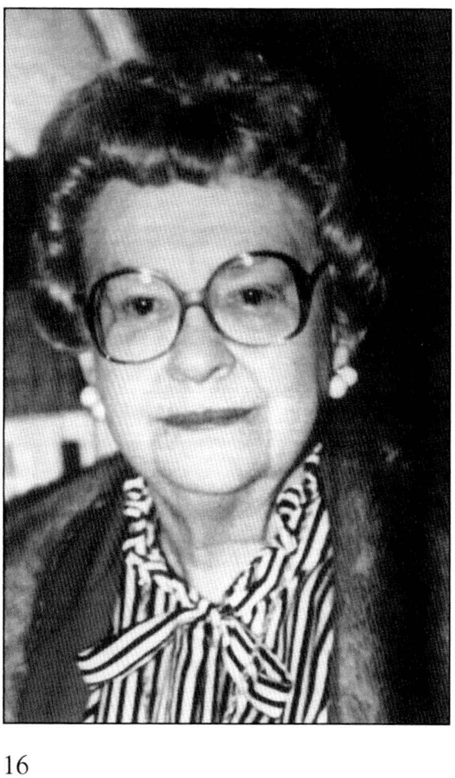

The youngest of six children, Mrs. Mildred Orf, daughter of Aaron and Margaretta (Meredith) Houtz, was born June 21, 1902, in Orwigsburg. The family lived at 111 North Balliet Street, where her father operated a grocery store. This building was destroyed in a fire in 1902, after which the family moved to Orwigsburg.

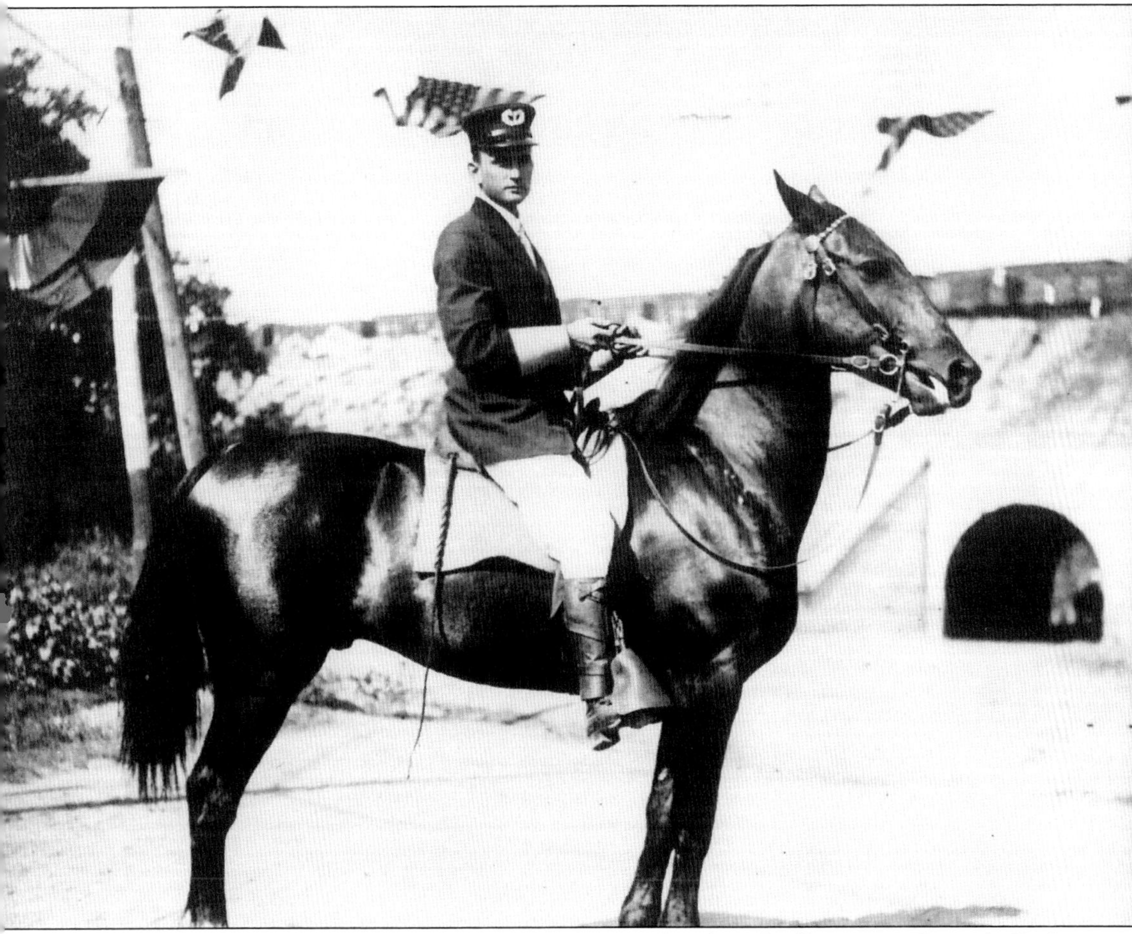

Pictured is Daniel Hannibal Frack, grandson of the founder of Frackville, as Grand Marshall of Old Home Week festivities in September 1914. Son of Daniel B. Frack and Sarah Seitzinger, Mr. Frack was born June 2, 1886, attended the Frackville schools, and was a blacksmith and distributor of horse feed to local coal companies. He married Esther Mae James on April 3, 1909, and they had two sons, Edward and Jesse. He died at the age of fifty-seven on November 12, 1943. His wife, who was born July 11, 1887, died October 8, 1964.

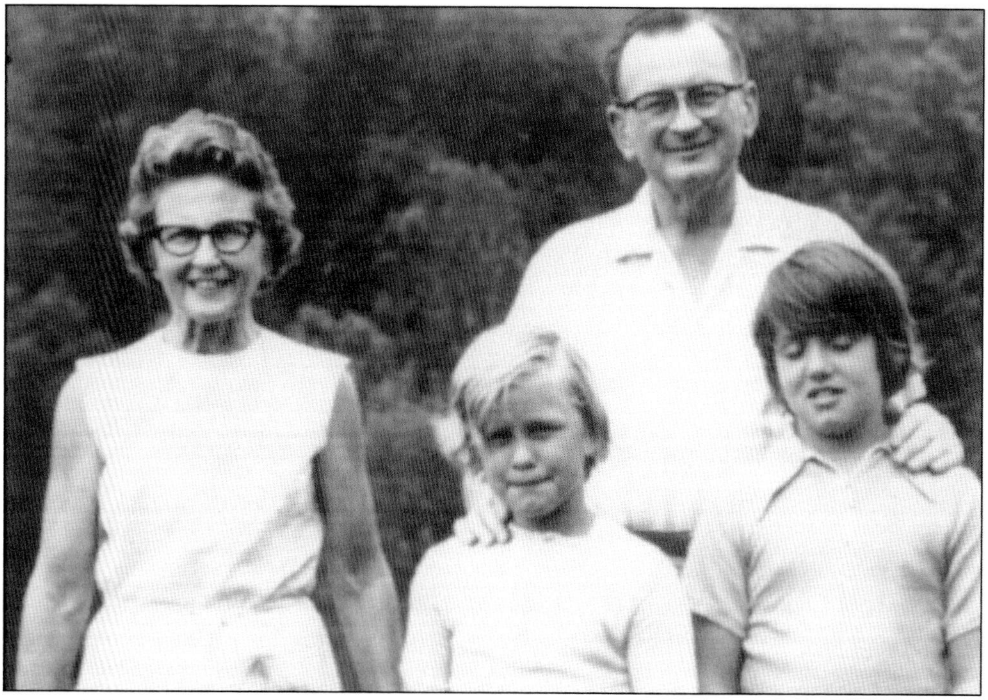

Mr. and Mrs. Edward Frack are pictured with their grandchildren. Mr. Frack was born January 16, 1910, attended the Frackville schools, and graduated from Bucknell University in 1933. During World War II, he served in Europe and the Pacific, reaching the rank of colonel. He was married to Reba Clark and died October 22, 1973.

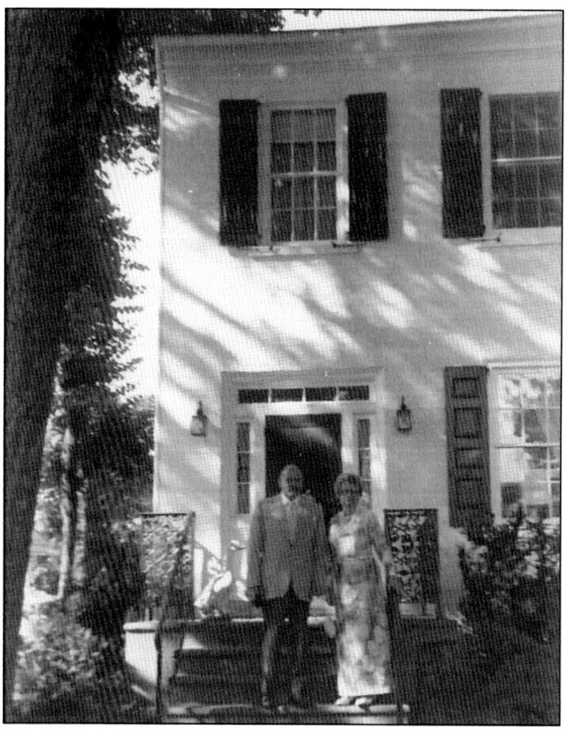

Shown are Jesse Frack and Mildred Orf, great grandchildren of Daniel Frack, standing on the steps of the original Balliet home at Ballietsville near Allentown. The towering trees were brought from France by Col. Stephen Balliet. The Balliet home is open for tours conducted by the Historical Society of Lehigh County.

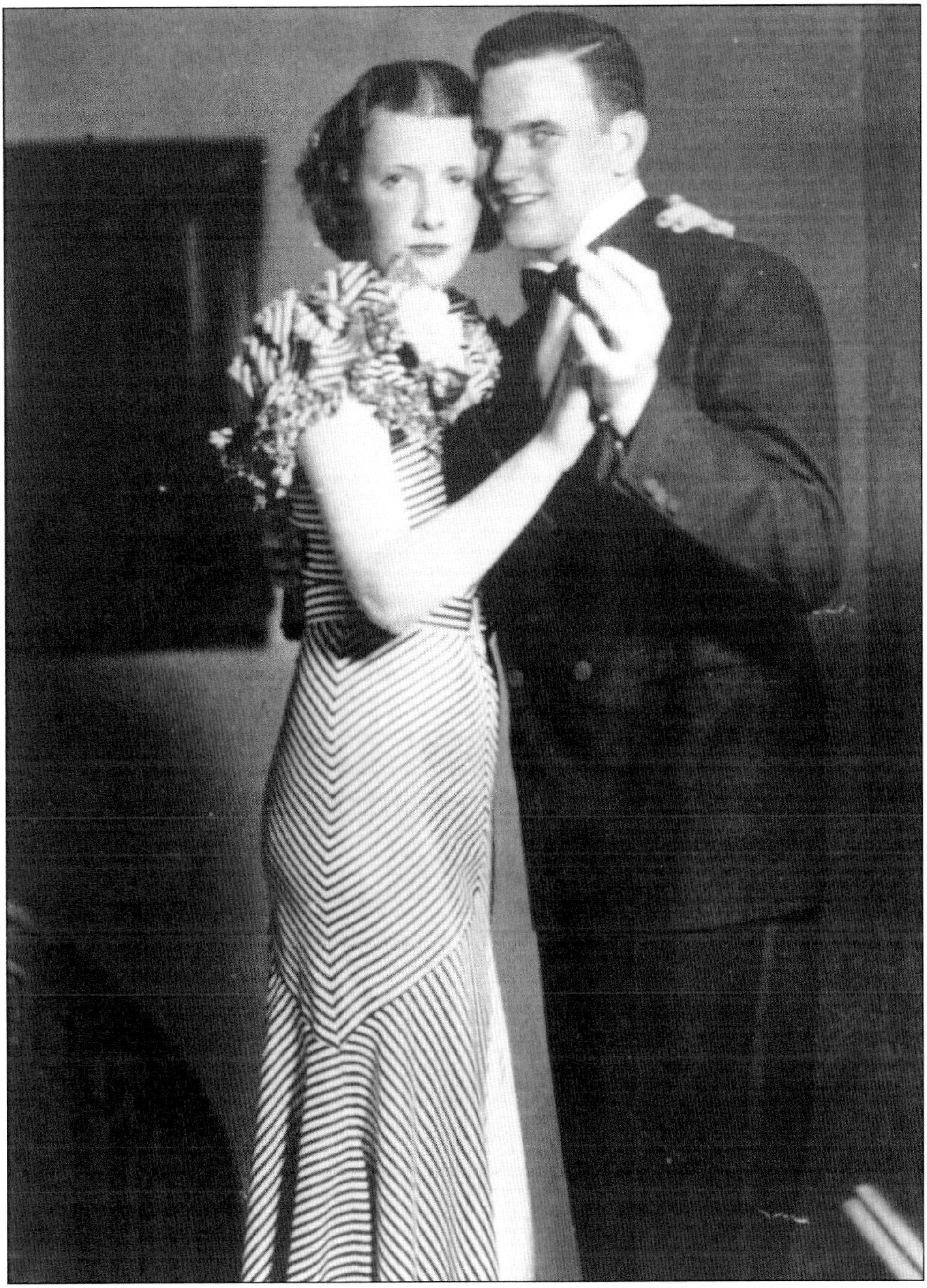

Eleanor Miller and Jesse Frack graduated from Kutztown in 1938. Although they didn't attend this dance together, they were best of friends, and this picture was in their college yearbook. The caption reads: "To those who know her on campus, 'Duchess' is appropriately named, for her charm distinguishes her as one of our loveliest and most sophisticated co-eds. A sturdy, man-sized, well-tailored athlete swooped down on Kutztown four years ago and made the name of Jesse Frack prominent in our football lineups."

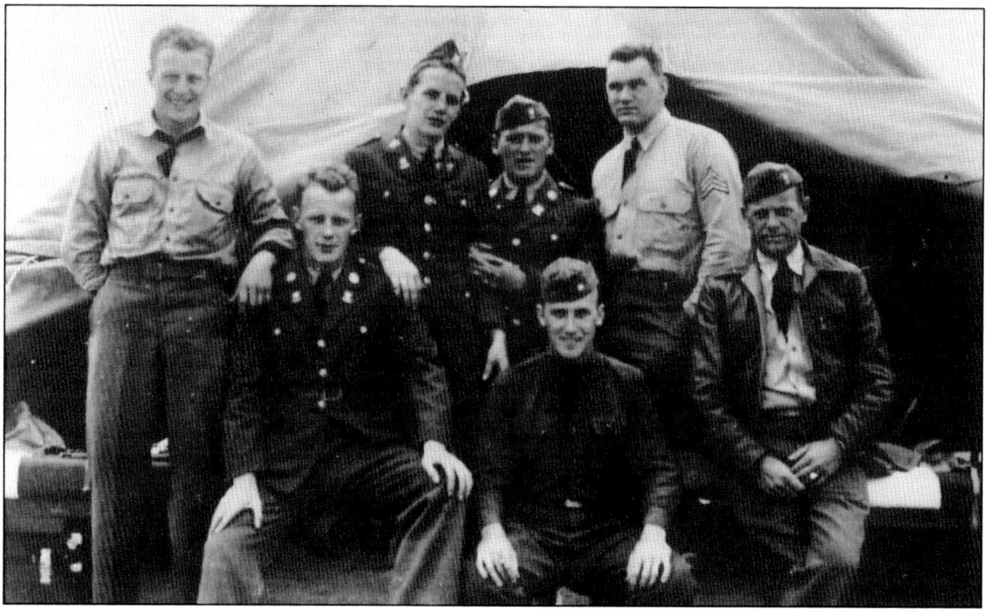

Jesse Daniel Frack was born June 26, 1916. He graduated from FHS in 1934, received his B.S. from Kutztown in 1938, enlisted in the National Guard in 1939, and was called to active duty in 1940 with the rank of sergeant. Pictured, from left to right, are as follows: (sitting) Matt Wylam, Sparky Carrol, and unknown; (standing) Jack Eisenhart, Howard Morgan, Robert Fellows, and Jesse Frack.

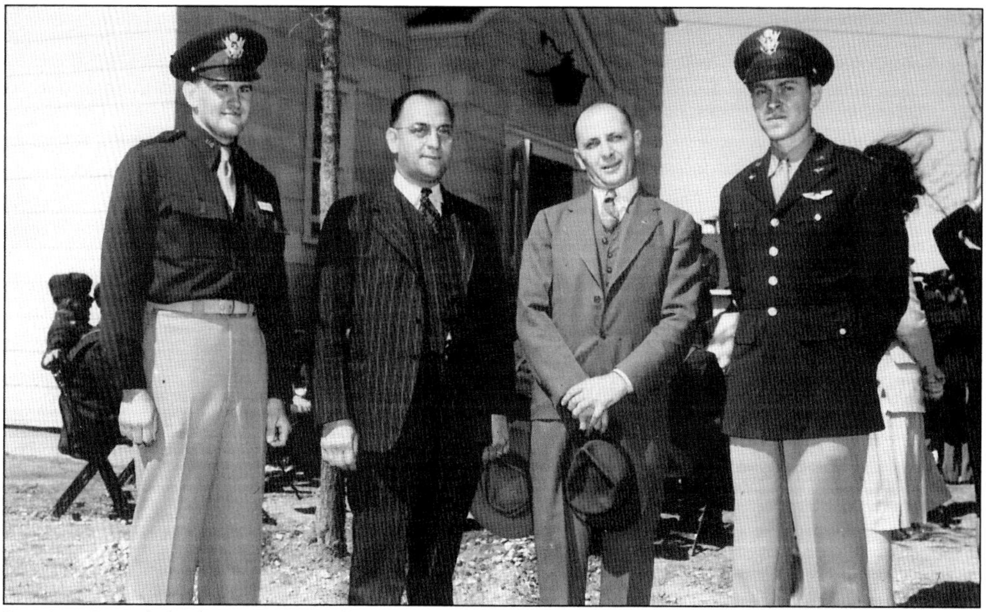

In 1941 Jesse left the Coast Artillery to become a cadet in the U.S. Army Corp. and attended Primary Flying School at Parks Air College, East St. Louis, Illinois; Basic Flying School at San Angelo, Texas; and Advanced Flying School at Houston, Texas, with the rank of 2nd lieutenant. He remained on active duty until 1950 and left the Air Force Reserve in 1957 with the rank of major. Pictured, from left to right, are Jesse Frack, Frank Palermo, Joe Strenkowski, and Henry Strenkowski.

Two

Old Home Week

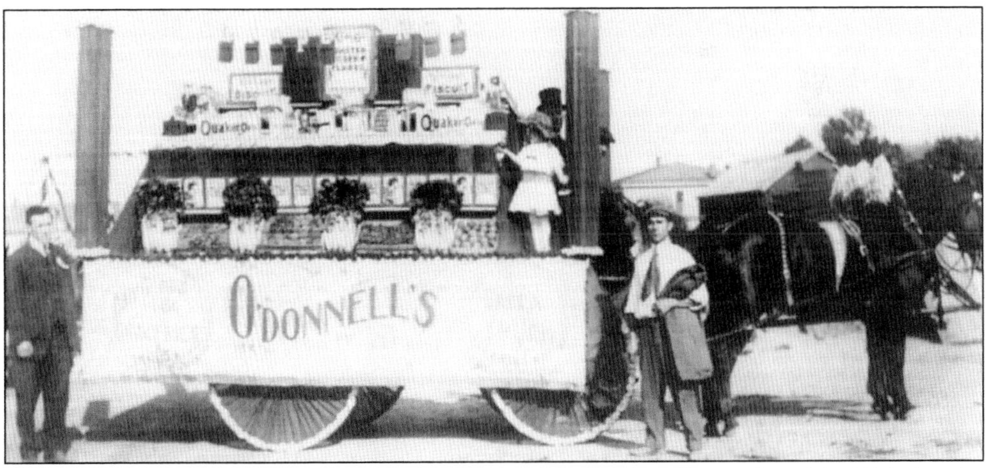

1914 News Release: "Old Home Week was opened Monday, September 14, 1914, by the ringing of bells and whistles. Night was turned into day by a flood of light which radiated from thousands of electric lights. Almost every citizen of town took part in the ceremonies and the crowds were augmented by hundreds of visitors from every town in the region. A week of activities was planned and special trains scheduled to handle the crowds. The Joseph Ferari Carnival Shows erected tents on the streets and had concession stands, peep shows, snake charmers, clowns, barkers, and a freak show featuring 'Minnehaha.'" Mrs. Bridget O'Donnell's Grocery float decorated with fresh vegetables and fruit won second prize, and her granddaughter Katherine is on the float.

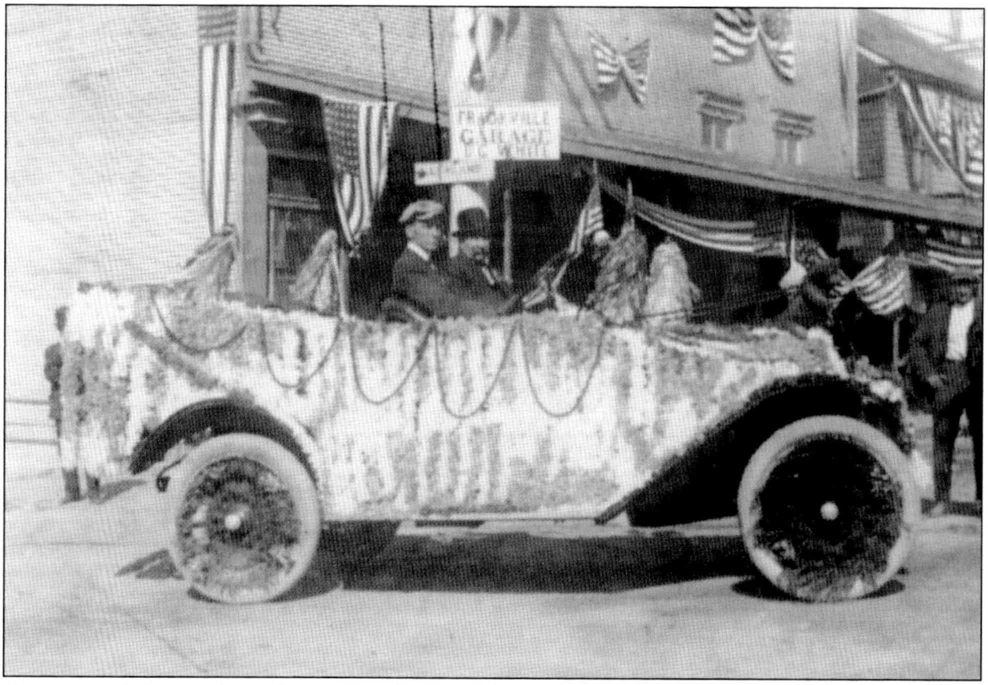

An automobile parade with one hundred and fifty cars participating was held. Jim White (in black derby) won $15 as second prize winner in this parade.

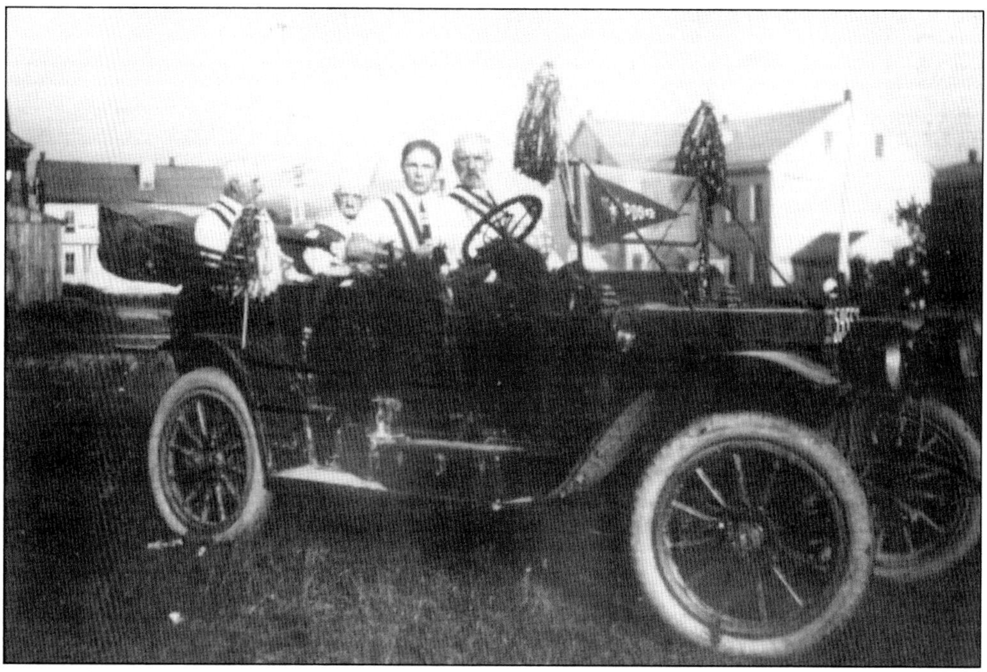

Pictured are members of the Patriotic Order Sons of America participating in the auto parade. In a fashionable Buick are Clarence Brosius (driving), Mr. Seitzinger (front seat), Reuben Trautman (right rear), and an unidentified gentleman (left rear).

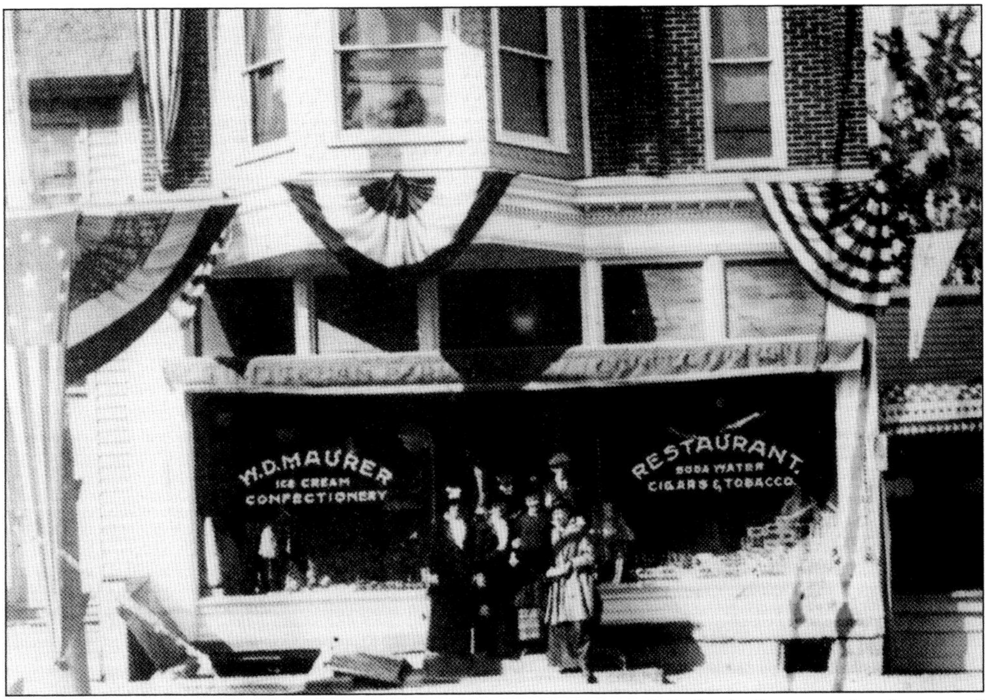

All businesses were decorated, and W.D. Maurer at 60–62 North Lehigh Avenue also decorated his store. The Maurer family is seen standing in front of the store, which in addition to being a restaurant, sold ice cream, candy, soda water, cigars, and tobacco.

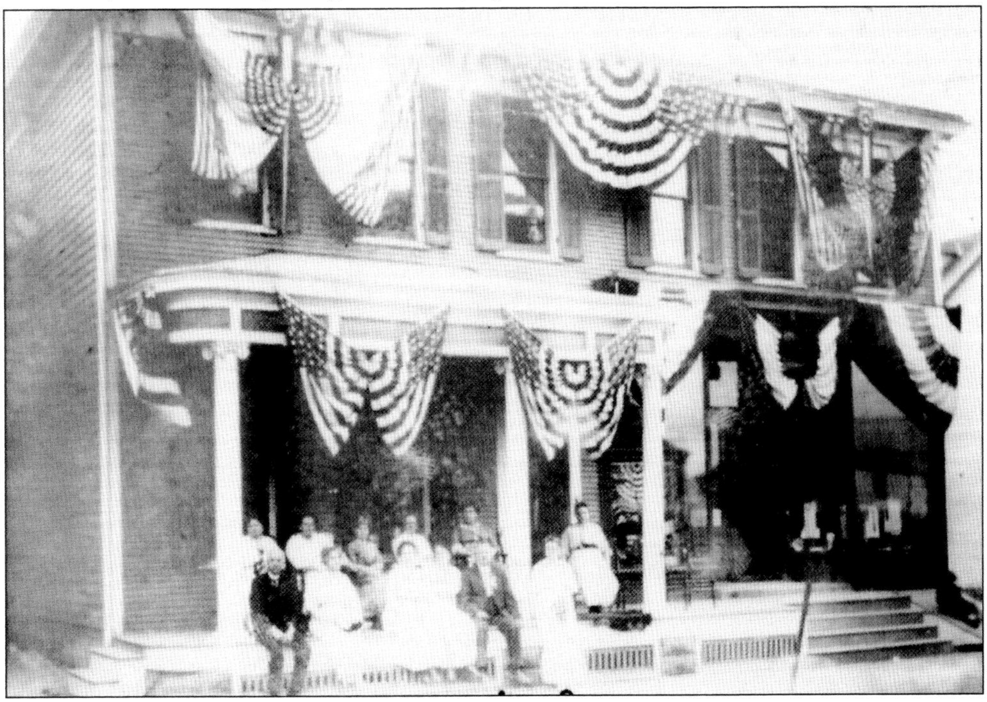

The Harry T. Evans General Store was located on North Nice Street. Mr. and Mrs. Evans and neighbors are waiting for the parade to pass.

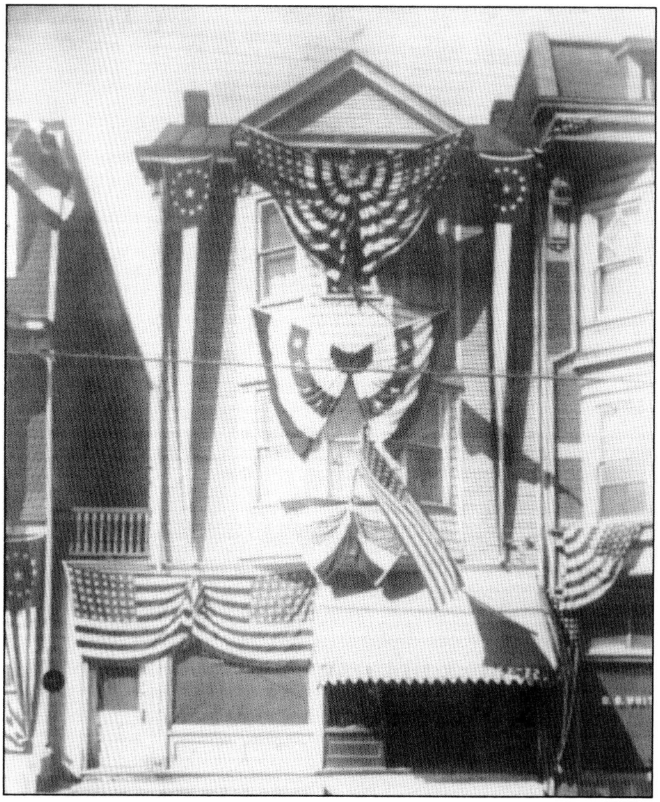

This building is located at 24 North Lehigh Avenue. The awning has "Haberdasher" across the front. This was later the Yarowsky Shoe Store, but is now demolished. The building on the right was Dave White's Pool Room with Bowling Alley in the rear at 26 North Lehigh Avenue. The J.Z. Appliance Co. is still located there.

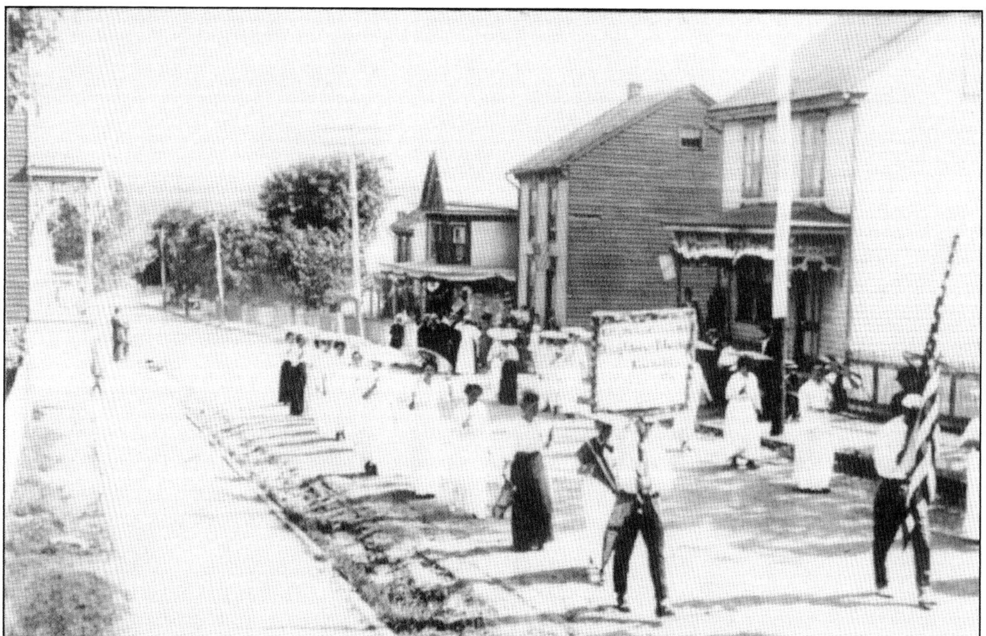

The sign reads, "Daughters of Liberty, Frackville, Penna." This group of well-dressed ladies are seen marching on South Balliet Street.

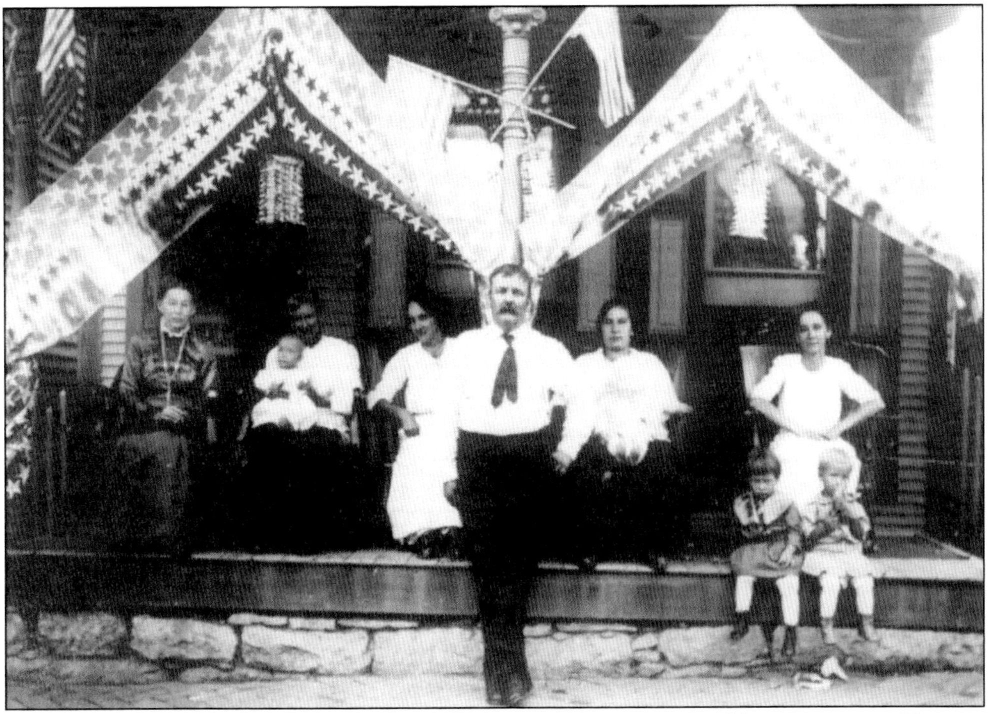

Another beautifully decorated home for Old Home Week was owned by Mr. George Ebert at 34 South Balliet Street. Shown are, from left to right: (seated in chairs on the porch) Sally Ohl, Mrs. George Ebert, Baby Alton, Deborah Alton, Mrs. Cora Colihan, Baby Thomas Colihan, and Mrs. Jennie Shiley; (sitting on porch) Evelyn Alton and Grace Colihan Dampman; and (standing in front) George Ebert.

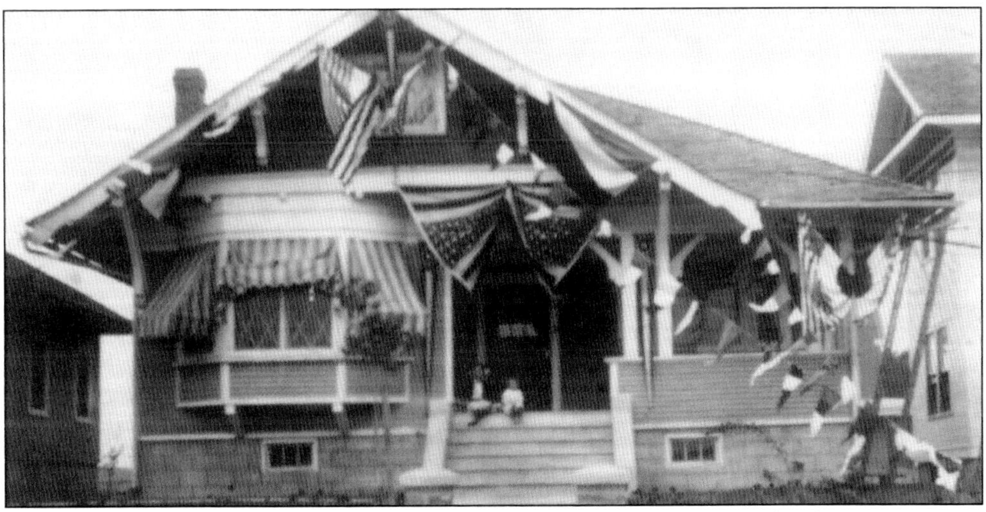

At the Robert Garrett residence, 58 North Centre Street, Elizabeth and Robert Garrett are sitting on the steps. During World War I, Mr. Garrett was appointed by the secretary of the United States Treasury to organize "The Four Minute Men," whose purpose was to sell Liberty Bonds to help support the war. He was the cashier of the First National Bank of town.

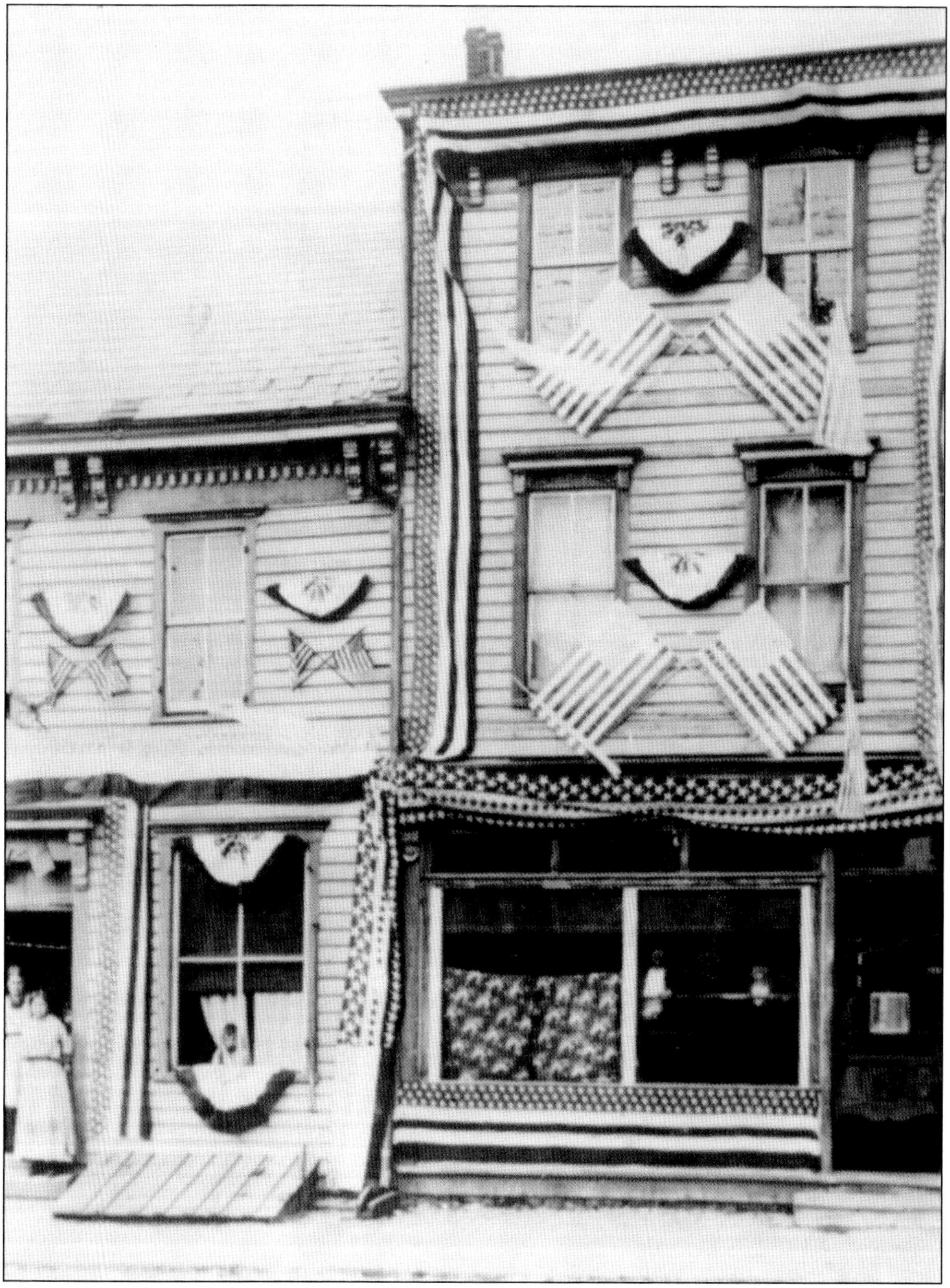

The Continental Hotel at 31–33 South Lehigh Avenue was built by John Shadel and later added to by Philip Prynn, both husbands of Barbara (Hay) Shadel. Pictured are Clara Seitzinger Shadel, with daughter Sara and son George, looking out the window. This picture shows the building decorated for Old Home Week festivities.

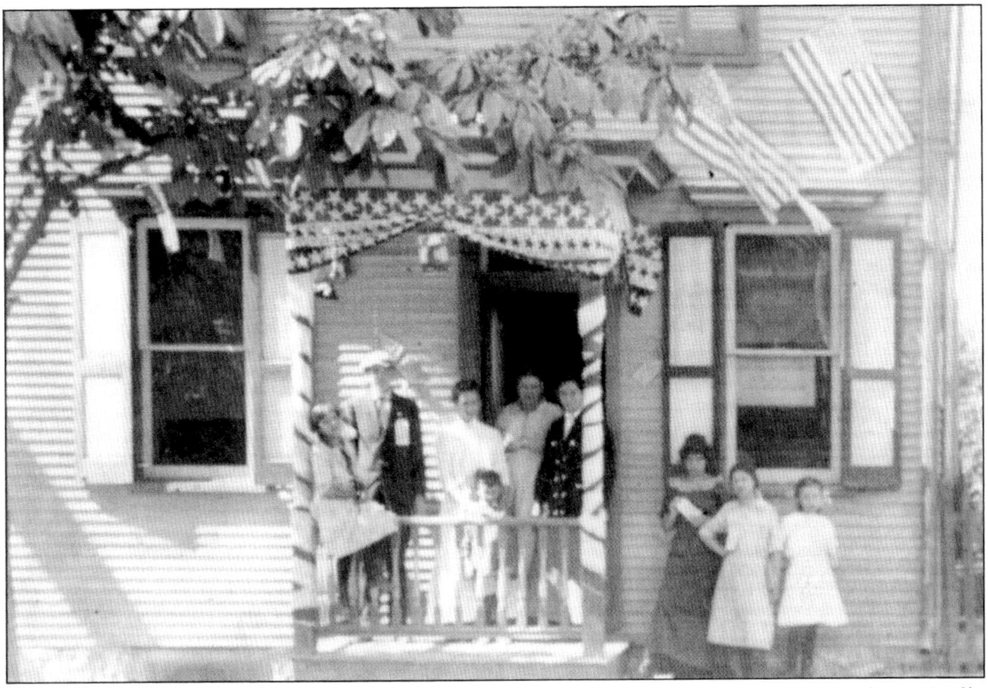

Shown at the Shadel residence, 112 South Lehigh Avenue, during Old Home Week are Stella (Shadel) Hoban, Carl Ardar, Pauline and Harry Shadel, Mary Kreitzer, two unidentified people, Mary (Shadel) Johnson, and Helen Shadel.

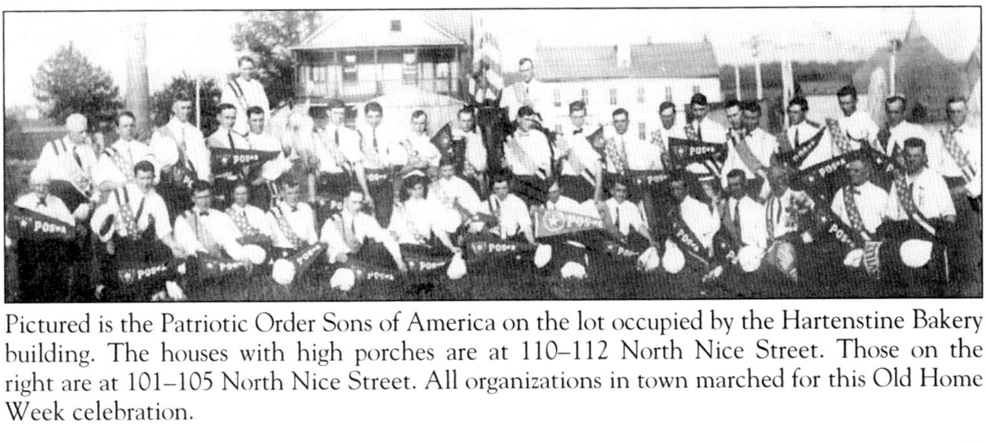

Pictured is the Patriotic Order Sons of America on the lot occupied by the Hartenstine Bakery building. The houses with high porches are at 110–112 North Nice Street. Those on the right are at 101–105 North Nice Street. All organizations in town marched for this Old Home Week celebration.

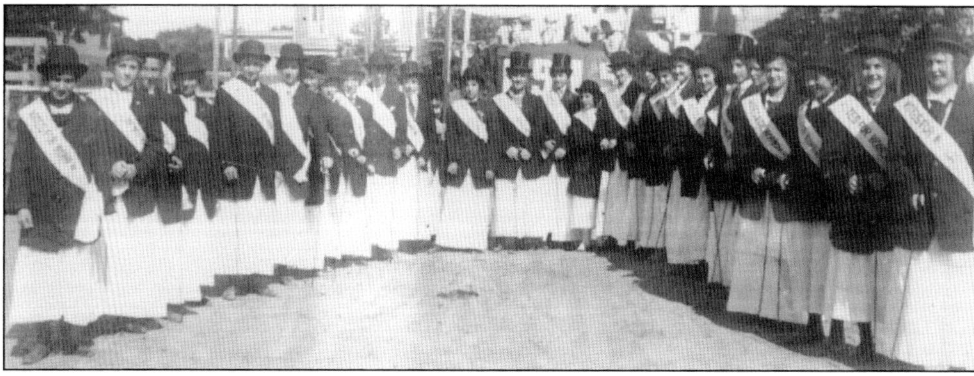

A group of suffragettes parade on West Frack Street in front of St. Joseph's Church. The banner reads: "Votes for Women."

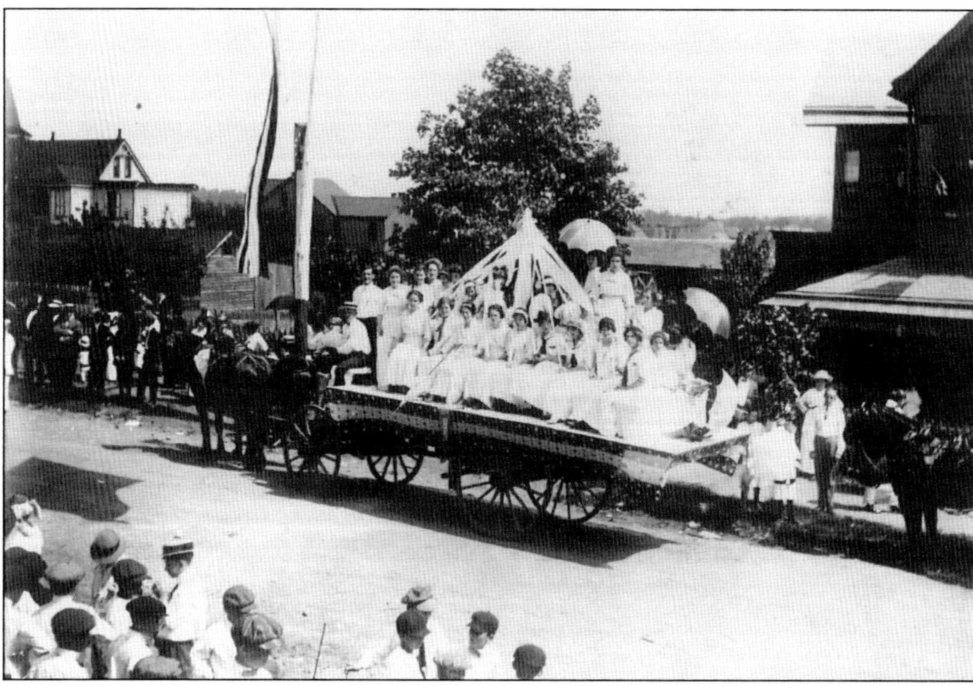

A news release from 1914 read: "The best float prize was awarded to the Daughters of Liberty Float. These lovely ladies, dressed in their best white dresses, sat on a horse-drawn float with maypole center."

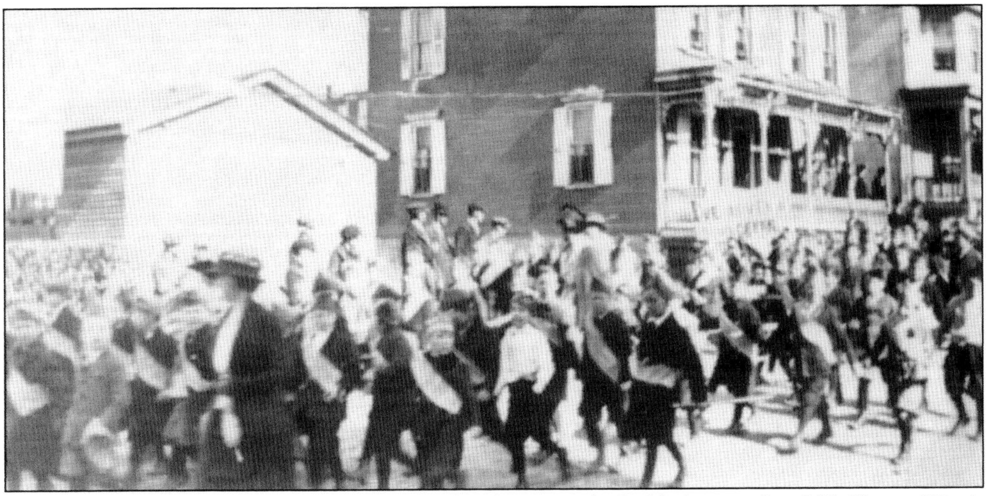

Eleven hundred children participated in the first parade held during the Old Home Week festivities. Many of them were dressed to represent historical events of the town. Here, young boys carry a sign stating, "I've never known defeat," as they march along East Frack Street.

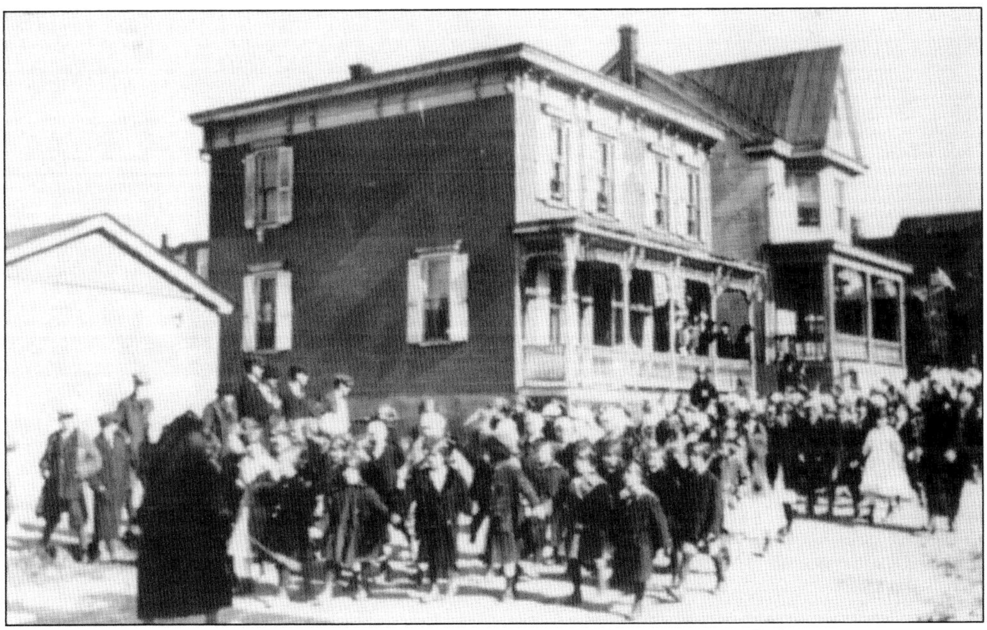

Another group of schoolchildren marched hand-in-hand along East Frack Street.

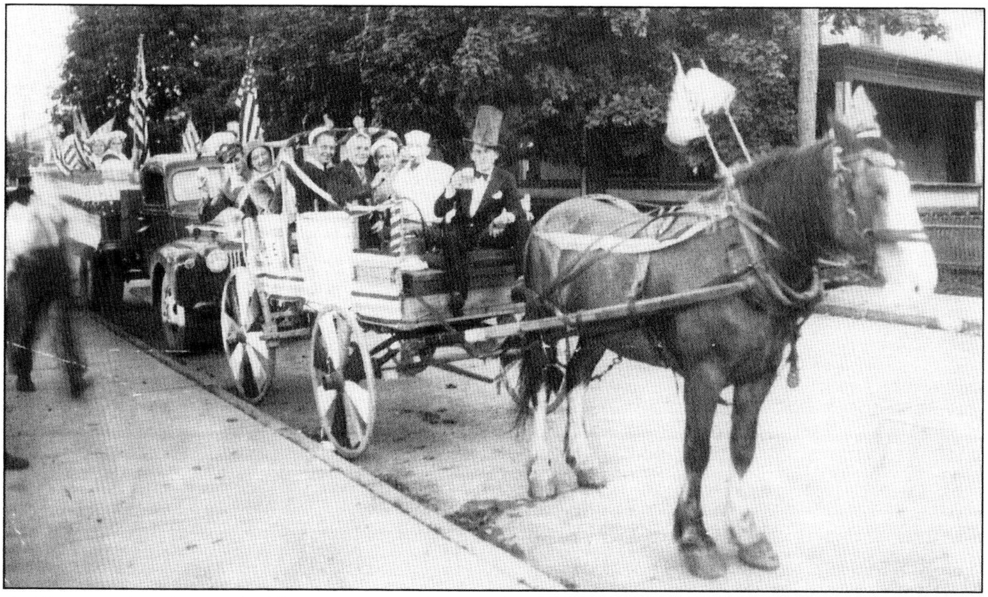

A Victory Parade was held in town on September 4, 1945, and this float carried veterans of several wars. Pictured are Stanley Andershonis and Frank Mekailek (Spanish-American War veterans), Ted Sanko and Joe Mekailek (World War II veterans), Gable Merlin (World War I veteran), and Bob Price (World War II veteran).

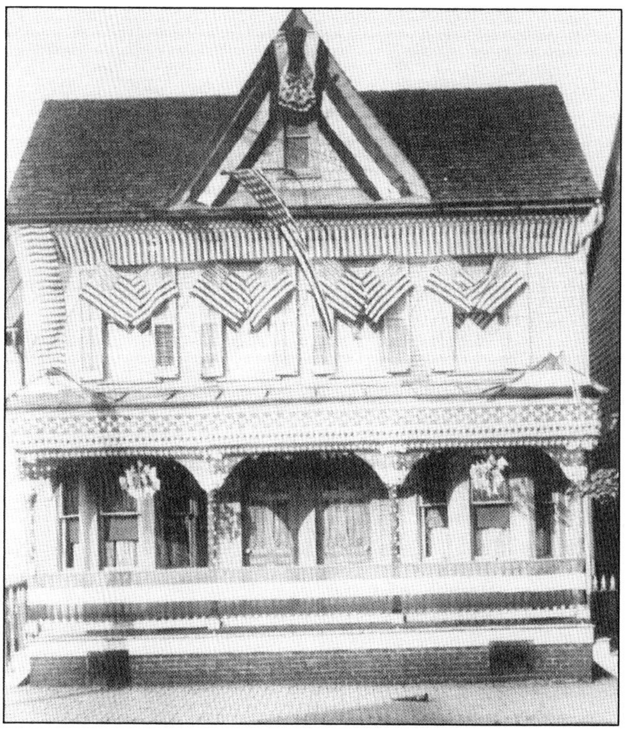

Pictured are houses at 39–41 South Lehigh Avenue decorated for Old Home Week, September 14–19, 1914. These homes were later made into an apartment building.

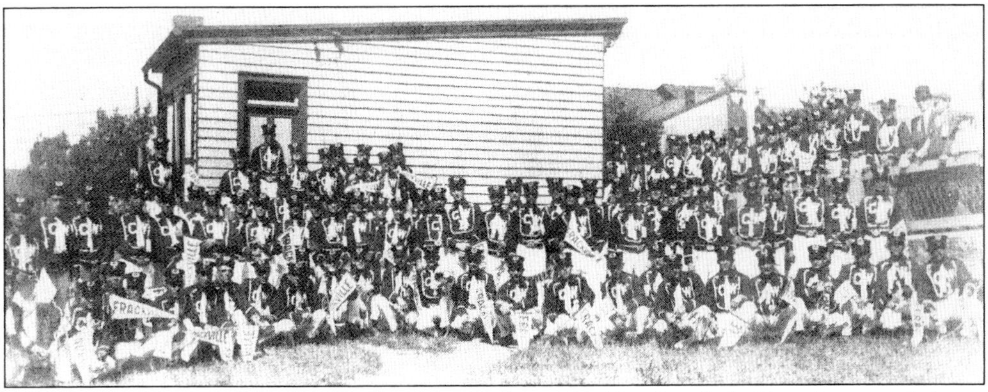

This picture was taken on East Oak Street on the side of Joe Roeder's Shoe Store and shows members of the Goodwill Fire Company carrying Frackville Banners.

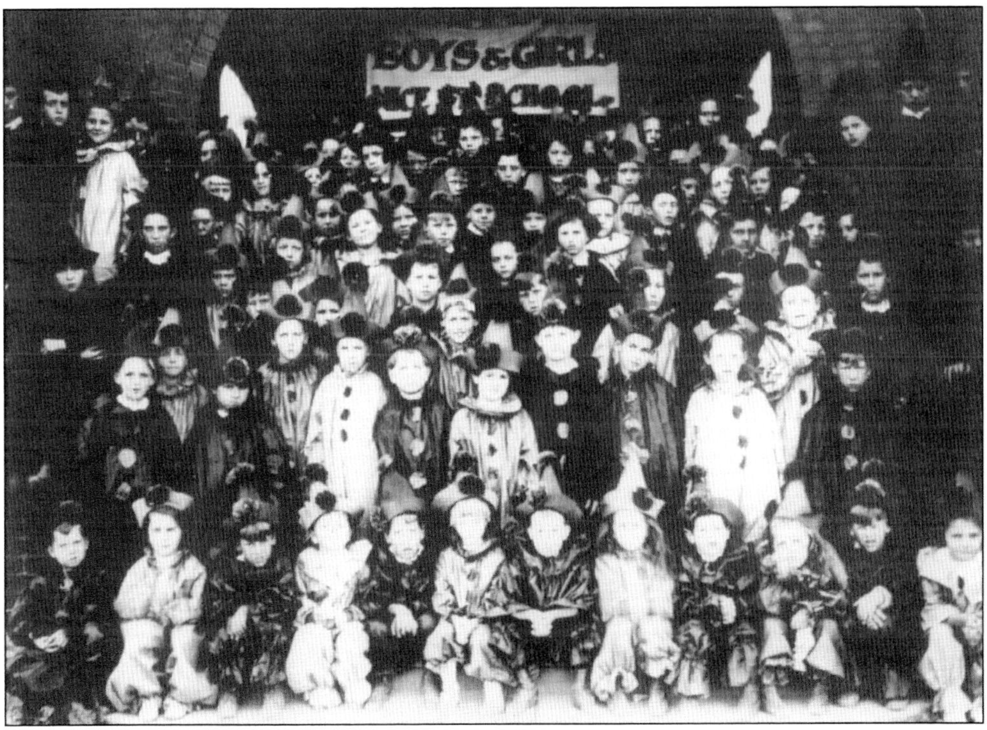

The sign reads, "Boys and Girls—Nice Street School." These were elementary schoolchildren dressed in clown costumes for the Old Home Week festivities. The Nice Street School was later renamed the Jefferson School because in 1925 all school names in town were changed to reflect a national patriot's name.

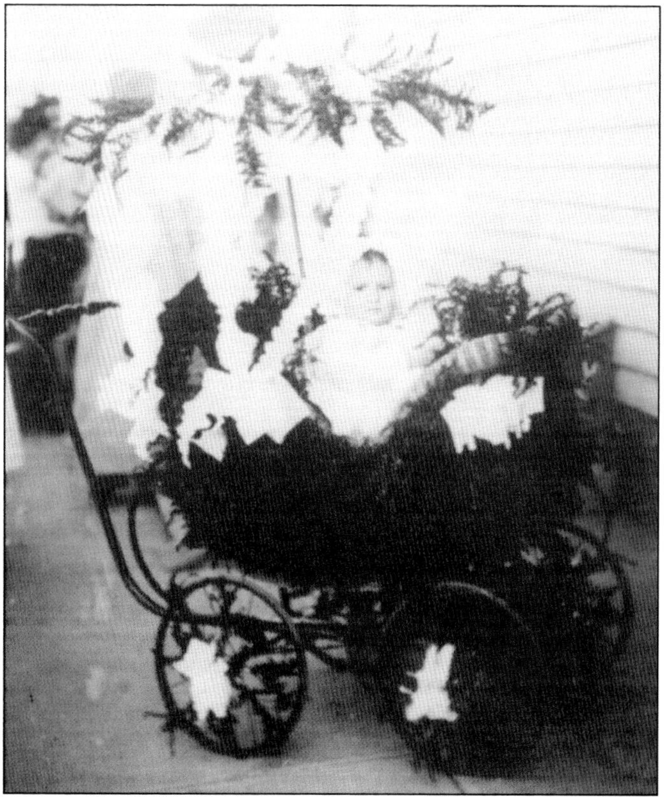

A 1914 news release read: "This cute little cherub was all dressed up for the baby parade in her beautifully decorated coach. Three hundred babies with proud mothers and fathers participated and a prize went to Edward and John McGrath, Pottsville, who were dressed in Irish costumes and were seated in a wheelbarrow filled with potatoes and pushed by Uncle Sam."

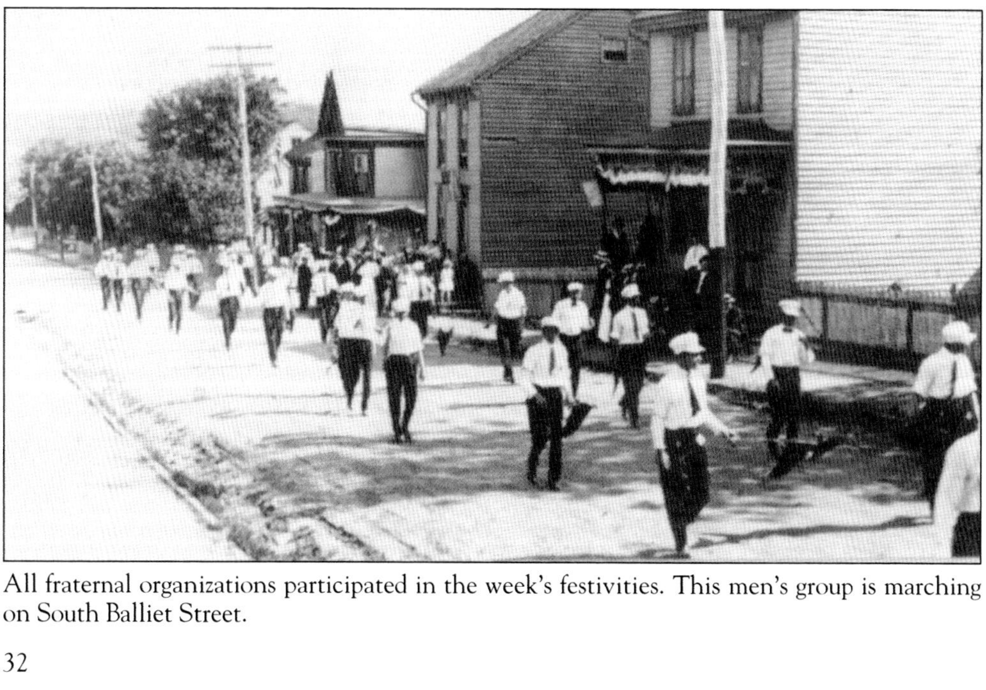

All fraternal organizations participated in the week's festivities. This men's group is marching on South Balliet Street.

Three

School Days

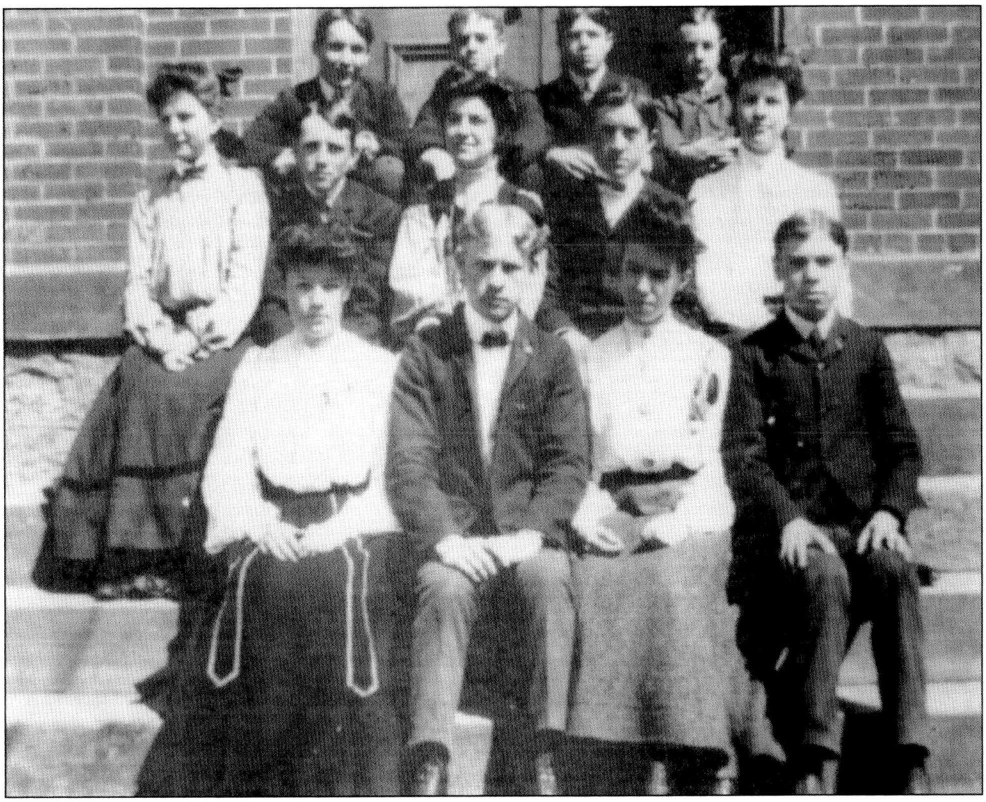

Members of the 1903 class at the Roosevelt School were, from left to right, as follows: (front row) Marion Fennelly, William Bracey, Kathryn Sanner, and Horace Price; (second row) Bertha Tayler, George Meck, Edna Miller, Claude Kramer, and Mary Minahan; (top row) Carl Sanner, Elmer Burchill, Louis Sanner, and John Hinks.

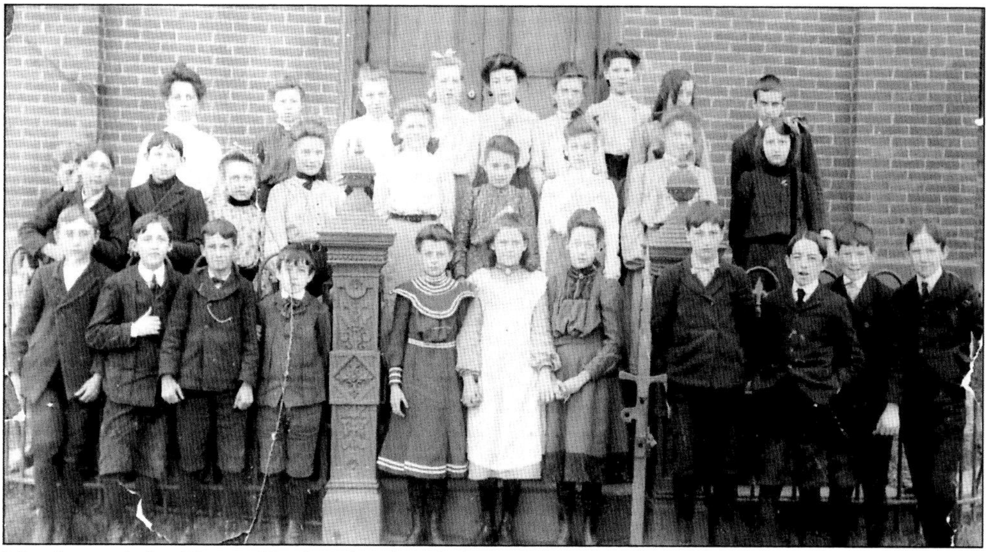

Members of the Town Clock School eighth grade class in 1904 were, from left to right, as follows: (first row) George Heim, James Speidel, Edward Monroe, Roy Sobey, Elis. Shaffer, Mary Curry, Sarah Hincks, John Monroe, Glen Sobey, Wm. Taggart, and Walter Pierce; (second row) Hoyt Leckler, unknown, Boyd Phillips, Verna Mervine, Margaret Kienzle, Sadie Rader, Emily Oerther, Pearl Sobey, Mamie Wilson, and Eva Rickards; (third row) Miss Lilly Beard, Marion Mowery, Nellie Evans, Margaret Miller, Kathryn O'Donnel, Agnes Curry, Dollie Krecker, Anna Wagner, and Paul Wascher.

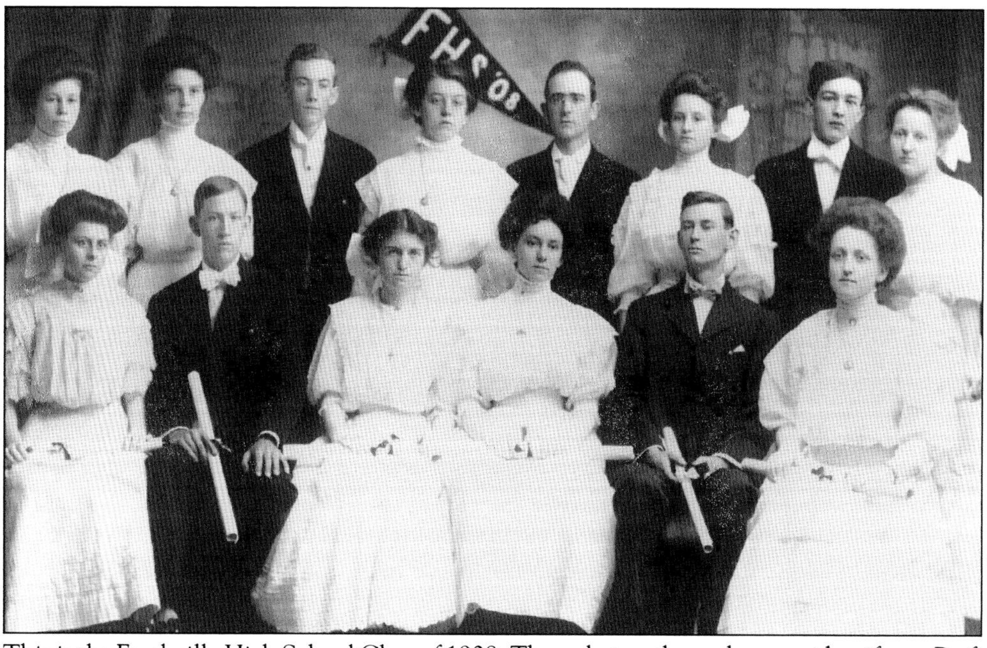

This is the Frackville High School Class of 1908. The only two the author can identify are Prof. Wm. R. Trautman (fifth person from the left in the top row) and Elizabeth Schaeffer (first girl on the left in the first row). Others are: Esther Billig, Harold Bauchman, Agnes Curry, James Dougherty, Bertha Fennesy, Harry McGinnis, Glenna Mengle, Marion Mowrey, Esther Orth, Walter Pierce, Pearl Sobey, and Eva Richards.

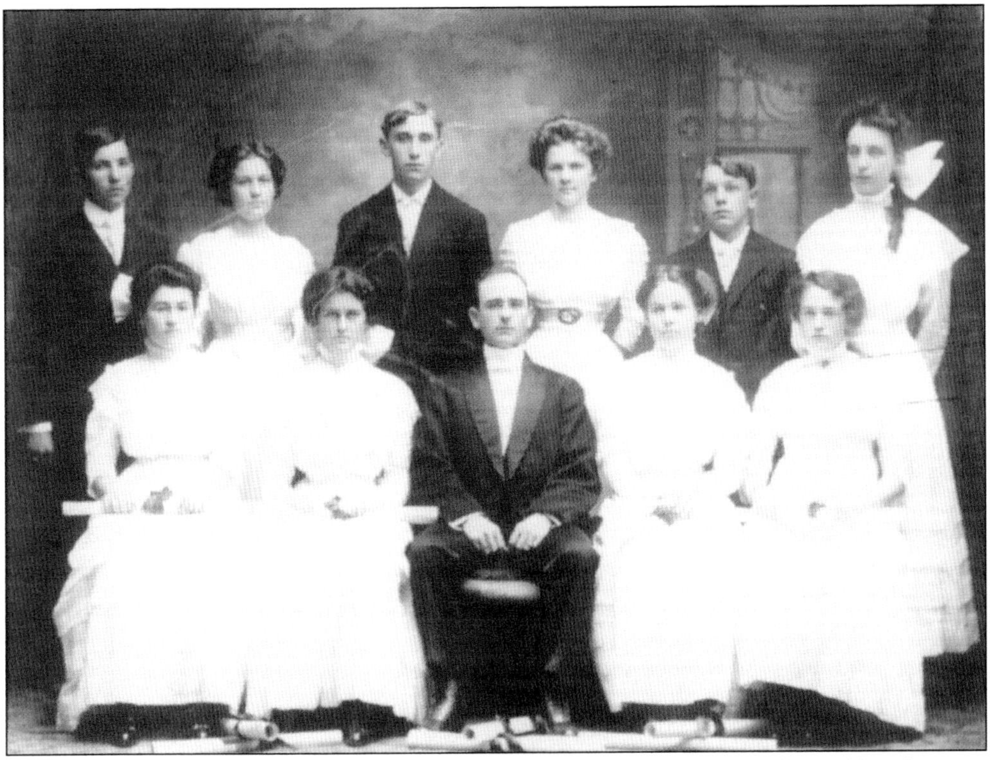

Schoolmates in the Frackville High Class of 1909 are from left to right as follows: (front) Mame Roberts, Mary Curry, Prof. Wm. R. Trautman, Florence Haughton, and Mercedes Fennelly; (second row) John Habel, Mary Wilson, George Heim, Sadie Reber, Allison Heywood, and Anna Wagner.

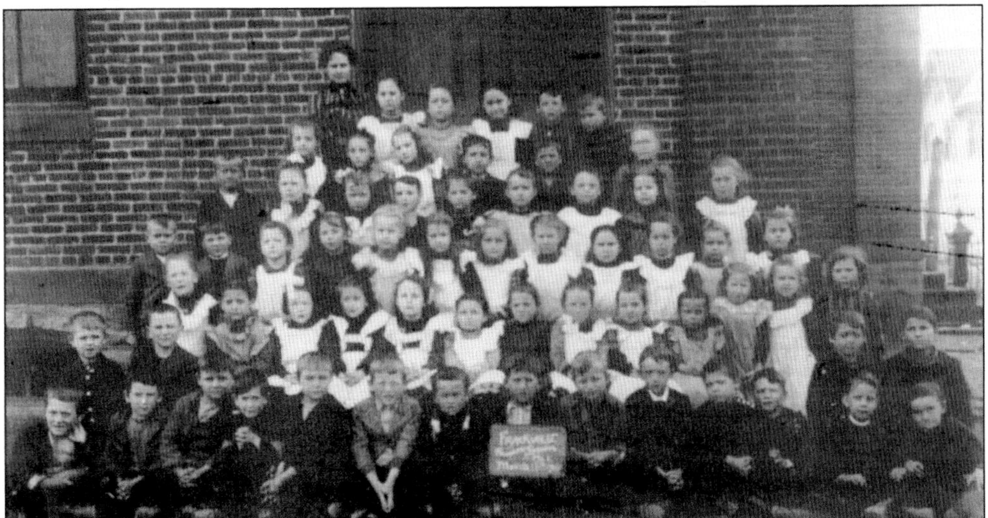

Pictured is the 1910 first grade class at the Town Clock School, which was renamed the Roosevelt School in 1925. The sign reads, "Frackville Elementary School No. 1, March 18, 1910." Miss Mildred Purnell was elected teacher, and Florence Haughton was elected substitute teacher at this time.

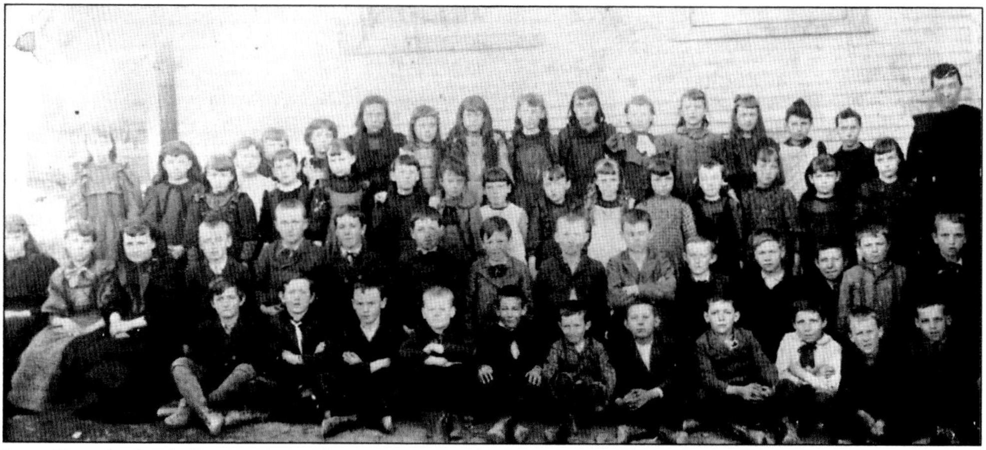

Jane Dingle (right) was elected teacher on July 4, 1898. The schools in Frackville in 1897/98 had eleven teachers and 739 scholars. In 1899 the school board purchased additional ground on the side of the Nice Street School at a sheriff's sale for $372.50.

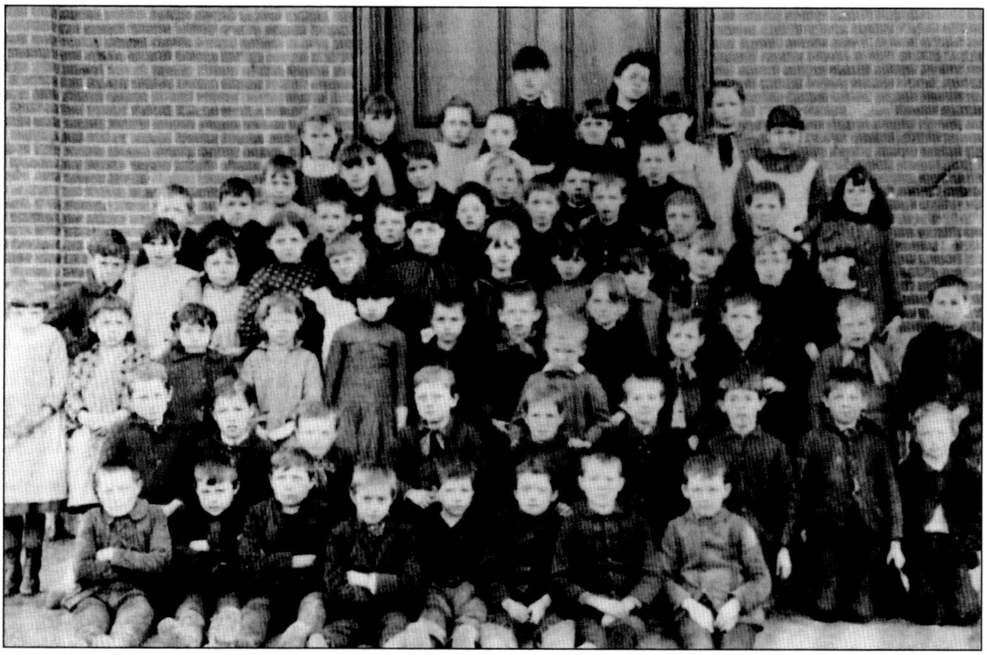

While the Town Clock School was being built, temporary schoolrooms were rented at the skating rink of Mr. Haupt at $300 for the season. The building was completed on September 6, 1888, at a cost of $11,400 with John D. Evans as the contractor. The school was renamed the Roosevelt School in 1925.

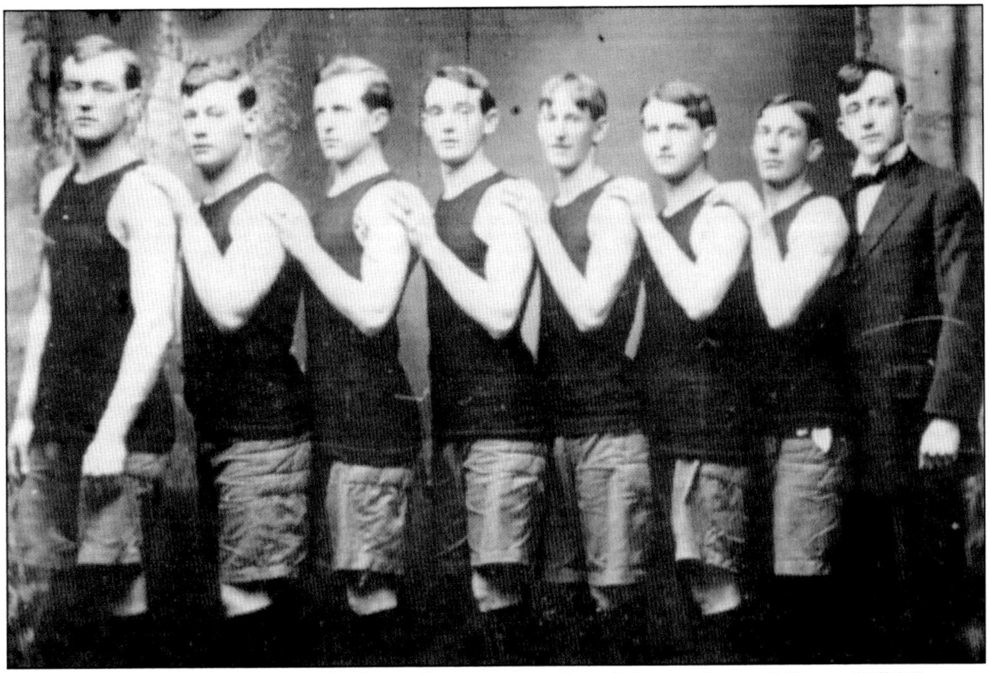

Players on Frackville's 1910/11 basketball team were, from left to right, as follows: Bill Wagner, Mart O'Donnel, Bill Taylor, Walter Guy, Bob Caton, Jack Brennan, Charlie Caton, and John Beddow (manager).

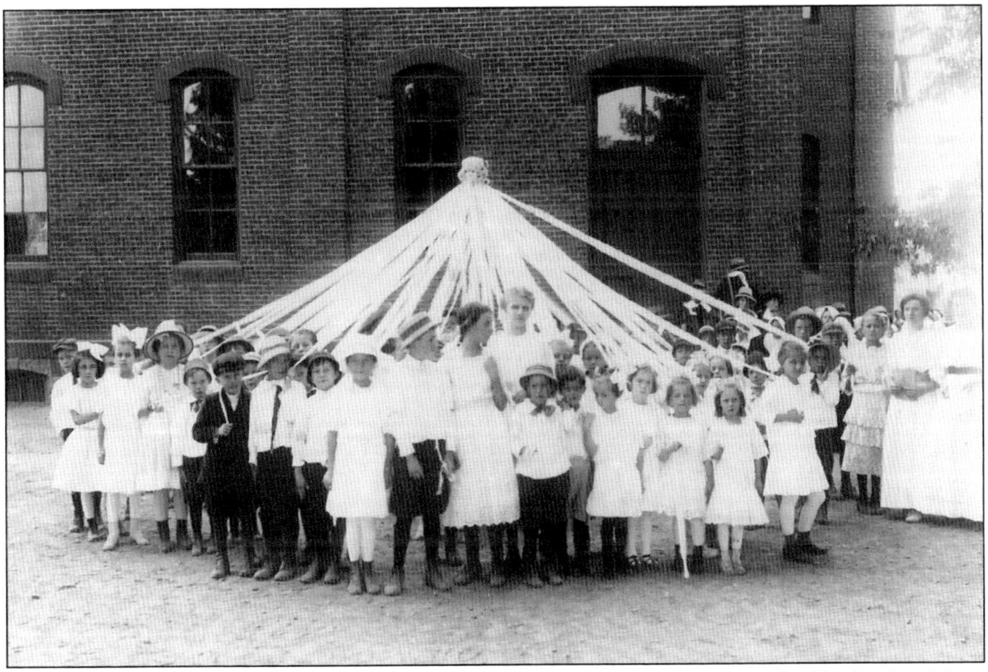

For several years the Frackville School District held May Day exercises with all schoolchildren participating. Pictured in 1912 are the Roosevelt School children dancing around the maypole. At far right are teachers Elizabeth Shaffer and M. Heywood.

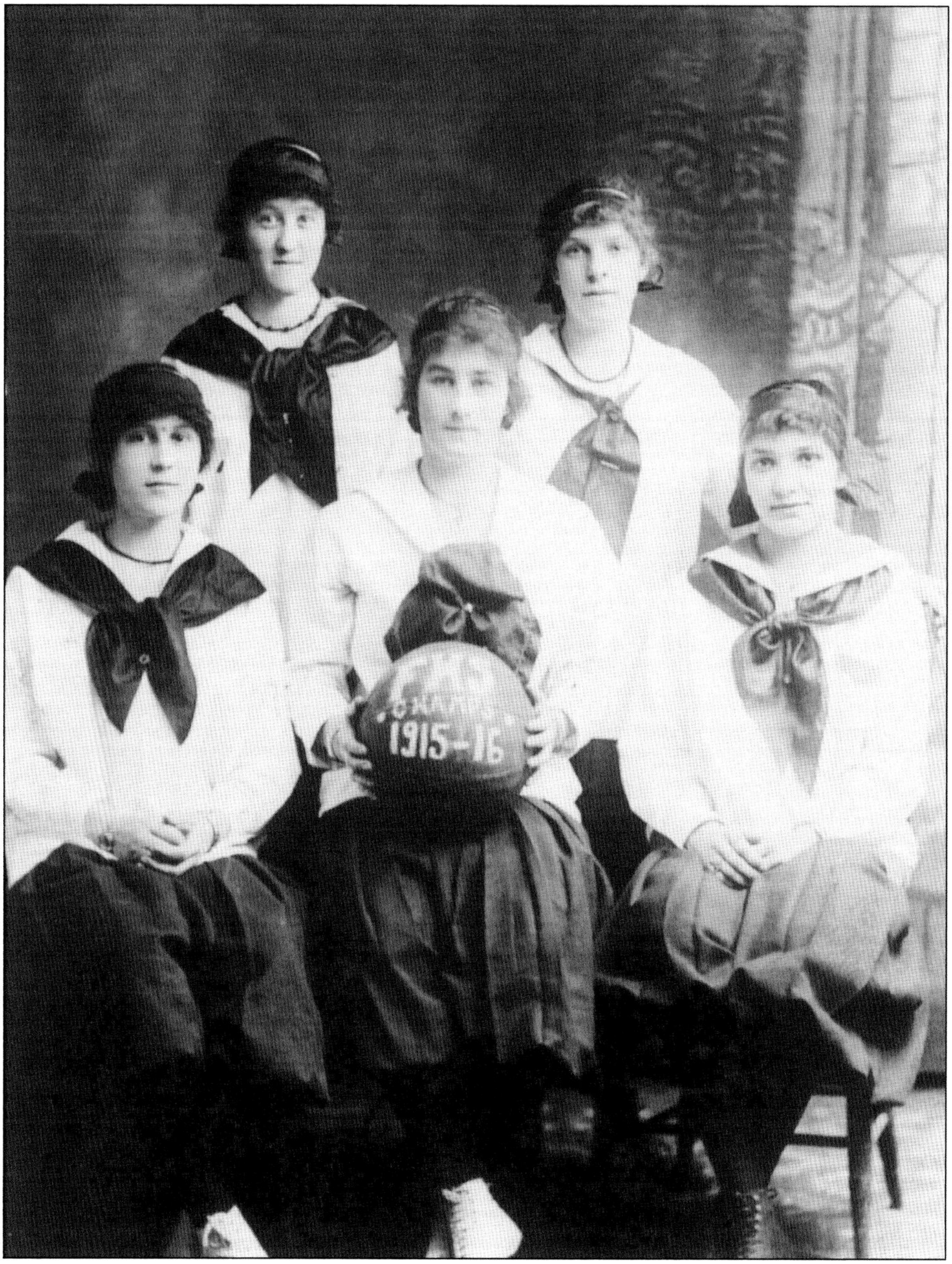

Players on Frackville's first girls' basketball team were from left to right as follows: (front) Ella Wagner Kaup, Beatrice Murphy, and Myrtle Forney Miller; (standing) Lillie Dudley Evans and Alma Berger Marshall. In 1917 Ella Kaup was valedictorian of her class of seventeen graduating students. She became the first female tax collector of Frackville in 1934 and held that office until 1949.

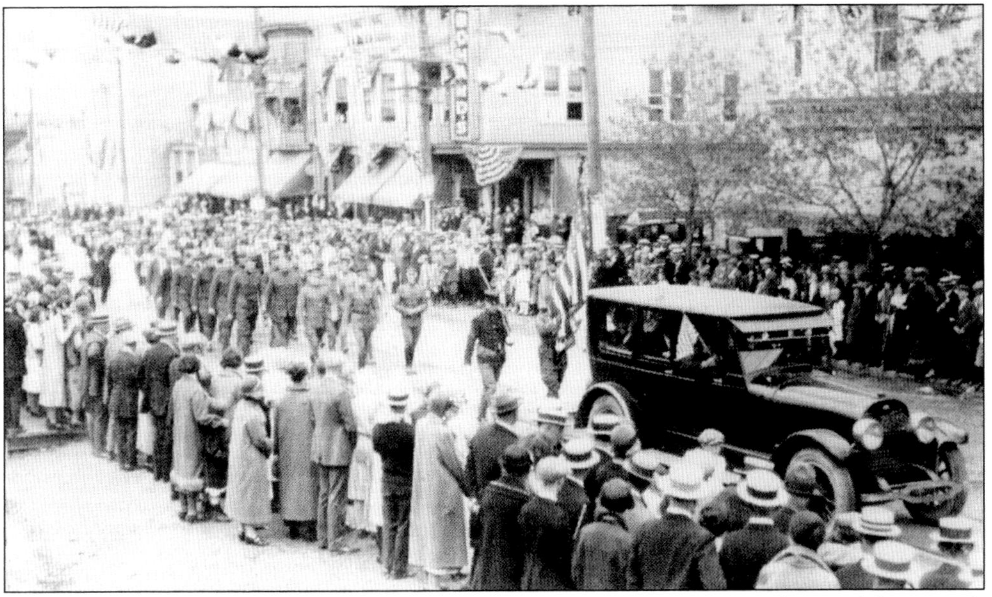

The dedication of the Washington School Building on May 30, 1925, was a huge celebration. A parade of six divisions marched with all the town organizations and schoolchildren participating. Frackville was beautifully decorated with archways of flags and bunting, and a history of the school was given by Supervising Principal W.R. Trautman.

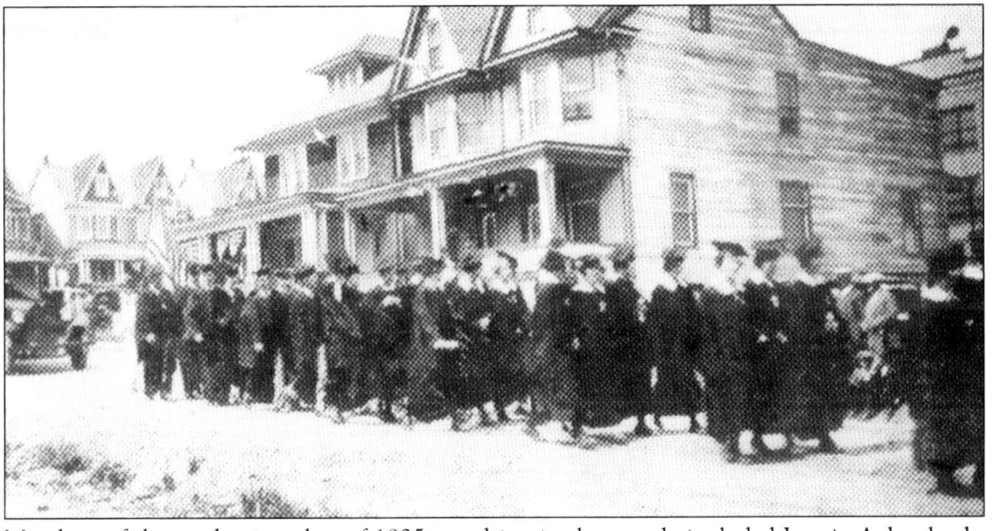

Members of the graduating class of 1925 marching in the parade included Jennie Achenbach, Elizabeth Atkins, Earl Berger, Arthur Birkelbach, Roberta Brosius, Lewis Burchill, Wilfred Coxen, Fred Craig, Elmer Dillman, Franklin Eyster, Sarah Eyster, Dorothy Gradwell, Elmer Hoffman, Grace Lindenmuth, Sylvia Maseritz, Tom McHale, William Moll, Thomas Morgan, Ada Moyer, John Moyer, Orval Palegrove, Millicent Parfitt, May Peterson, Harriet Phillips, May Reed, Mildred Reed, Alberta Semrod, Frances Timmins, Roy Wertz, Earl White, Elizabeth Williams, Lois Wonn, Alma Wood, and Marion Dillman.

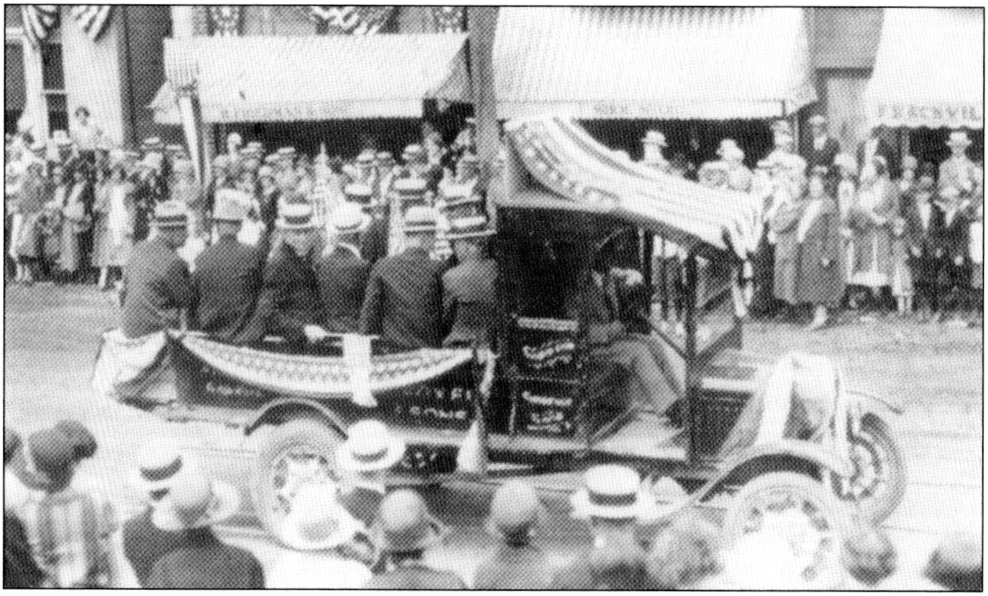

The Class of 1864 with teacher, H.D. Berkheiser, rode in the Washington School dedication parade in May 1925. Mr. Berkheiser laid the cornerstone of the building during the services held that afternoon.

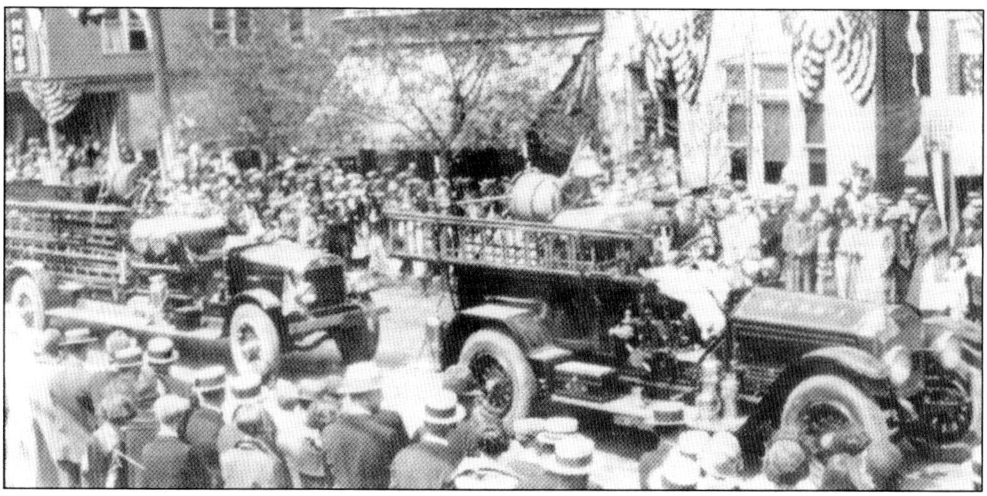

The Goodwill Hose Company paraded in the Washington School dedication in May 1925. They were first organized in October 1910 after a citizens' meeting was held in Shadel's Hall on Mahanoy Avenue. In 1911 the company assumed occupation of the Goodwill Hose Company on East Oak Street. This building was erected by the Frackville Borough Council.

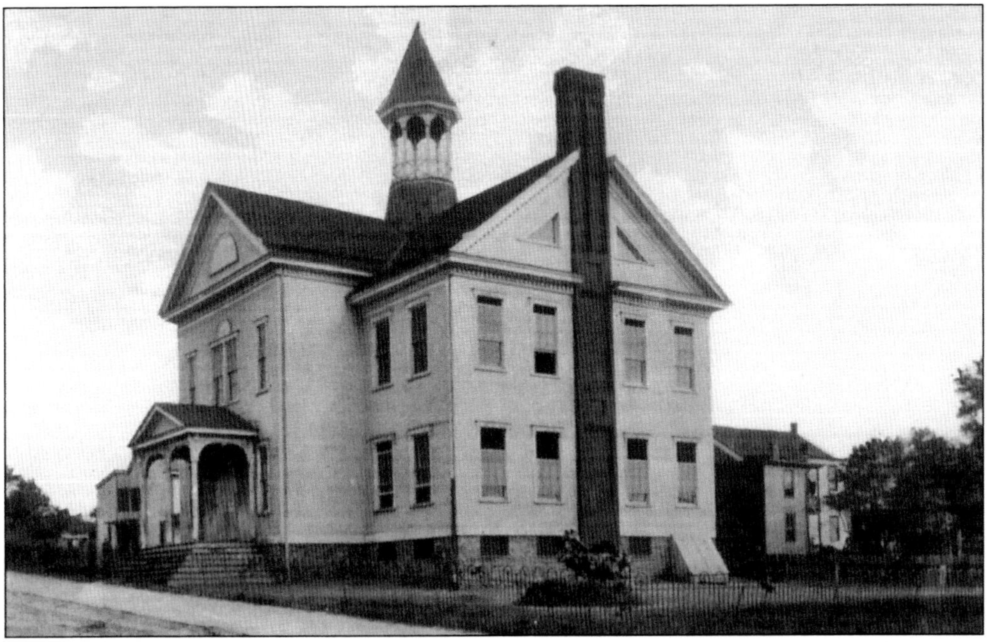

On March 29, 1893, two lots of ground were purchased from Samuel Parfitt for $1,000 to erect the East Side School. The contractor for the building (which cost $5,640) was P.J. O'Neill of Port Carbon. In 1925 the school was renamed the Franklin School, and the annex was added in 1918.

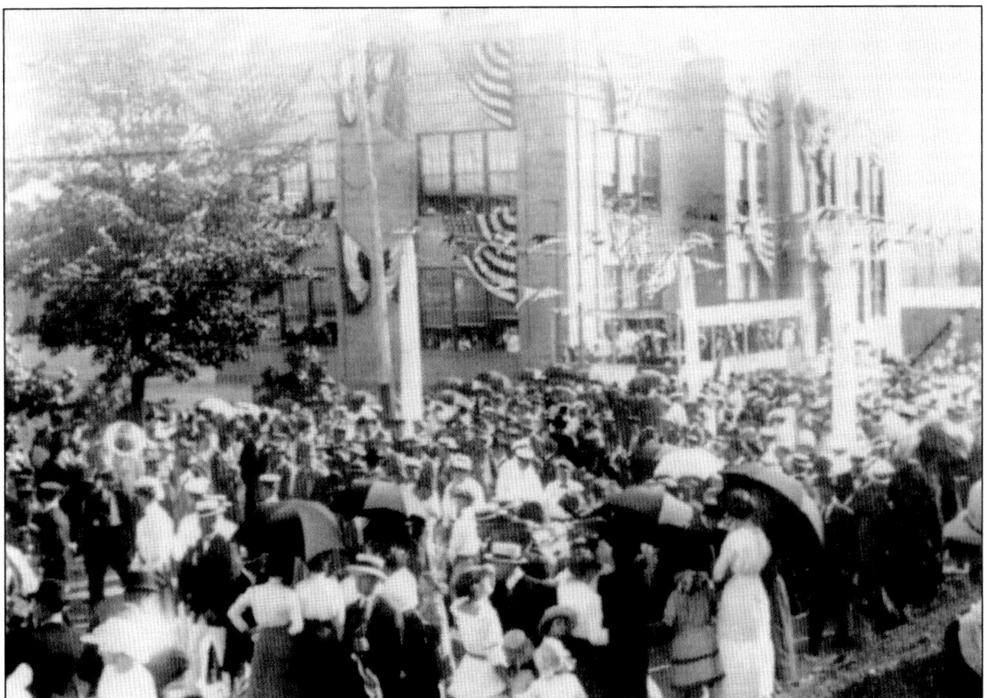

This was the scene at the dedication of the Frack Street School on May 30, 1914. It had fourteen classrooms, and the name was changed to the Lincoln School in 1925.

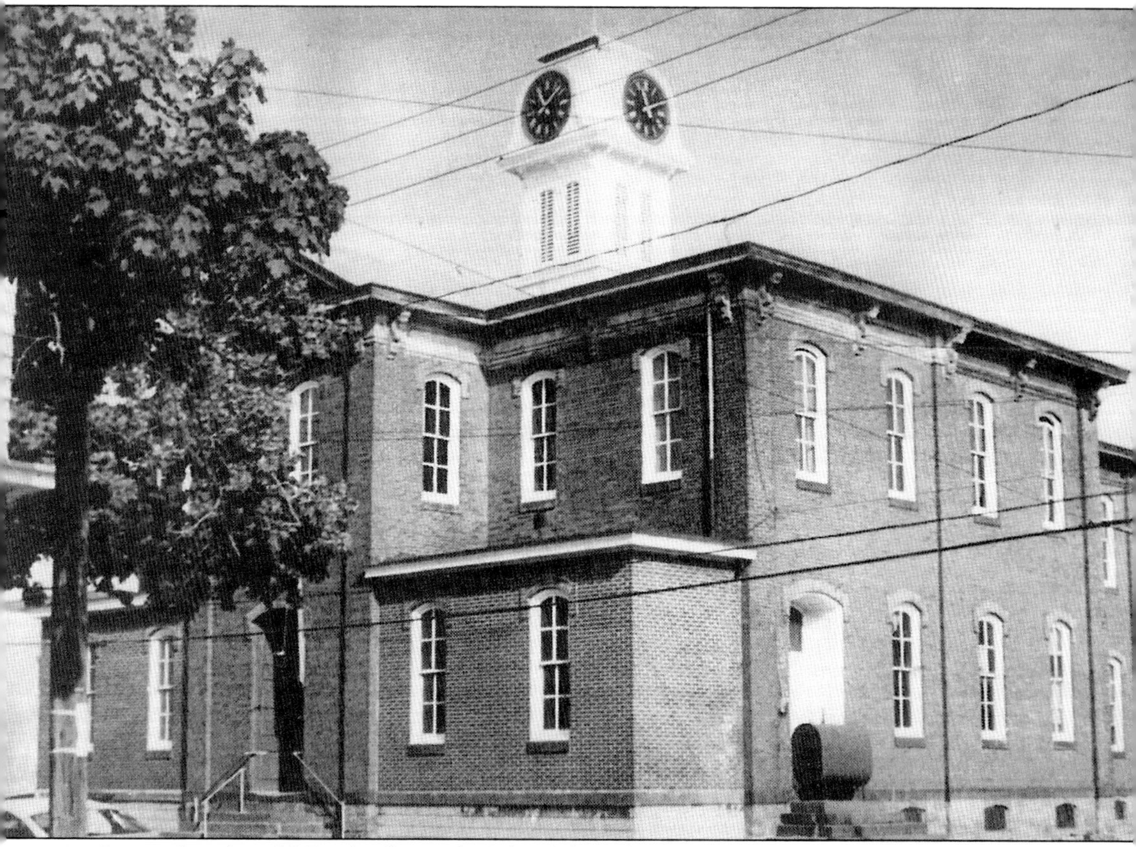

Pictured is the old Frackville High School, later known as the Roosevelt School and more popularly known as the Town Clock School. In 1886 there were 508 scholars and six teachers in the school system. On May 5, 1886, Mr. Seaman made a motion to build a good and solid, six-room building with a stone foundation and steam heat, which was the beginning of the plans for a new school. The building was built by John D. Evans of Shenandoah at a cost of $11,400 and was completed on September 6, 1888. The Borough Council presented the clock as a gift to the school, and the wooden casing around the clock was built by Peter S. Klinger of South Lehigh Avenue. The school was demolished in 1986, and a Medical Arts Building is now located there.

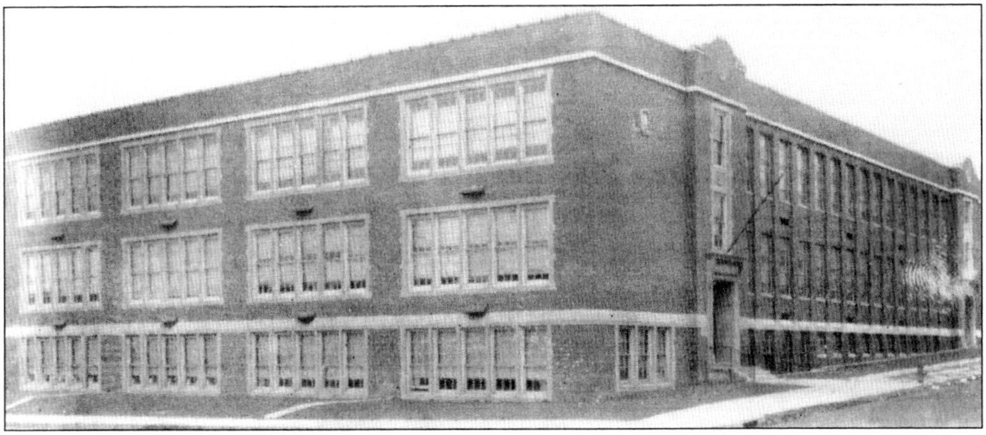

The Washington School was dedicated on May 30, 1925. A parade was held, and one thousand four hundred and forty-four 8" x 12" flags were bought for the schoolchildren to carry in this parade. Grace Madara, Viola Hoffman, Beatrice Knopf, Kathryn Moyer, Esther Taylor, and Harold Speidel were elected to the faculty.

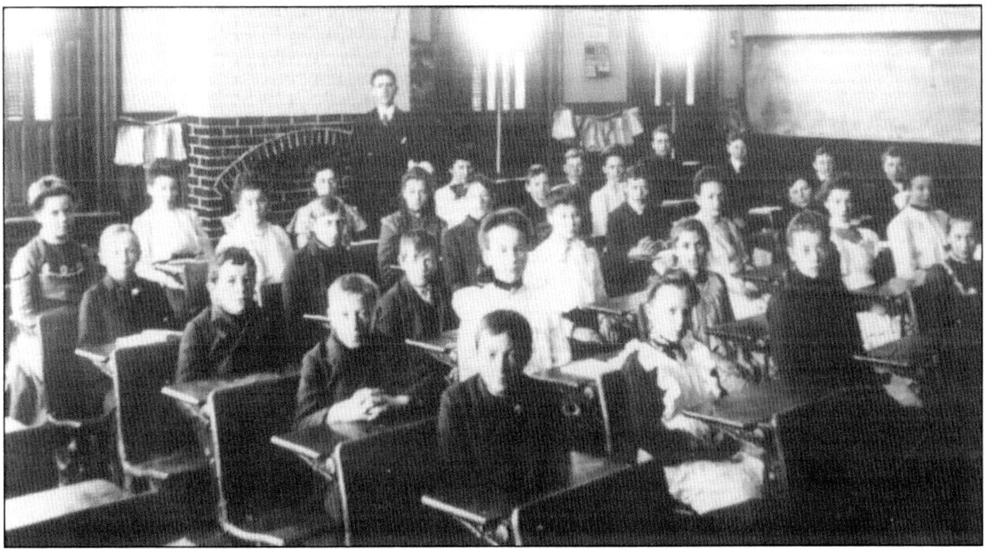

Sam Moyer was supervisor of the carpenters of the Franklin School in 1893. Some of the carpenters were John Hartenstine, David Lloyd, Eugene McGovern, J.H. Haupt, and Ben Bretz. Herb Ranck was the painter, Morris Heckman built the chimney, and Charles and James Leibeg did the plastering. Pictured is teacher W.R. Trautman with his class at the Franklin School.

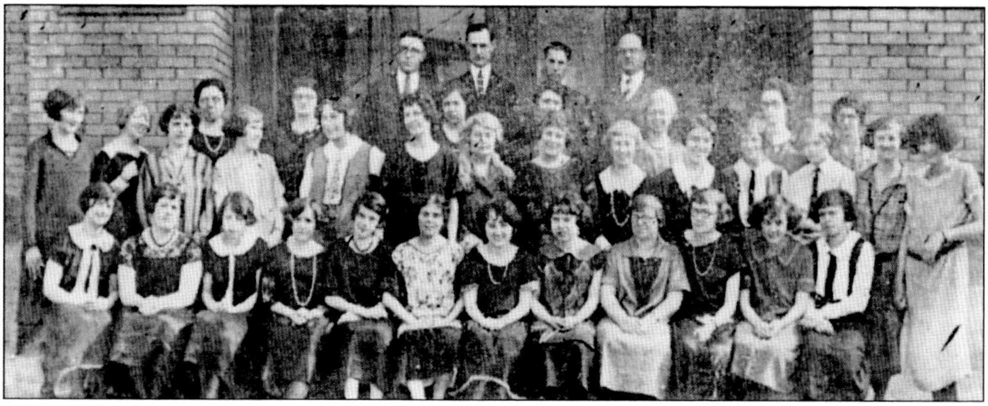

The Frackville School District teaching corps in 1925 included, from left to right: (first row) Sara Reed Farley, Grace Madara Trautman, Viola Hoffman, Arminta Handelong, Pauline Fennelly, Eliz. Schaeffer, Gladys Taylor Haldeman, Helen Price Segnar, Martha Heywood, Myrtle Purnell, Emily Williams Haldeman, and Olive Kimmel Phillips; (second row) Mary Connelly, Gladys Roberts Haupt, Esther Burchill, Grace Burchill, Grace Wonn, Ivy Kershener, Alice Burns, Elva Berger Hoffsommer, Mia Frew, Dorothy Guy Campbell, Edna Bailey Dando, Alice R. Morgan, Frances Gotschall, and Blanche Williams; (third row) Jane Dingle, Gladys Leddicoat, Edith Rosser Speidel, Lettie Clark, Lillian M. Beard, Edith Hampton, and Verna Hampton; (top row) Principal Charles Drumm, Ross Rhine, Rolin Kline, and W.R. Trautman.

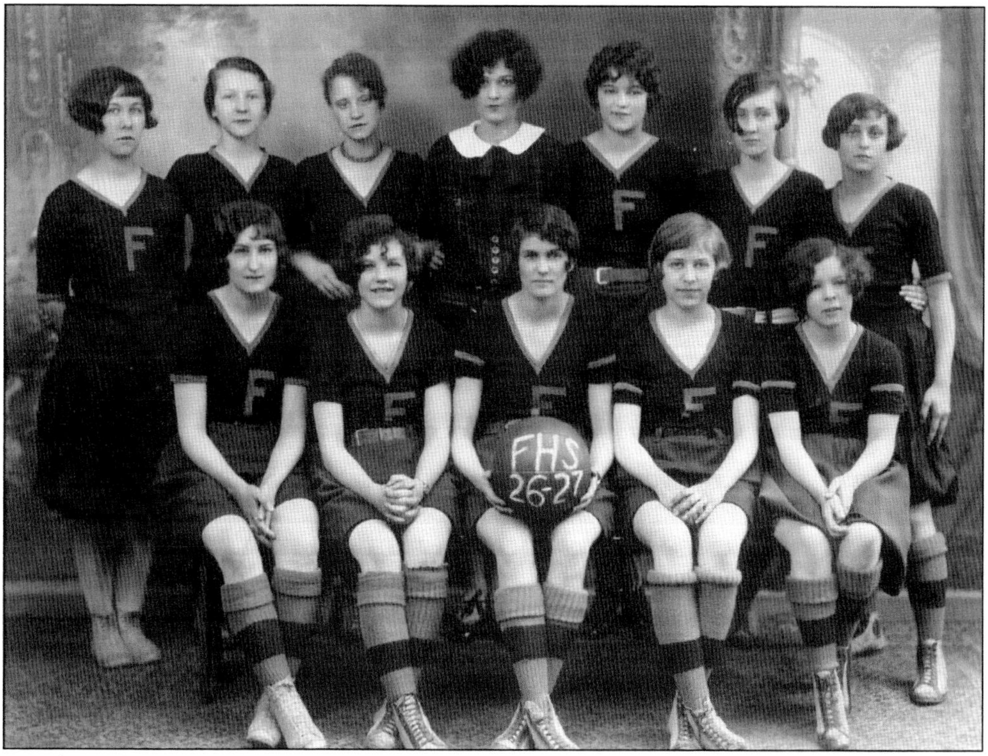

Members of the FHS 1926/27 girls' basketball team included, from left to right, the following: (front row) Hazel Jones, Marge Cope, Annabelle Foltz, Ruth Beddow, and Ruth Habel; (back row) Ruth Wagner, Nellie Povalitis, Jean Taggert, Blanche Williams (coach), Connie Picklinge, Jean Connelly, and Ann Konopka.

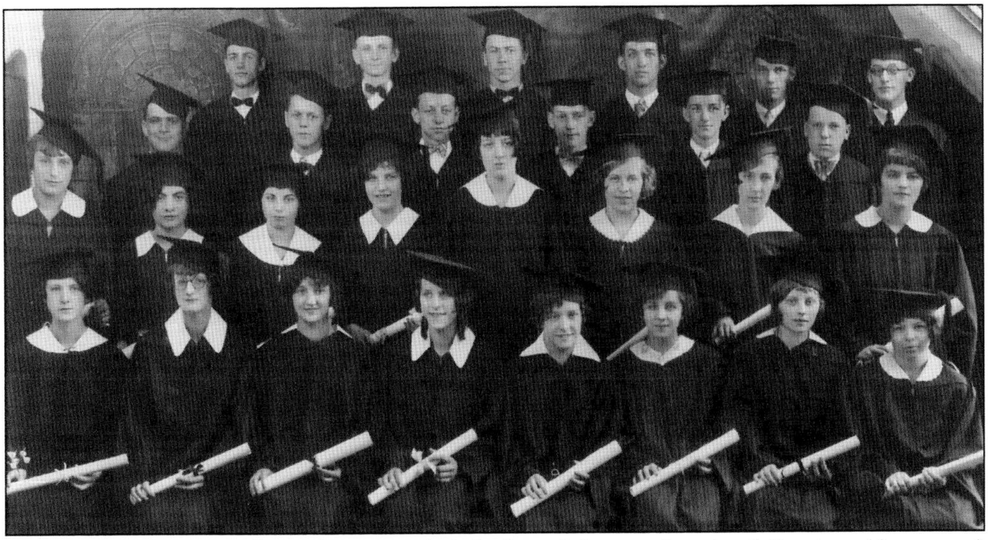

Students in the FHS class of 1928 included, from left to right, the following: (front row) Margaret Wagner, Catherine Sebold, Susan Walesky, Helen Milutis, Marion Witter, Dorothy Pierce, Anna Grish, and Ruth Habel; (second row) Stella Pascavage, Dora Friedman, Mary Brunner, Marge Cope, Ruth Williams, Ruth Beddow, Jean Connelly, and Connie Picklinge; (third row) David Richards, Michael Kryba, George Hoffman, Calvin Grafton, Edgar Davies, and Willis Williams; (top row) Robert Garret, Wilbur Gough, John Muscalus, Connie Guditas, Warren Guy, and Francis Dampman.

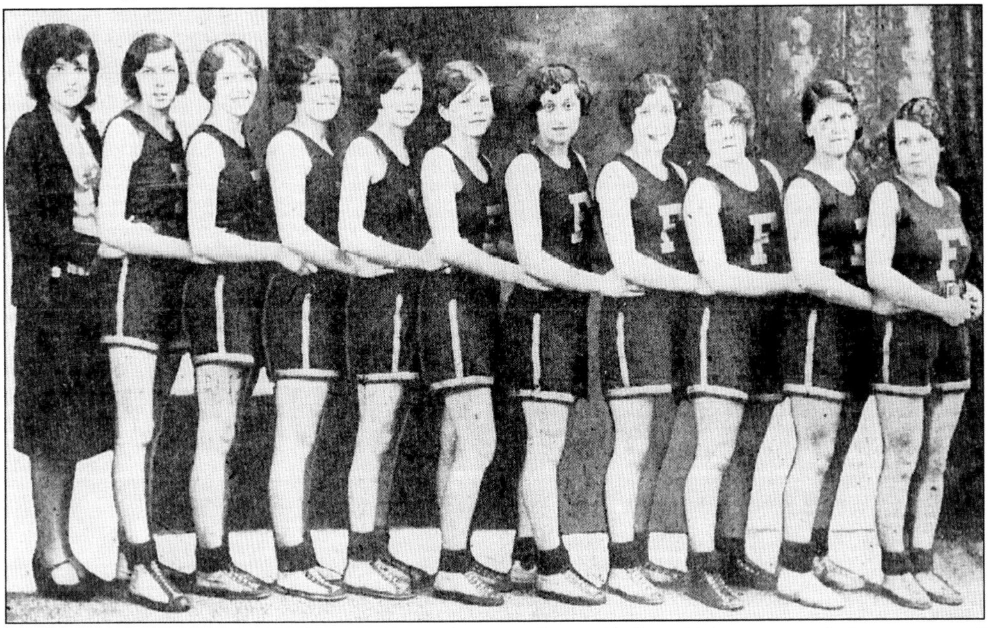

These Frackville lasses were champs in 1930, when they rolled up 442 points to their opponents' 92 points in eleven games. In March 1930, a special train was engaged to take the team and all their fans to the game in Philadelphia. Young women pictured are, from left to right, as follows: Blanche Williams, Helen Miller, Nellie Povilaitis, Elma Henry, Helen Shirey, Blanche Timmins, Anna Konopka, Josephine Povilaitis, Kazymere Karuktis, Josephine Walters, and Anna Coveluskie.

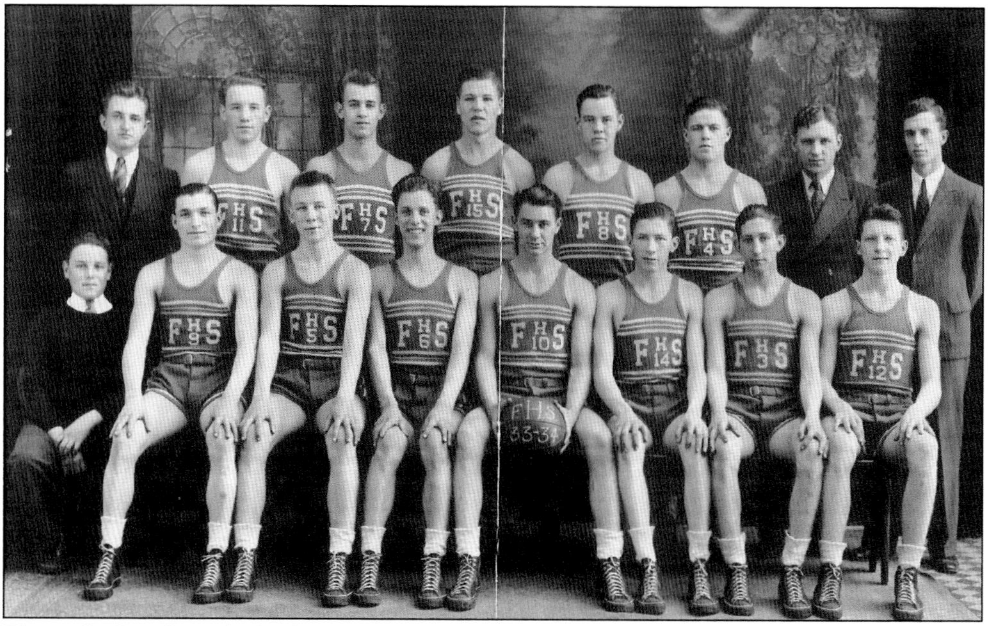

This is the FHS boys' basketball team of 1933/34. Team members pictured are, from left to right, as follows: (first row) Bob Hoppes (manager), Frank Hreshko, John Pilconis, Peter Haberle, Walter Wasilewskie, Charles Caton, Cyril Copeland, and George Povilaites; (second row) Bob Reese (manager), Stanley Slovak, Walter Heim, Joseph Pakenas, Ted Burchill, Lee McGeough, Charles Dunkleberger (coach), and Chester Timmins (faculty manager).

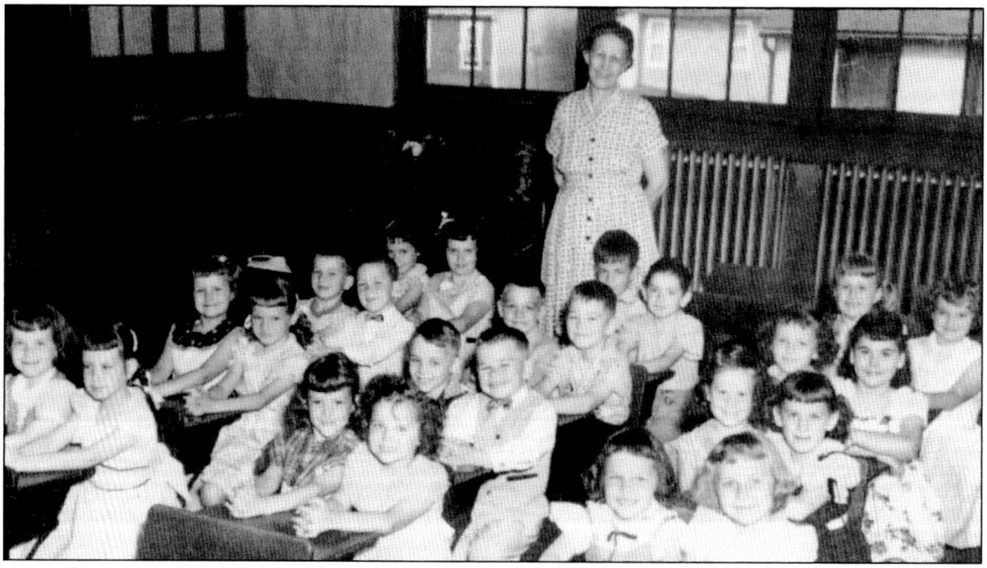

The first grade class in 1954 at the Lincoln School was the last taught by Mrs. Ivy Kershner. Classmates are, from left to right, as follows: (first row) Ruth Craig, Judy Snyder, Helen Berg, Joanne Troyanoski, Linda Luckey, and Florence Prock; (second row) Sandra Fellows, Linda Rupp, Lynn Luckey, Robert Runkle, Josephine Paisley, and Lynn Thomas; (third row) John Zaylskus, Robert Wagner, David Boyer, Lester Harter, Sonia Yastishok, and Patricia Powanda; (fourth row) Sandra Tatusko, Carol Mekailek, Thomas Williams, Charles Yeager, Linda Lash, and Winifred Etherington.

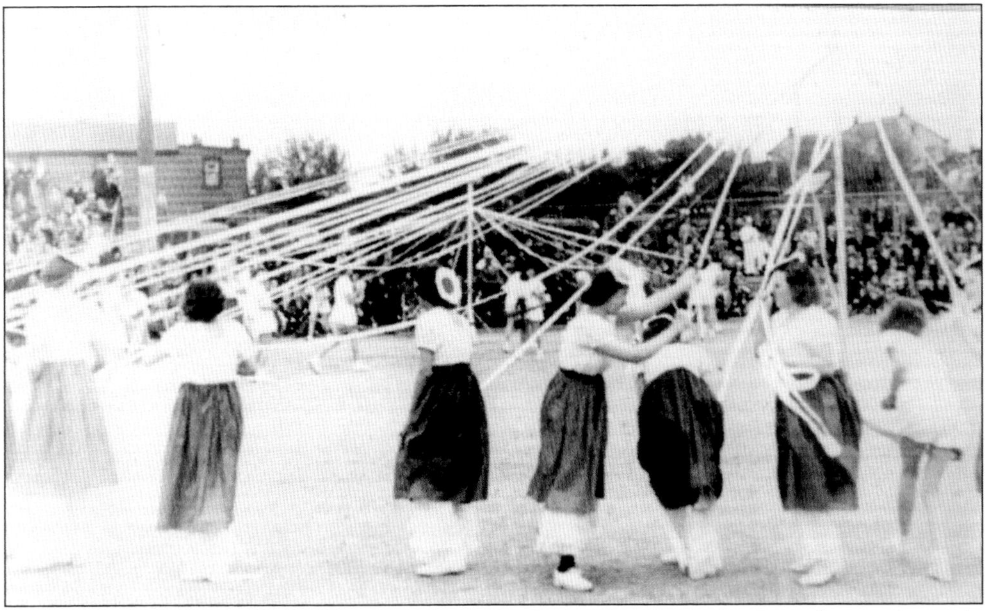

The second annual May Day festivities were held on May 18, 1938. Five thousand people witnessed this grand May gathering, and all grades participated in this Mother Goose story. There were eleven maypoles and the older students, dressed in pink and white costumes, danced around each one.

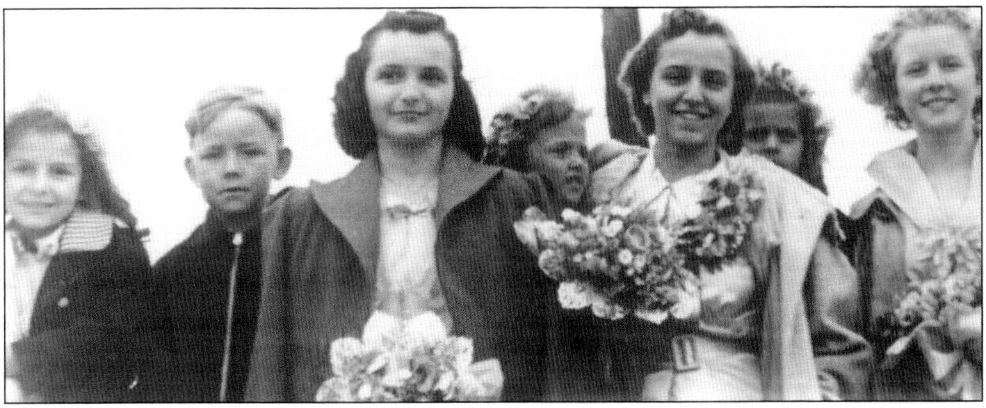

At the May Day festivities held on May 18, 1938, princesses Betty Klitch (center) and Marie Stec (far right) were in the queen's court.

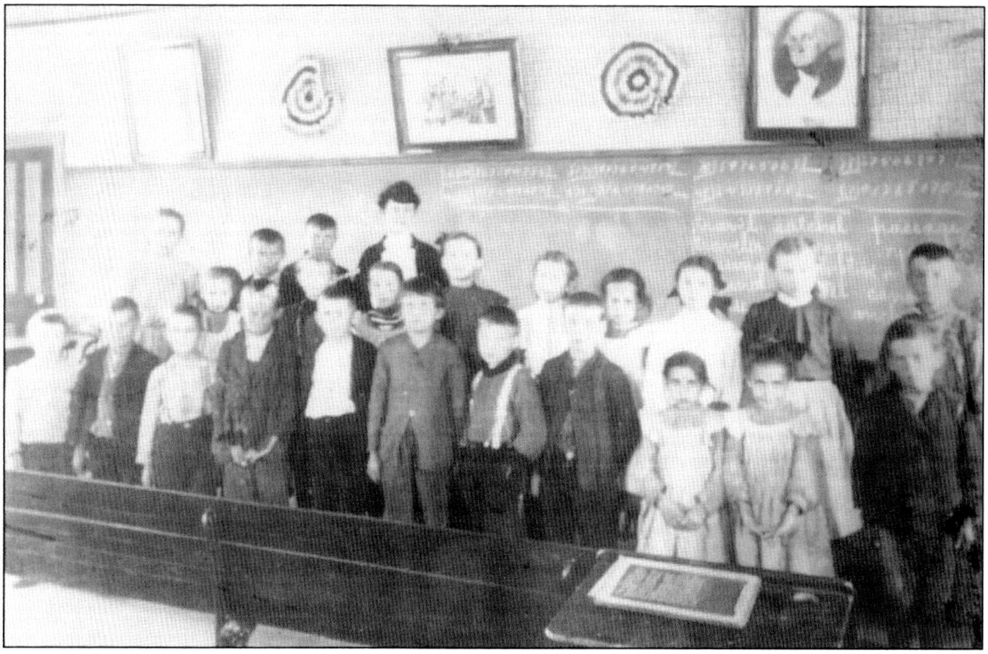

Pictured is a schoolroom of long ago in Frackville. Note the recitation seat in the front of the room where scholars were seated while awaiting their turn for recitations, while the remainder of the class stayed at their desks. Also note the slates on the desks.

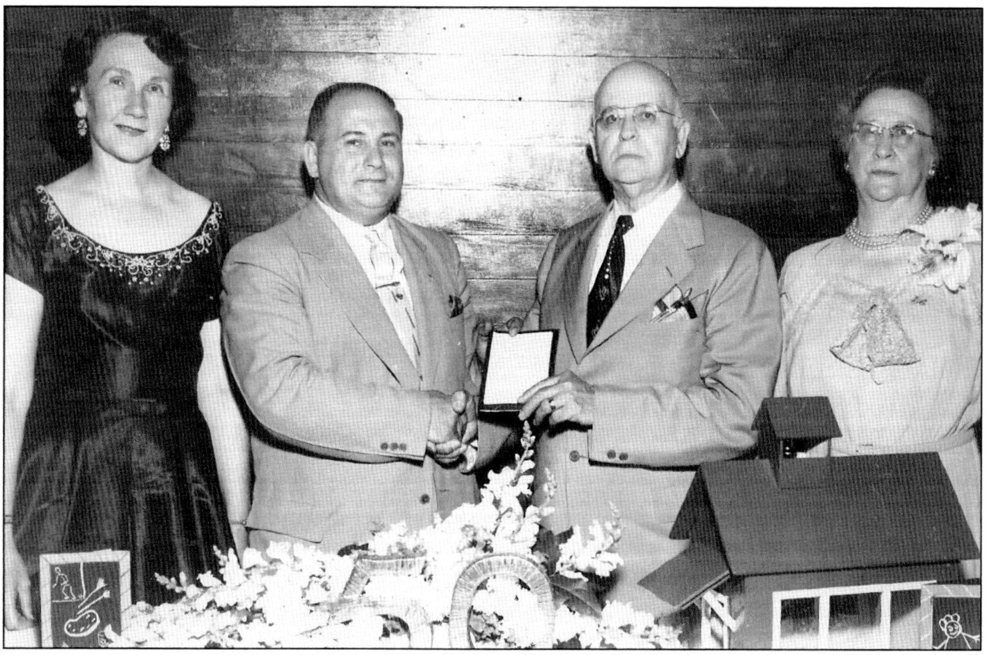

William R. Trautman, Frackville school head, retired after fifty years of service and is shown being honored at a dinner of the Teacher's Association in May 1953. He is the second person from the right, receiving his certificates for a lounge chair and life membership in the Retired Teachers Association from Franklin Wolfe, the head of the teachers' group. Looking on are Mary Connelly (at left) and Mrs. Trautman (at right).

Four

Earning a Living

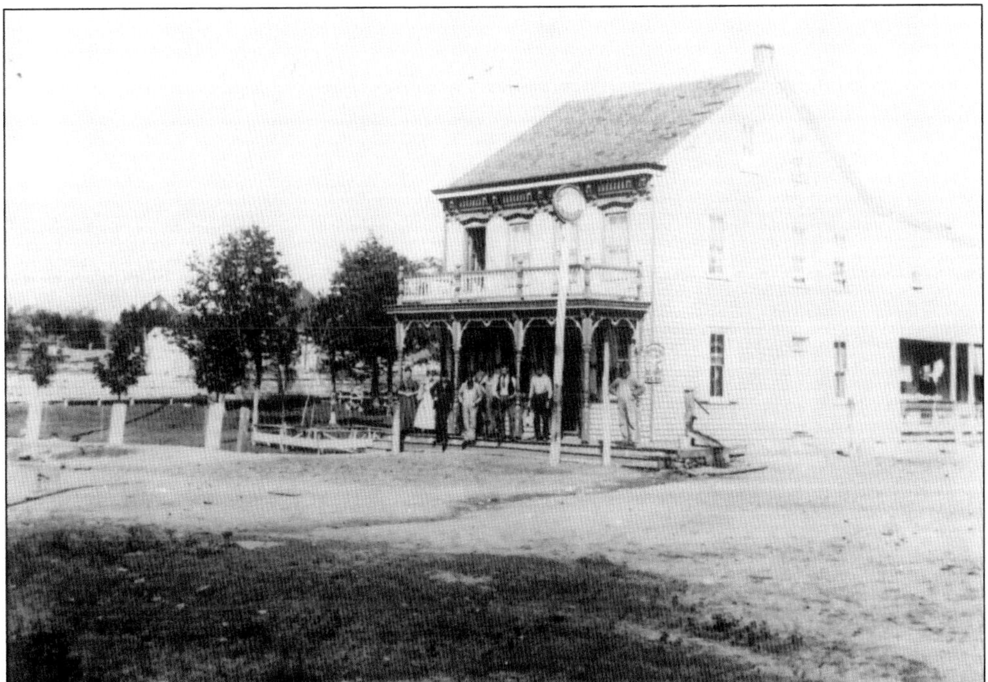

The Valley House was a Frackville hostelry located at 405 South Lehigh Avenue in 1892. Pictured are, from left to right, Mrs. S.A. Rauch (owner), Lizzie Rauch, Chick Bachman, Hiram Newman, Jacob Pauly, William Rauch, Harry Hostler, and Daniel Kramer. The Dutch Kitchen is now located here.

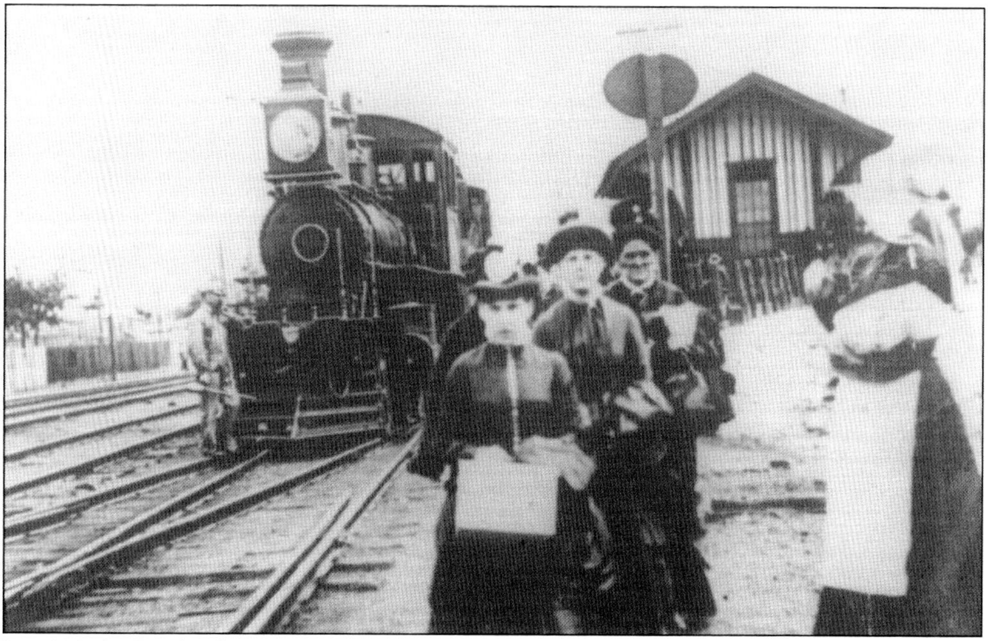

In 1888 the Frackville Passenger Station was a busy place. Since few residents had cars, they traveled by train. Harry Berkheiser Sr. was the ticket agent for many years, and Richard Davis was the telegraph operator. In 1925 a new brick station was erected on this site.

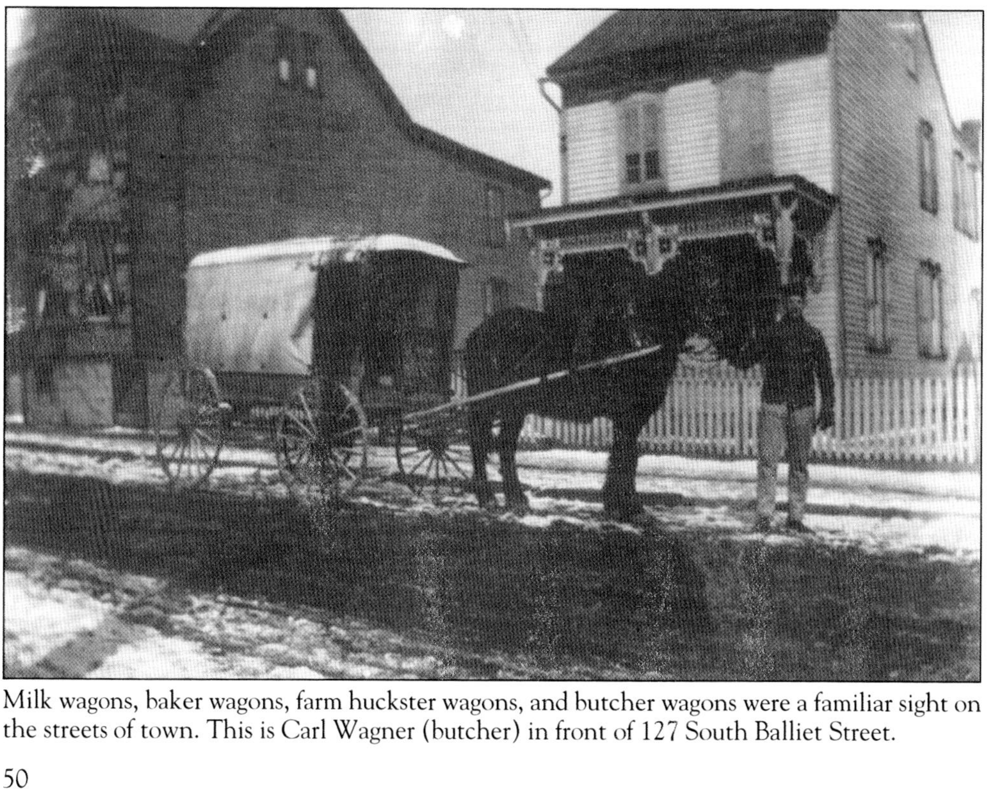

Milk wagons, baker wagons, farm huckster wagons, and butcher wagons were a familiar sight on the streets of town. This is Carl Wagner (butcher) in front of 127 South Balliet Street.

Pictured are John N. Pauly (center, bottom) and friends enjoying their favorite beverage, Yuengling beer. The Yuengling Brewery is the oldest brewery still in existence in the United States. Mr. Pauly was a beer and liquor agent at 23 South Lehigh Avenue from 1895 to 1926.

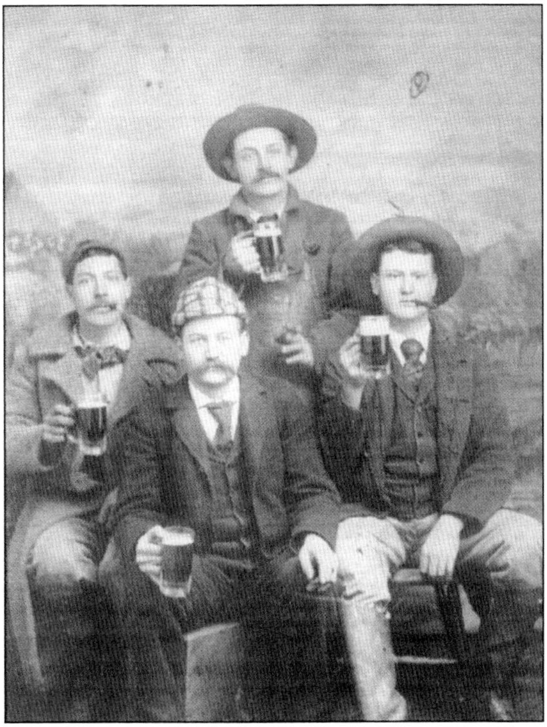

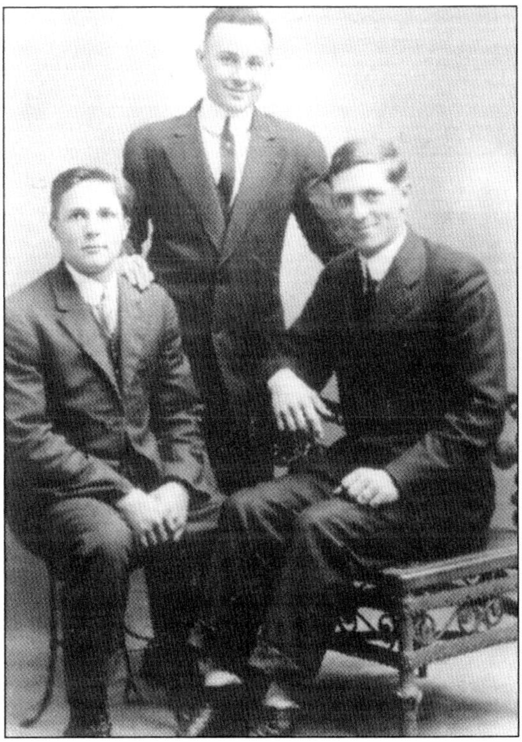

The year is 1916. Do you remember these men, from left to right: Clarence Brosius (local builder), L.K. Stoner (the Pottsville tile man), and George Sebold (local plumber)?

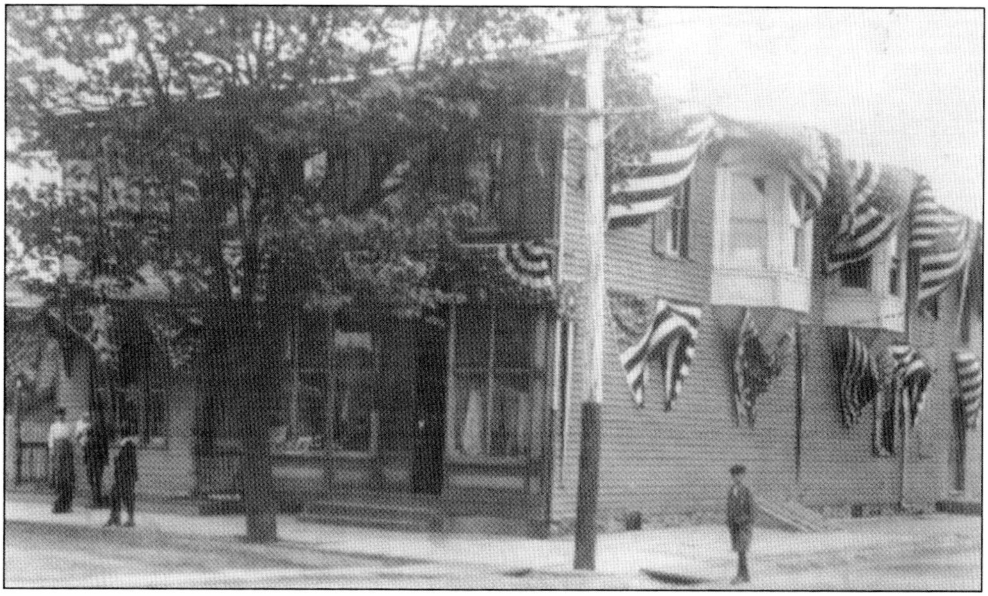

Do you remember Scott's General Store on the corner of Frack and Lehigh Avenue? This building was moved to the rear of the lot and is now the Law Building. Alex Scott is holding Caroline Dooling, who often shopped there with her mother, Mrs. Florence Caton. The First National Bank was built on this corner, but is now the CoreStates Bank.

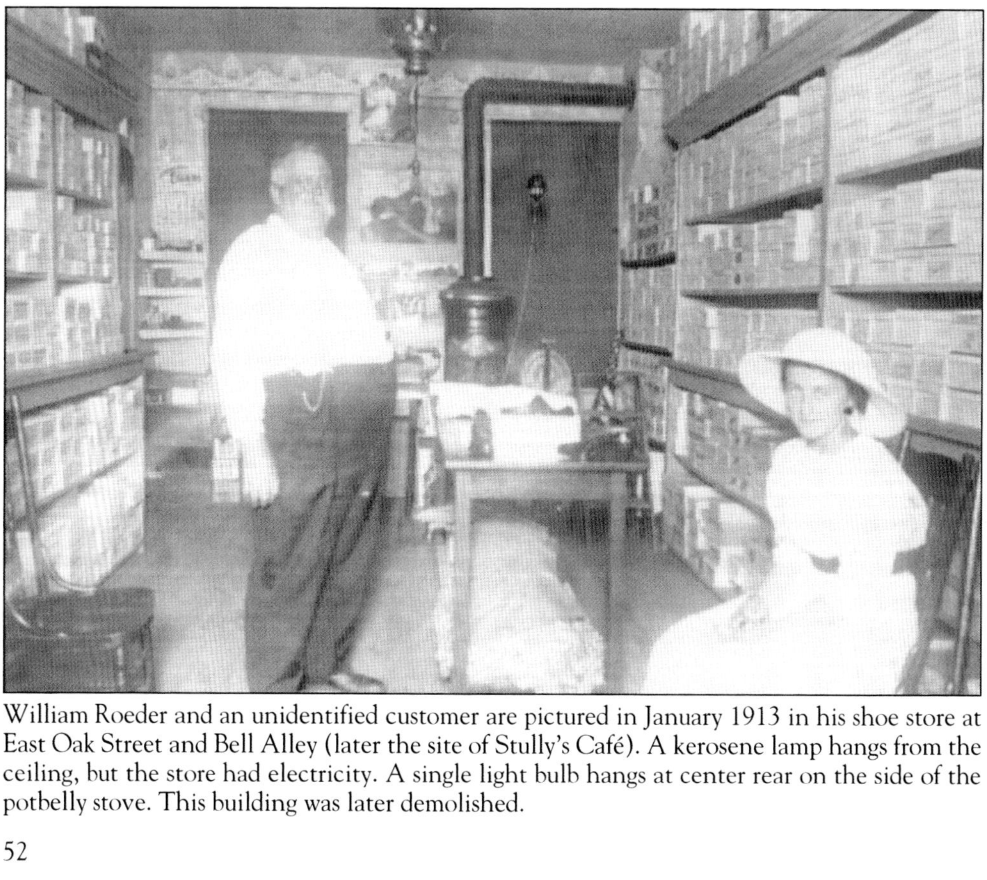

William Roeder and an unidentified customer are pictured in January 1913 in his shoe store at East Oak Street and Bell Alley (later the site of Stully's Café). A kerosene lamp hangs from the ceiling, but the store had electricity. A single light bulb hangs at center rear on the side of the potbelly stove. This building was later demolished.

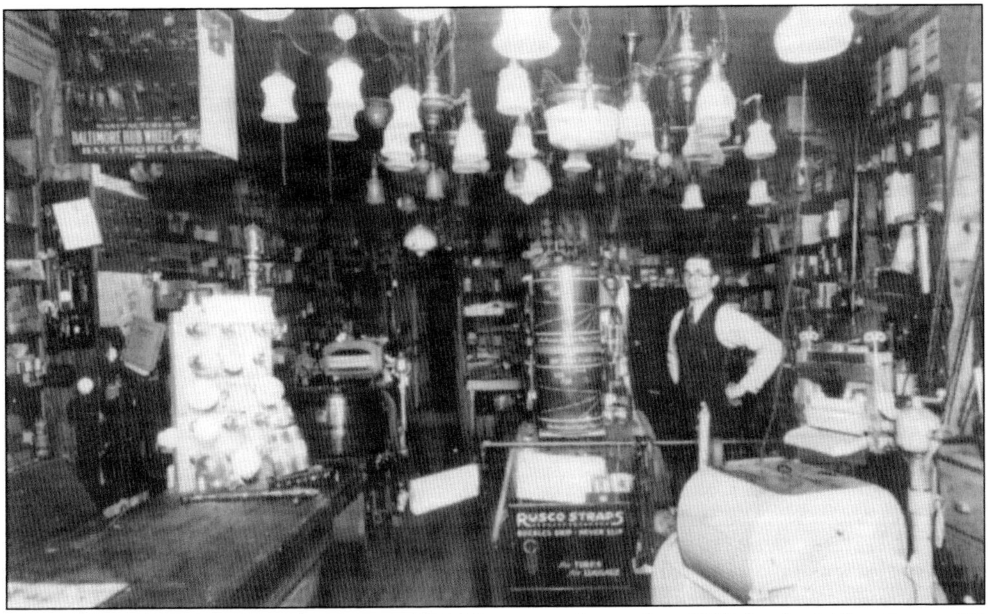

The Electrical Store owned by Gus and Ed Heine was located at 128 North Balliet Street. Ed conducted business in the store, and Gus did the furnace installation. At that time, the 200 caloric (hot air) furnace was popular.

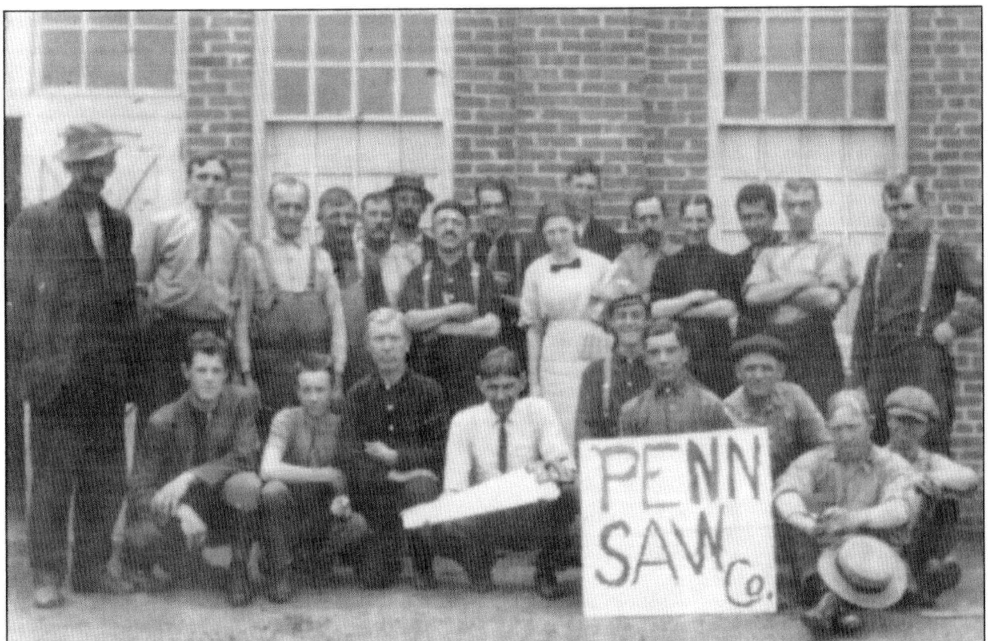

Workers at the Saw Factory are pictured here. Herbst Dellecker is at the lower left, and Sally Hicks (center) is the office clerk. Others are: Pat Murphy, Ralph Miller, William Reich, Charles Berger, George Bracey, Jim Richardson, Bill Griffiths, Elmer Koch, and James O'Neill.

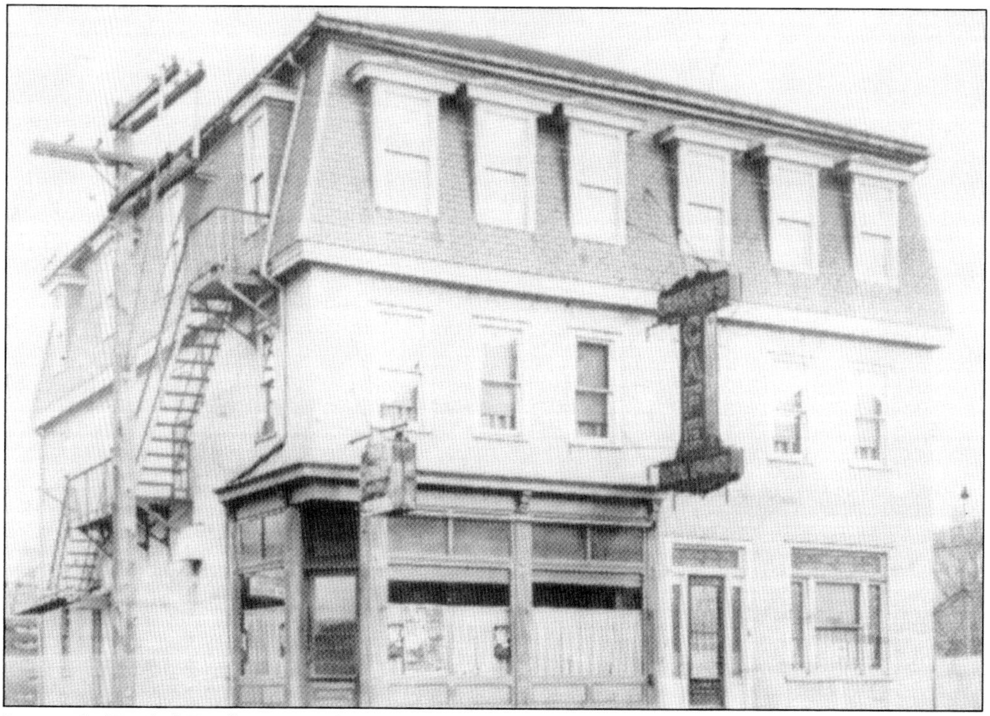

Jeremiah (Darby) Foulk operated this spot for many years as a hotel at 65 North Lehigh Avenue. Mr. Kirelawich bought the building in 1920, added the third story, and ran a hotel there until 1939. His son, Bill, became the operator until 1942, when he sold it to Charles O'Donnell. Today, it is the site of Giorgios.

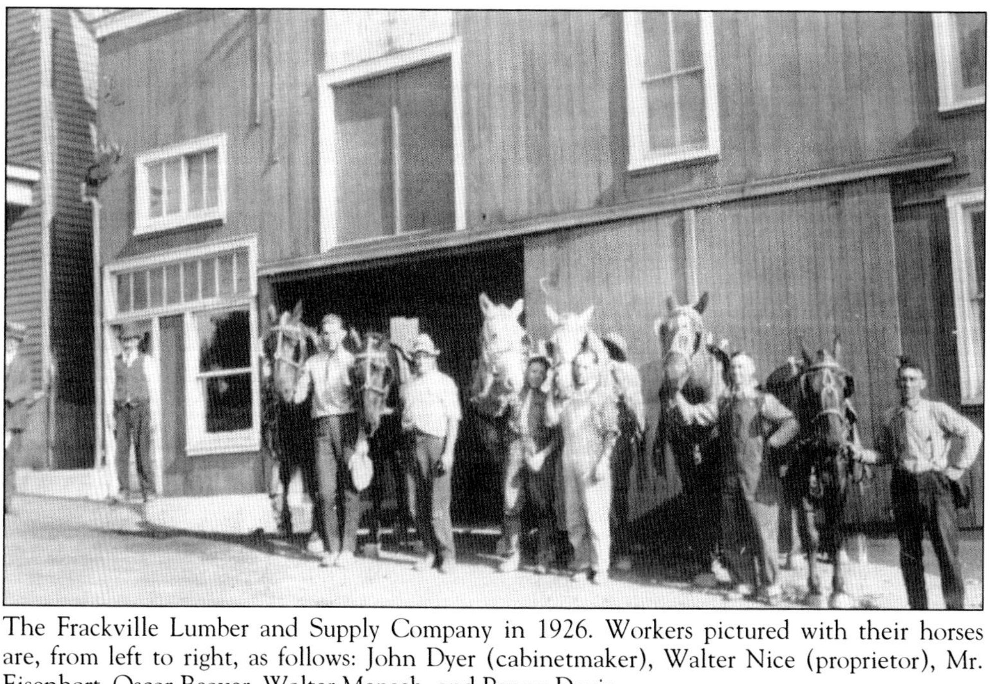

The Frackville Lumber and Supply Company in 1926. Workers pictured with their horses are, from left to right, as follows: John Dyer (cabinetmaker), Walter Nice (proprietor), Mr. Eisenhart, Oscar Beaver, Walter Mensch, and Penny Davis.

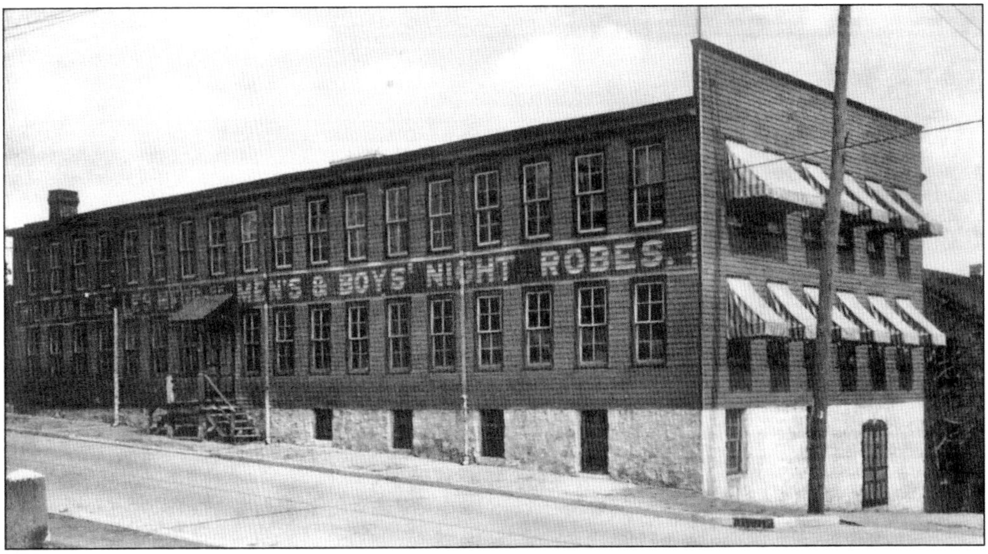

The William E. Bellas factory was located on West Oak Street. Men's and boys' robes were manufactured here and sent all over the world. Oscar Wagner was foreman on the first floor, and Mr. Reichley was foreman on the second floor. Mr. Bellas kept pigeons in the basement, and the building was heated by steam heat which was also used for the steam irons.

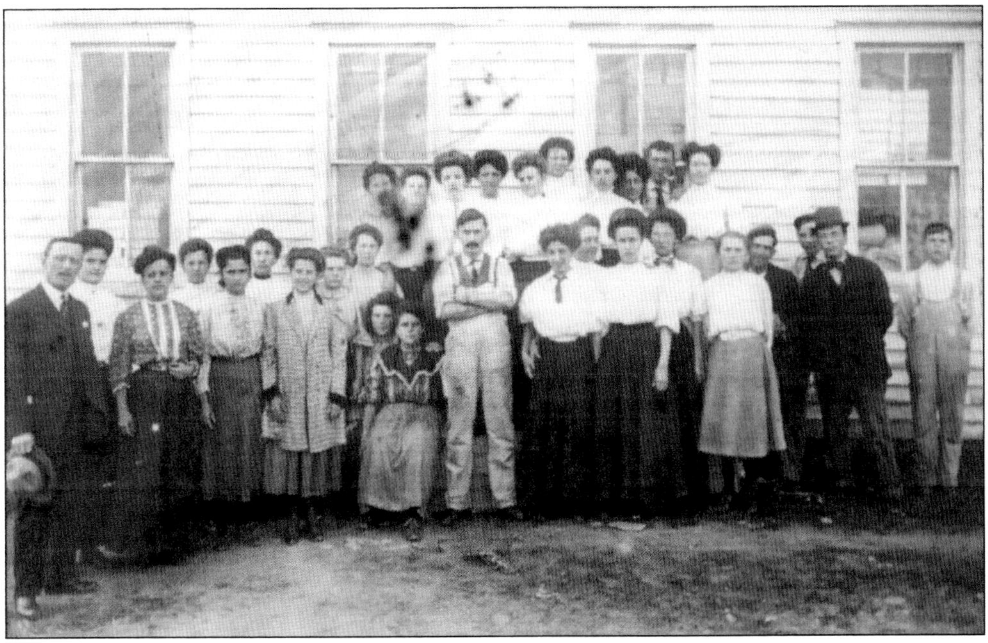

Pictured is William E. Bellas (far left), owner of the Bellas factory on West Oak Street, with his workers. Mr. Bellas was first listed in the Boyd's Directory of Businesses in 1919.

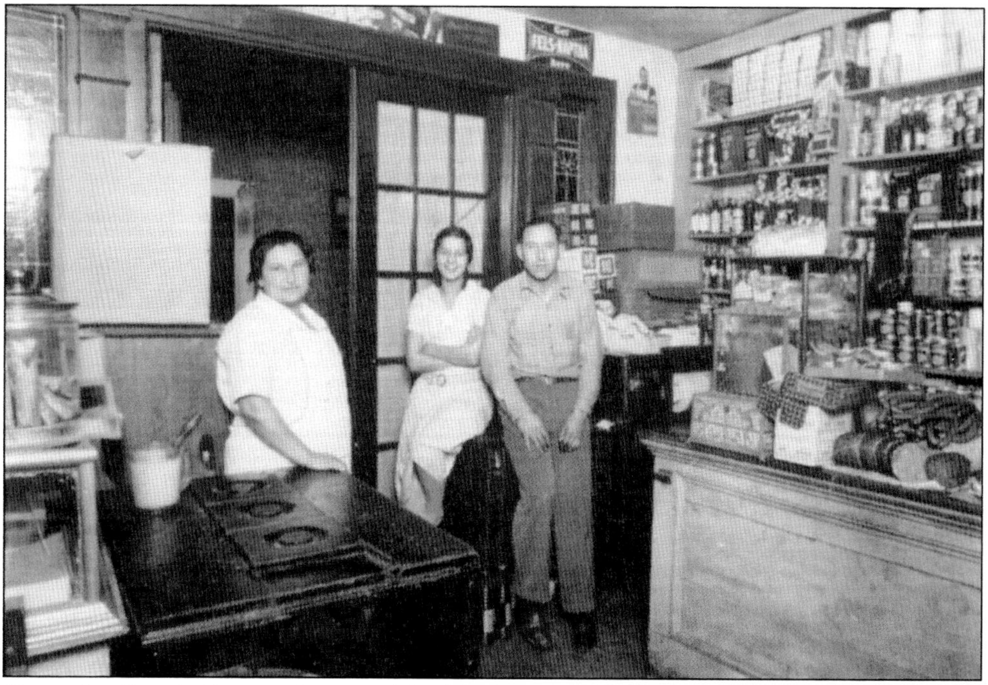

Pictured at Sarra's Grocery Store are Mrs. Theresa Sarra (left), Mary (her daughter), and Paul Squierdo (Mary's husband). Mrs. Sarra specialized in Italian items, and county people came to buy from her. Large blocks of Italian cheese, loose spaghetti sold by the pound, cheese freshly grated by Mr. Sarra, and Italian spaghetti sauce made and jarred by Mrs. Sarra were favorite shoppers' items.

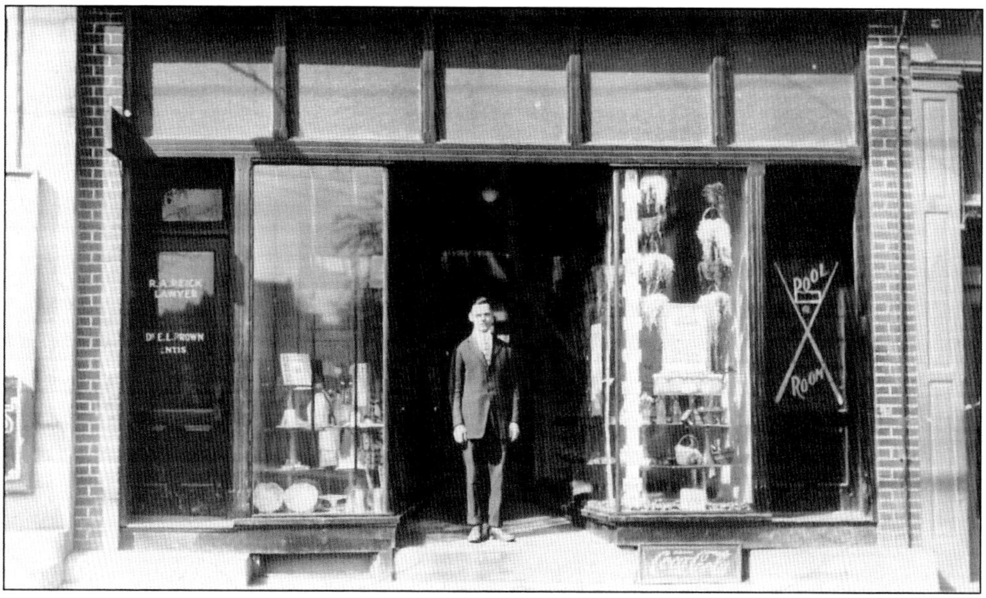

This 1925 photograph shows Alexander Polanchyck in front of his 5 & 10 at 60 North Lehigh Avenue. This store is remembered for the small mirror and comb holders made here, as well as the dances held in the basement hall. In 1938 the store moved to 44 South Lehigh Avenue and remains in the same family, with Russell Polanchyck as proprietor.

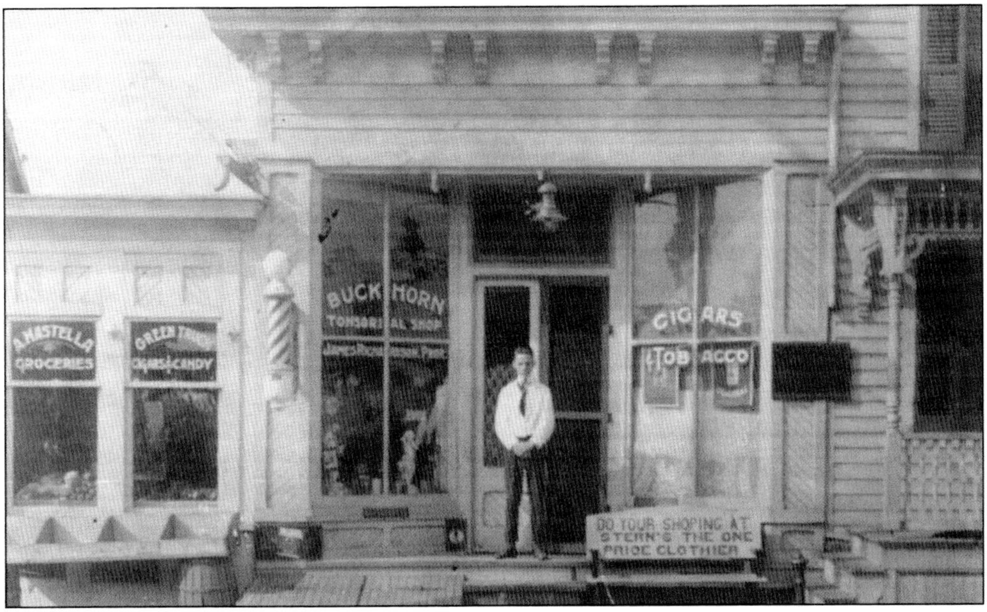

Jack Richardson's Buck Horn Tonsorial Shop is pictured in 1914. At left was Mastella's store, which sold groceries, cigars, and candy. The bench at right was sponsored by Stern's One Price Clothier. Roy Thomas is the gentleman in the photograph. These buildings were later dismantled, and the Alexander 5 & 10 is on the site.

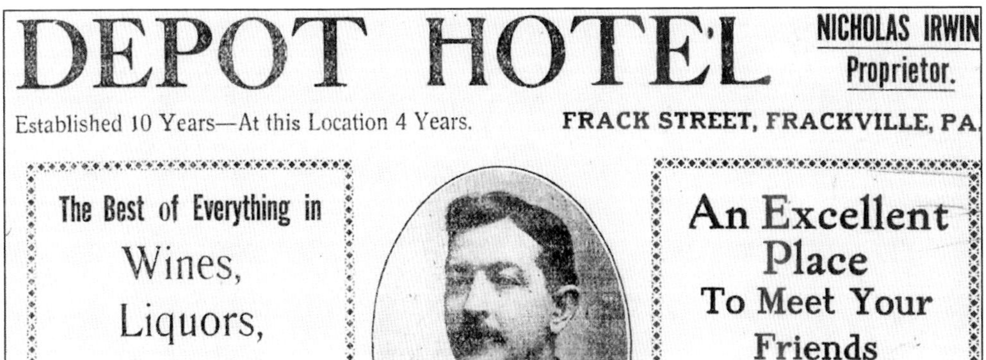

Do you remember the Depot Hotel on West Frack Street? The hotel was located to the rear of the Bohard building and has since been demolished. This advertisement appeared in the January 16, 1915 edition of the *Evening Herald*.

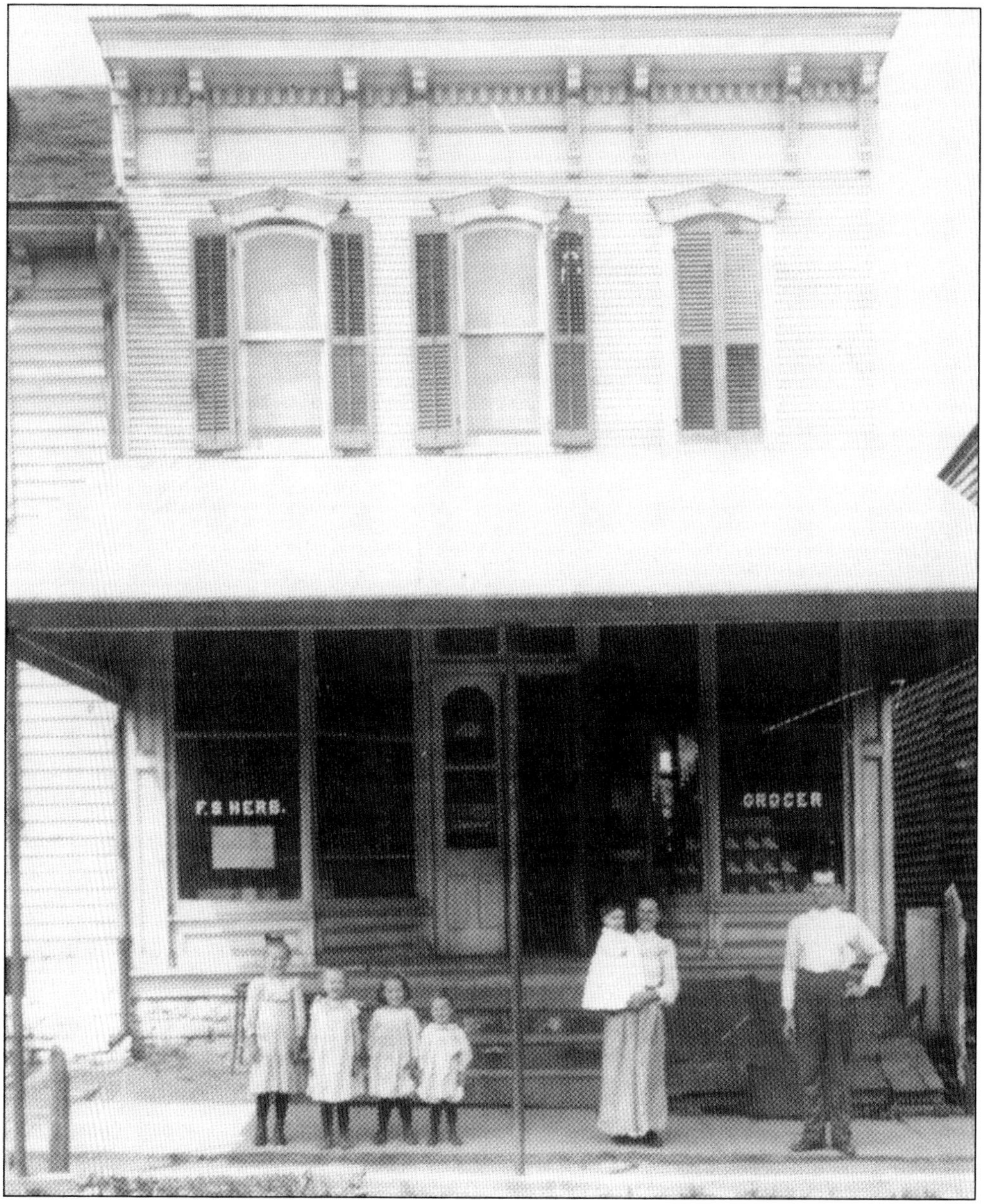

The F.S. Herb Green Grocery Store is shown in 1901 at 24 South Lehigh Avenue. Pictured, from left to right are the following: Pearl, Mae, Bessie, Jennie, Mrs. Frank Herb (holding Helen), and Mr. Frank Herb.

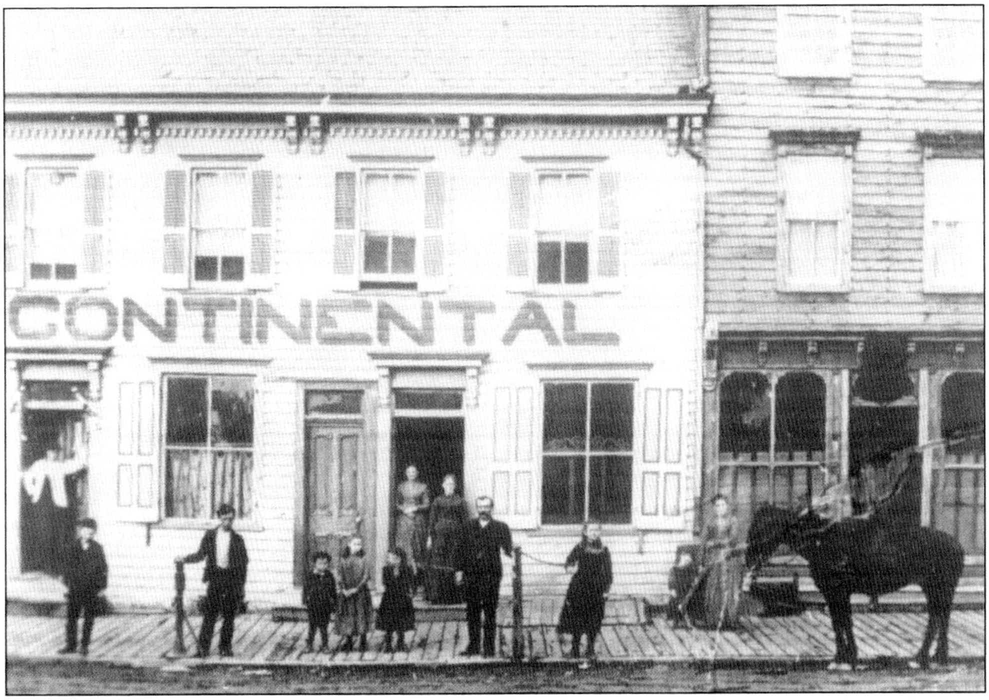

The Continental Hotel at 31–33 South Lehigh Avenue was built by John Shadel and added to by Philip Prynn, both husbands of Barbara (Hay) Shadel. Residents pictured are, from left to right, Harry, Robert, John, Philip, Bernetta, Jennie, Margaret Ann Shadel, Grandma Hay, Philip Prynn, Lillie Shadel, Silas Shadel, and Barbara Prynn. Note the water pump on left side, the hitching post in center and right side, and the sidewalk made of boards.

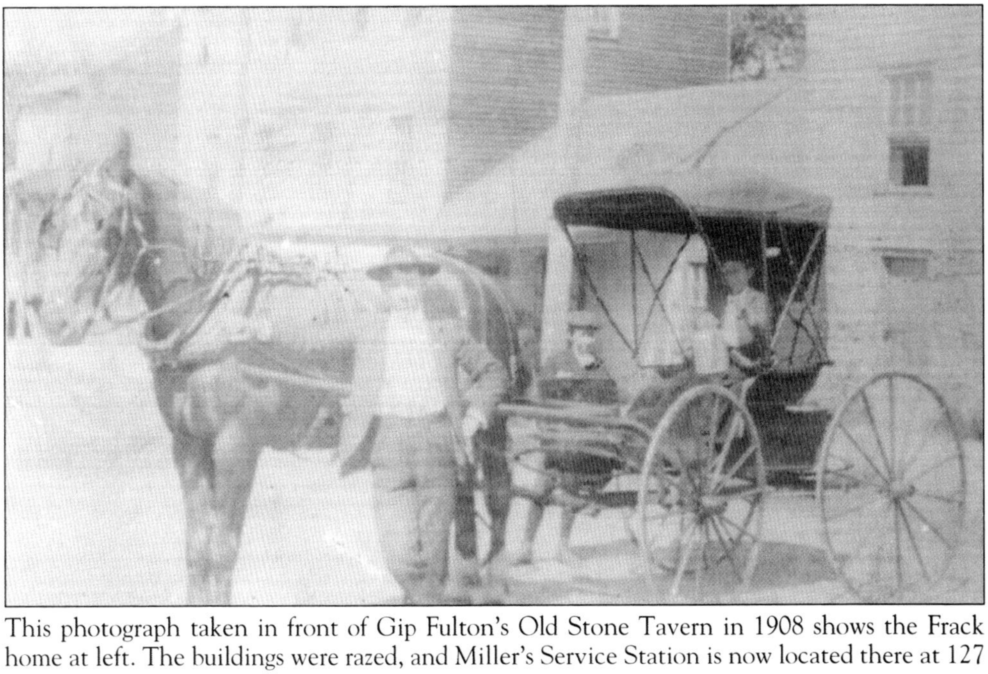

This photograph taken in front of Gip Fulton's Old Stone Tavern in 1908 shows the Frack home at left. The buildings were razed, and Miller's Service Station is now located there at 127 North Lehigh Avenue.

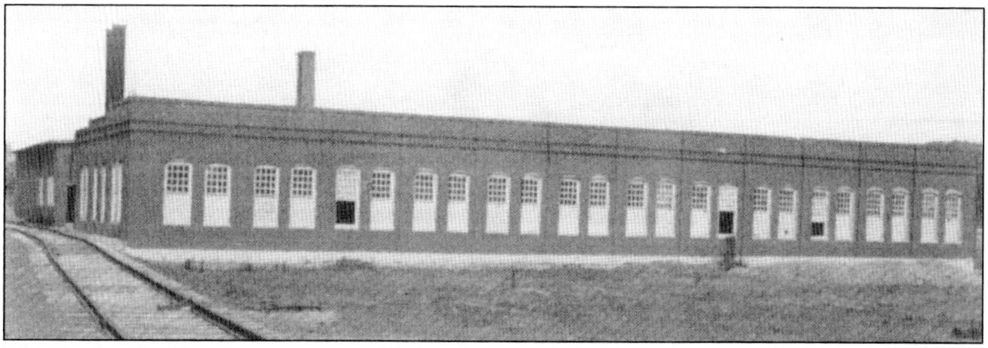

The Frackville Saw Factory on South Broad Mt. Avenue is where the Robbins Door and Sash Company was later located. When the building was dismantled, many residents used the bricks for their homes and garages. The plant made some of the best saws, and they shipped them all over the world.

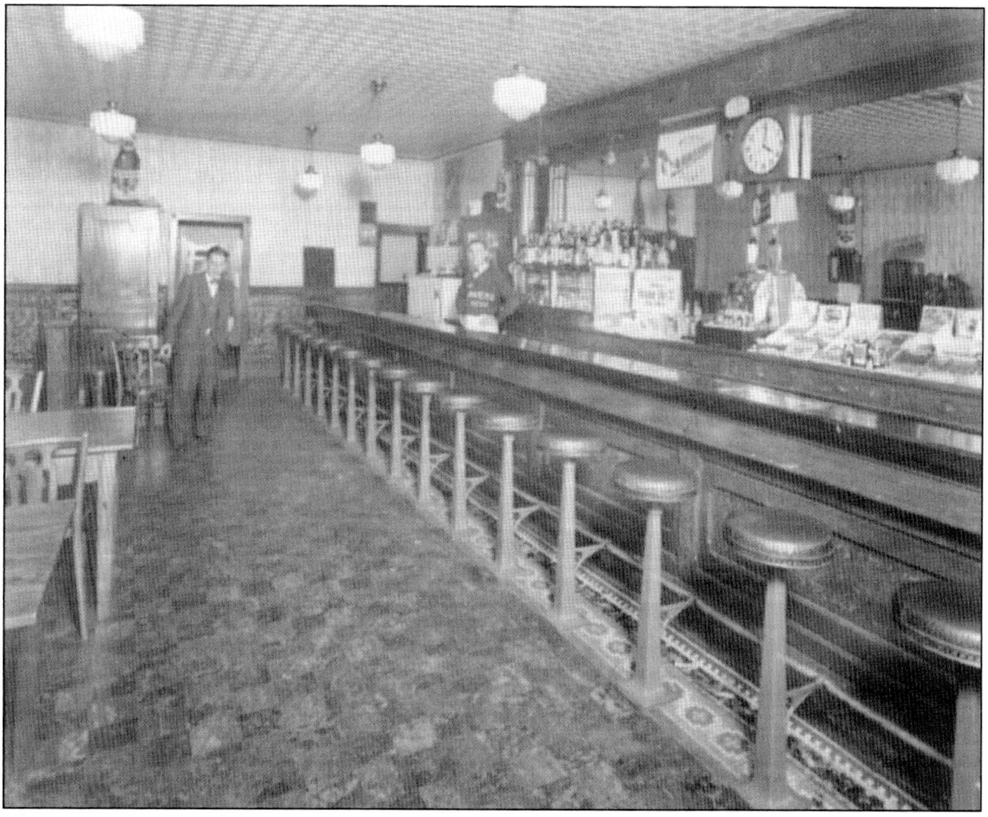

This 1934 photograph of the Charles Kirelawich Cafe, located at 64 North Nice Street, brings back many memories to the residents of town. Pictured are: Joe Kirelawich and a customer Bill White.

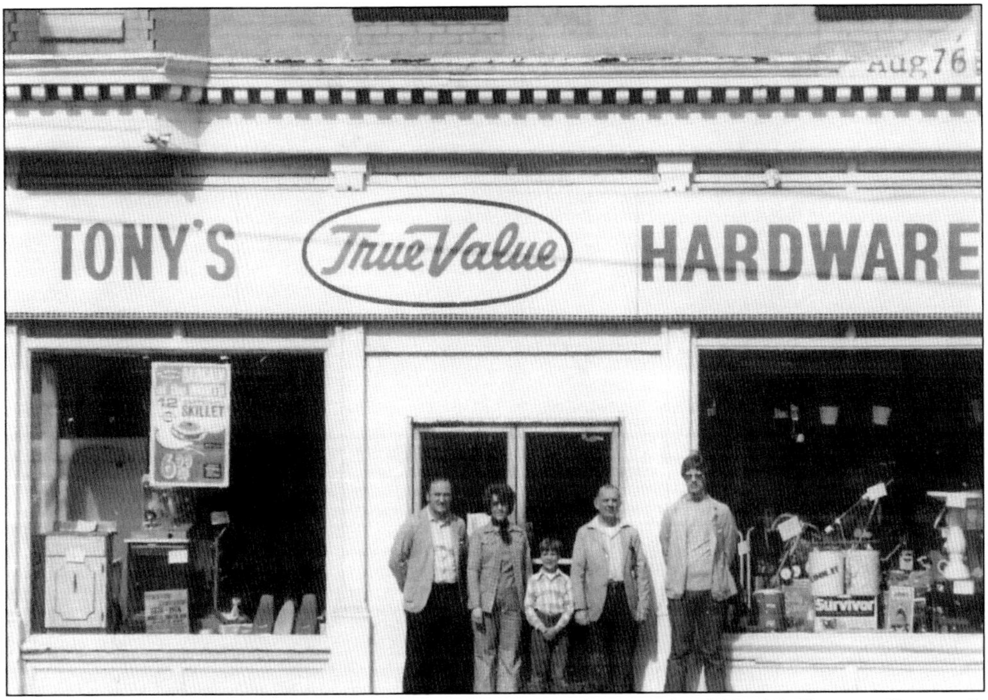

Tony's True Value Hardware Store is pictured in 1976. This was the Alfred S. Seaman Drygoods Store in 1904 and was later owned by the Madeira Hill Company and then by the Veterans of Foreign Wars. Pictured are, from left to right: Mr. and Mrs. Tony Bolinsky, their son Anthony, and clerks Leonard Brazausky and Joseph Kretulskie.

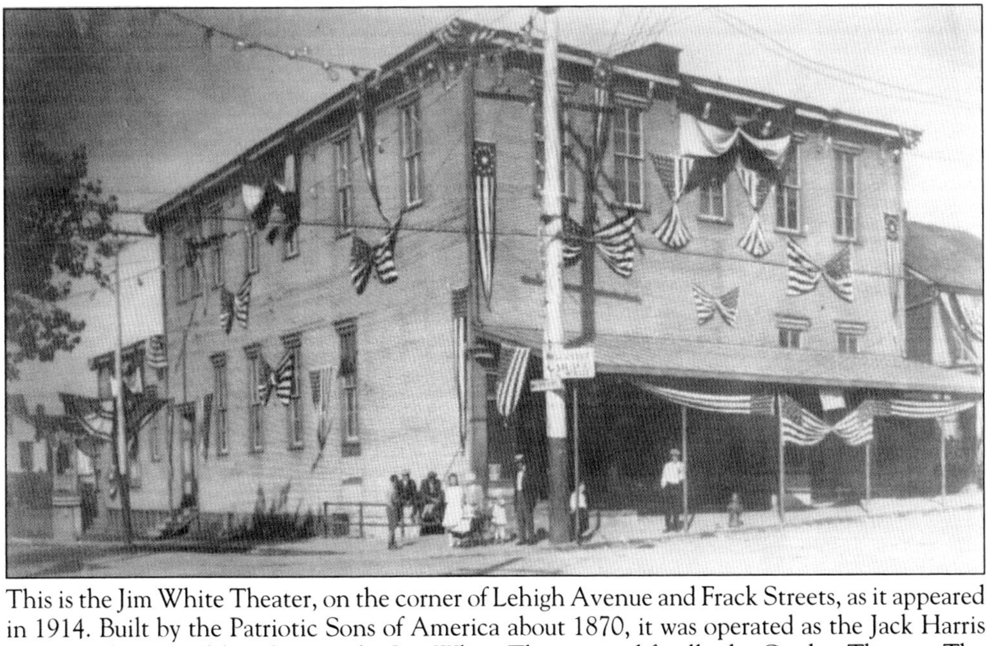

This is the Jim White Theater, on the corner of Lehigh Avenue and Frack Streets, as it appeared in 1914. Built by the Patriotic Sons of America about 1870, it was operated as the Jack Harris Theater, the J.J. Kehler Theater, the Jim White Theater, and finally the Garden Theater. The last picture shown here before the theater was torn down in 1968 was *Dr. Zhivago*. The Hess Gas Station is now on this location.

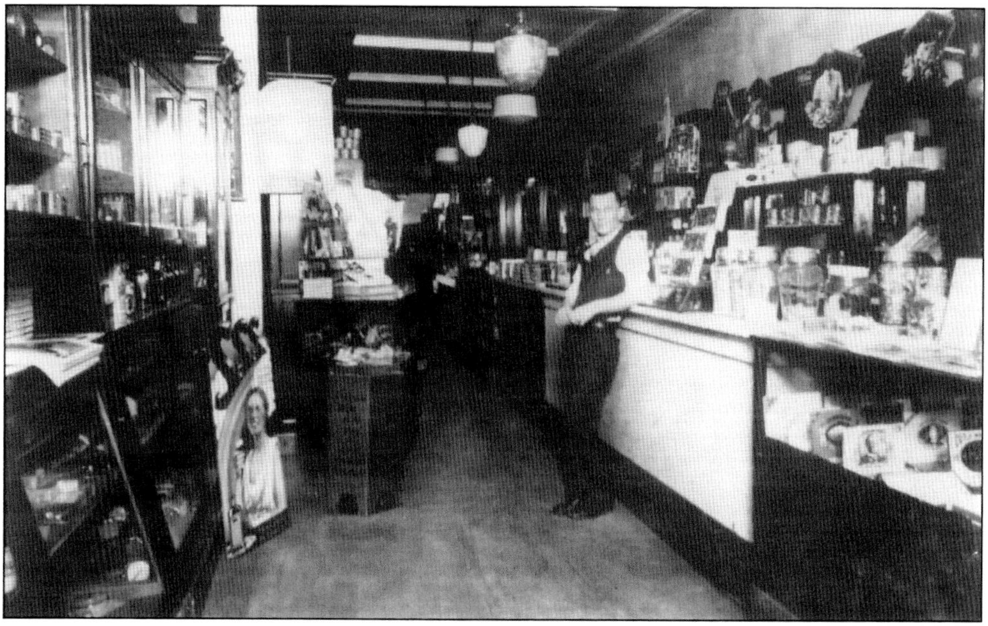

Edward Zemaitis Sr. is pictured in the early Depression years at the counter in his drugstore at 14 South Lehigh Avenue. Notice the floor poster at left center advertising SSS tonic (the Geritol of that era) and a poster at right that reads, "In Hollywood, 76 of our 80 leading beauty shops recommend Palmolive."

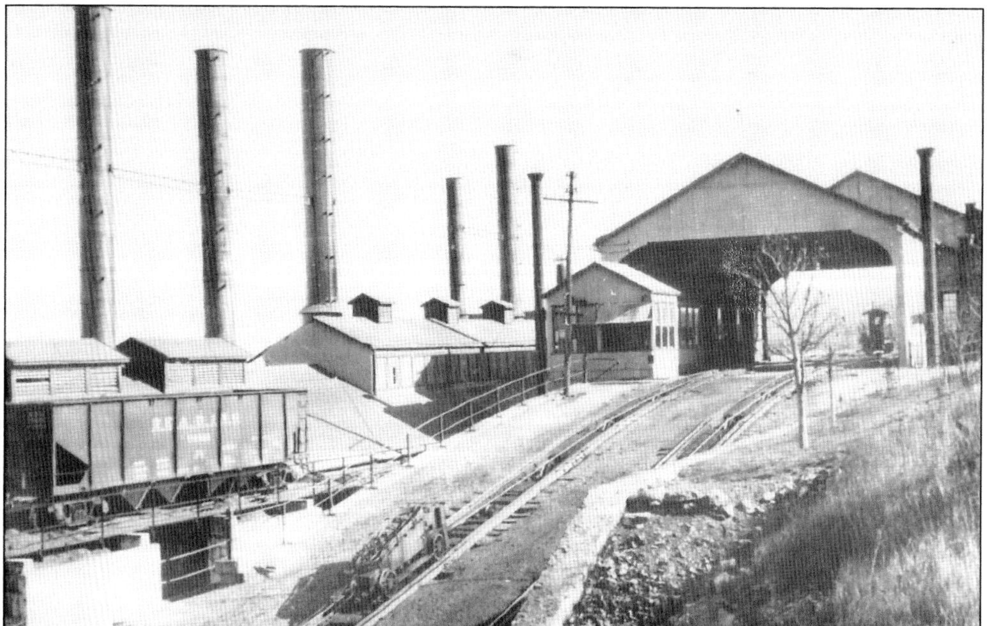

The Mahanoy Plane, one of the county's historic landmarks, was in operation for seventy years. Coal was first hoisted May 30, 1862, and the plane was last operated February 24, 1932. The largest steam engines in the world were used here, and during the course of the plane's operation, the lives of 148 men were claimed and another five hundred men were injured. The plane was dismantled in 1952.

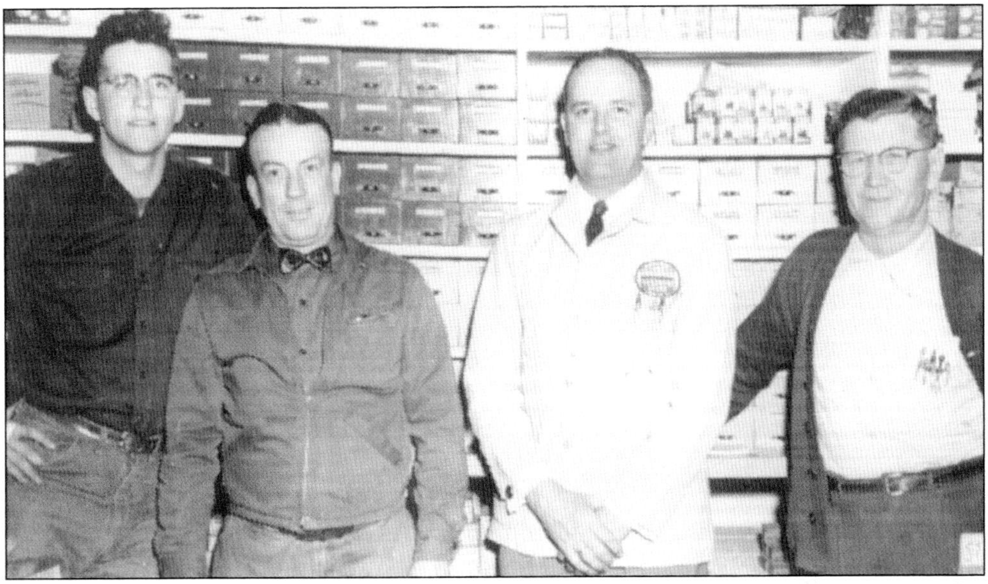

Do you remember the Baney and Herwick Hardware Store at 2 North Lehigh Avenue? This picture, taken April 14, 1955, shows, from left to right, Joseph Yatcilla (truck driver and bottle service), T. David James (salesman and gas service), and Edgar Herwick and William Baney (partners).

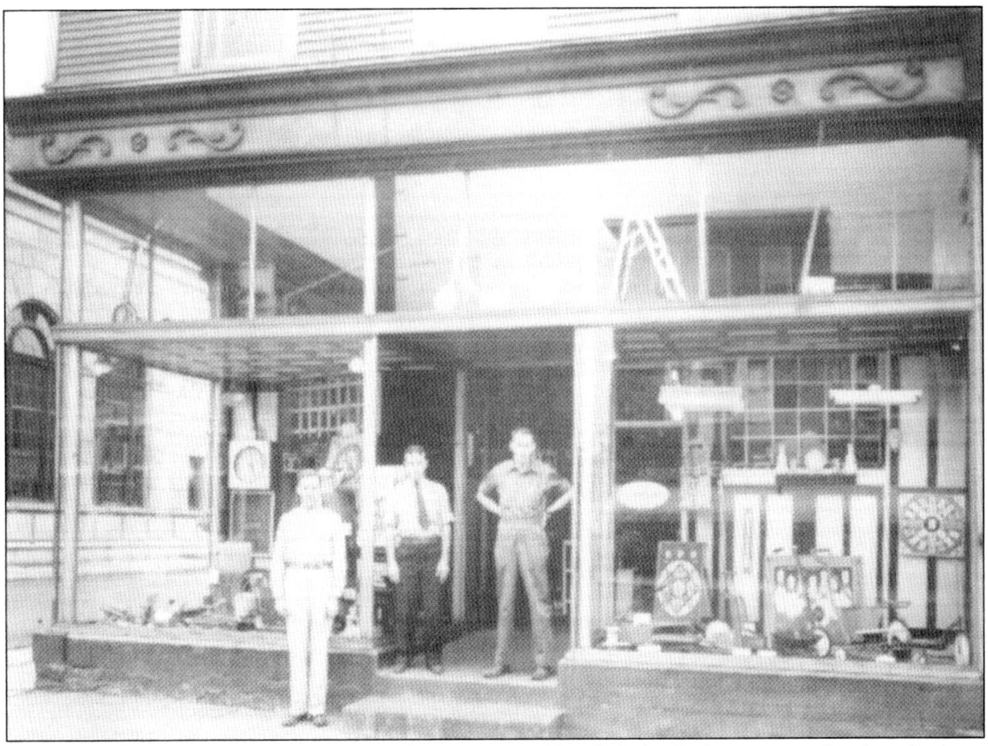

Hock's Hardware Store was a familiar business at 2 North Lehigh Avenue in the decade from 1937 to 1947. Shown are, from left to right, George Hock, Red James, and Herb Hock. This building is now demolished.

AT AUCTION

50 HOUSES—
100 LOTS

FRACKVILLE, PA. 1928

TUESDAY, JULY 17

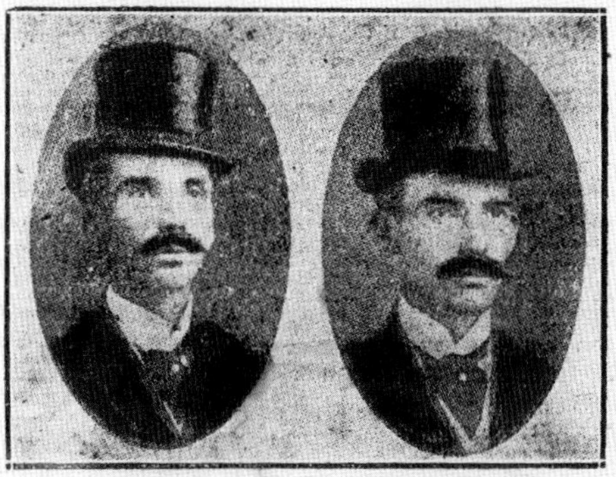

Sold by Penny Bros., World's Original Twin Auctioneers

10:00 A. M.

Fifty Houses located on Chestnut, Howard, Morris, Laurel, Frack, Second and Fourth Streets. All of these houses are practically new—some have all modern conveniences. All rented.

3:00 P. M.

One Hundred Lots on Laurel, Arch and Second streets. These are well located home-sites. Frackville is a fast growing town and you can make no mistake by investing in some of this property. Frackville has more than doubled its size in the past few years and continues to grow rapidly. There have been a number of new enterprises for Frackville in the past twel. e months.

MAKE YOUR ARRANGEMENTS TO ATTEND THESE SALES

Valuable Prizes Given Away

Everyone Present Will Have An Equal Chance

SOLD ON EASY TERMS
HEAR OUR PRIVATE LIVE WIRE BAND AND TENOR SINGER

—SALE CONDUCTED BY—

PENNY BROS., World's Original Twin Auctioneers

AMERICAN LAND CO., Promoters, Greensboro, N. C.

G. A. Haupt, Jr., Owner

This is an advertisement from 1928.

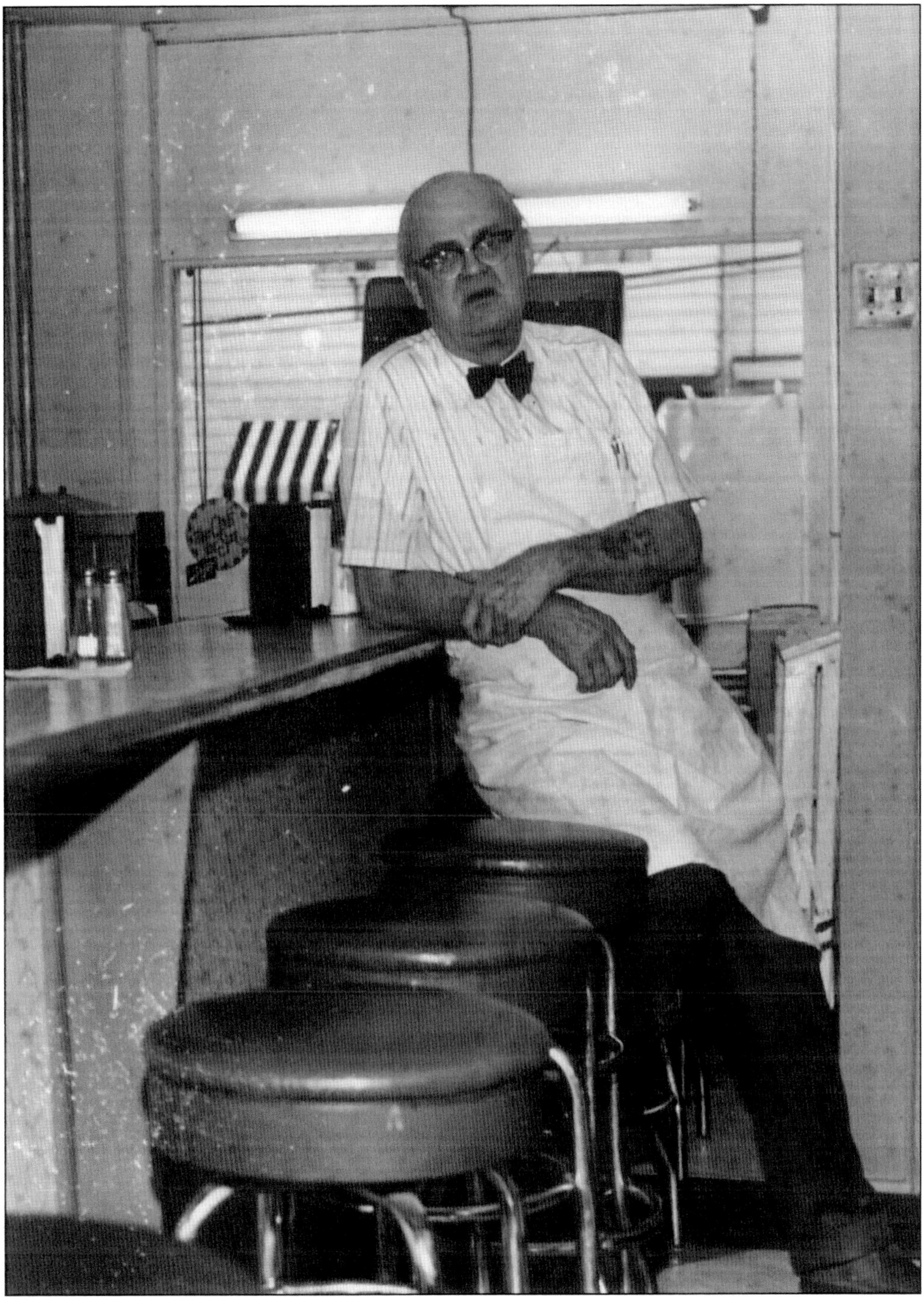

"Insults and Lunch"—That's what you got at Polish John's Restaurant at 48 North Lehigh Avenue, a gathering place for many residents in town. It was a place where the problems of the world were solved; football, baseball, and basketball games were replayed and political events were always a popular topic. It was also a place where the game of wits was played every day as each customer tried to outwit John (who, by the way, was hard to beat).

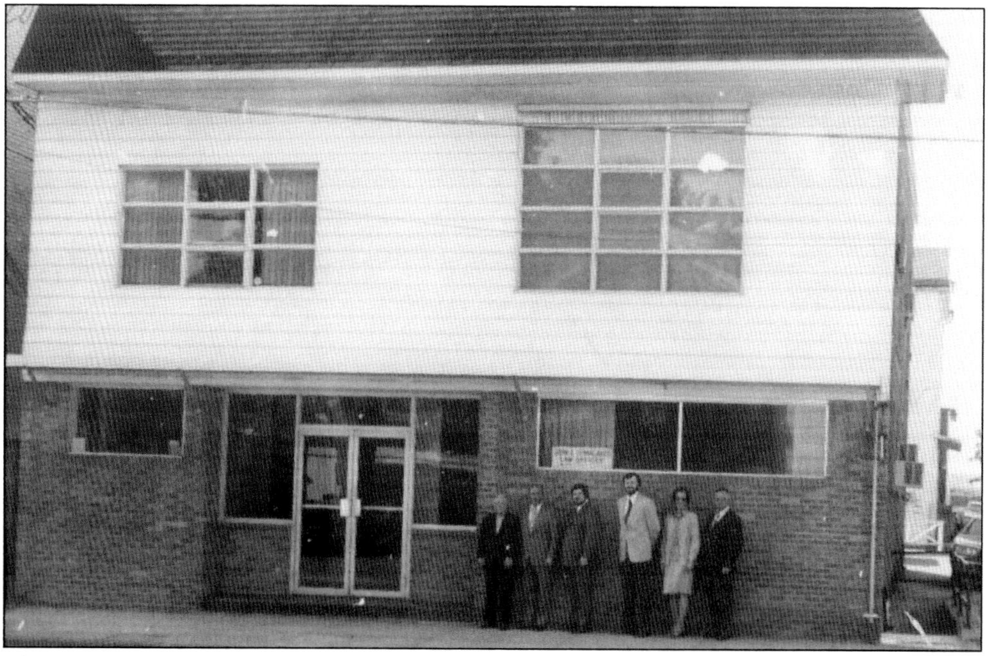

This was the Alex Scott General Store, located on the corner of Lehigh Avenue and Frack Street. In 1925 the American Bank wanted to build on this lot, so the building was moved to the rear of the lot at 14–16 West Frack Street and is now the Law Building. Pictured in 1976 are, from left to right, G. Harold Watkins, Wilbur Rubright, John Domalakes, Charles Miller, Lorraine Stanton, and John Domalakes Sr.

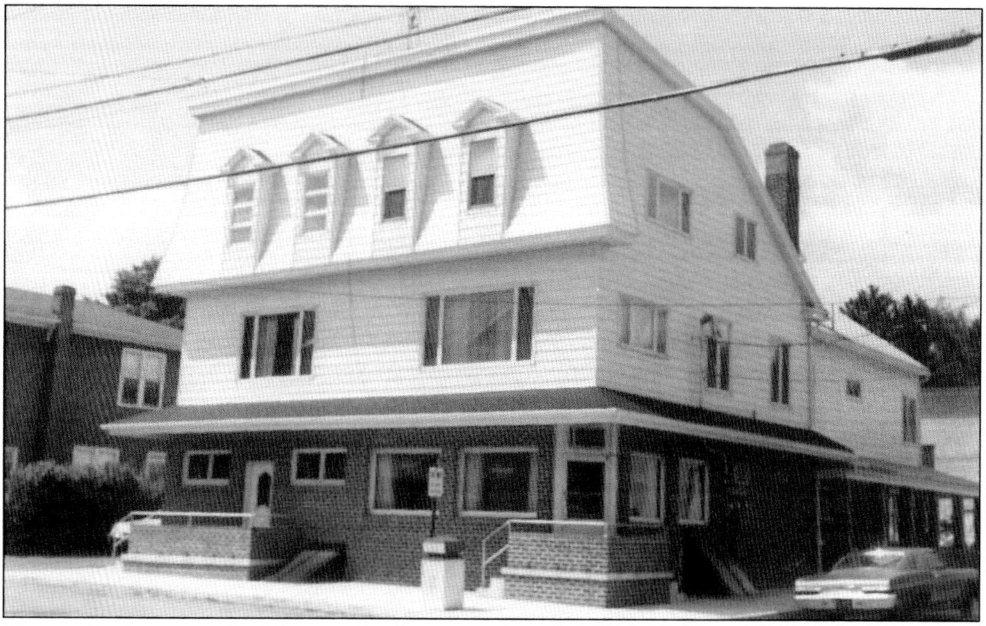

This is the homestead of Samuel R. Haupt at 64 North Nice Street. It was only a two-story building at that time; however, when Charles Kirelawich bought the building, he added the third floor. In the early 1900s the Moose Club met on the second floor and held dances in the hardwood ballroom.

Five

Reflections in Time

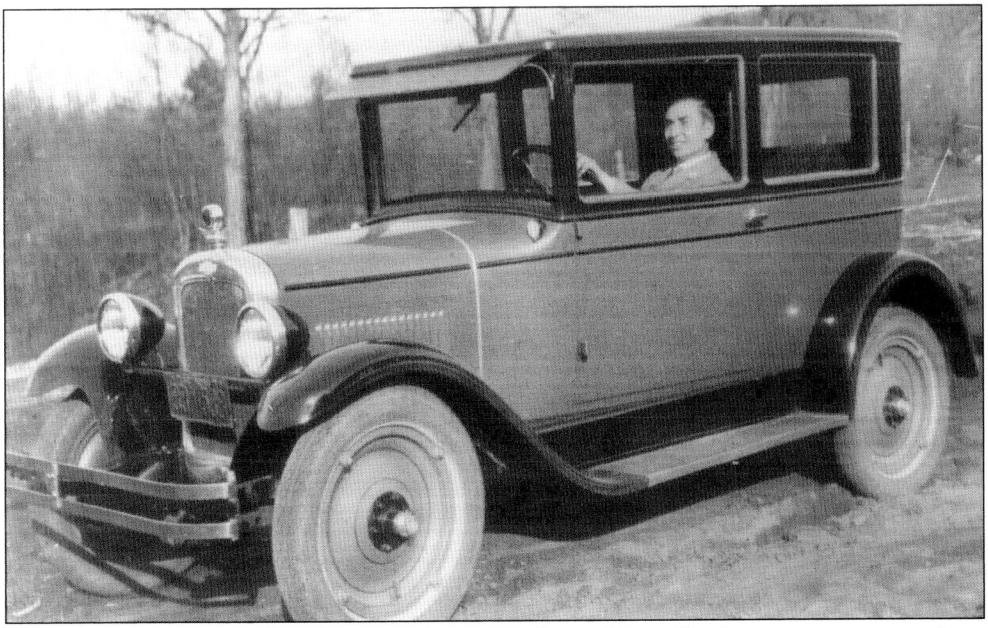

There's no mistaking that look of pride on the face of Pete Kowker, a young man about Frackville, as he sat behind the wheel of his brand new Chevrolet automobile on an early spring day in 1927. That year Pete was voted the most handsome salesman for the Metropolitan Life Insurance Co.

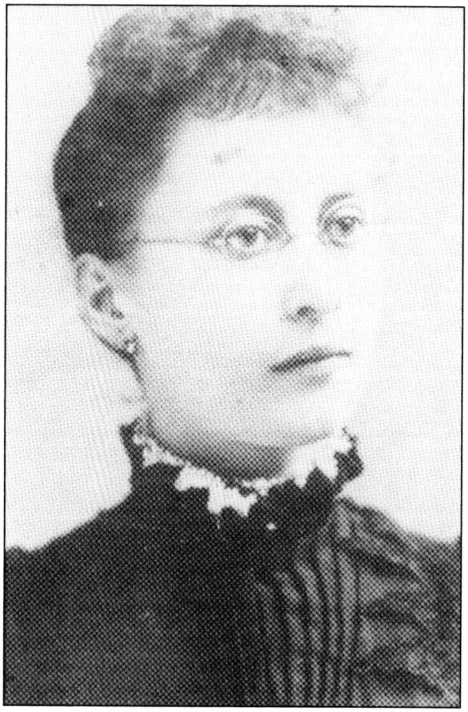

Susan Lydia Haupt was born September 27, 1869, graduated in 1888, and was a teacher in the Frackville schools. She died at the age of twenty-seven on October 30, 1896.

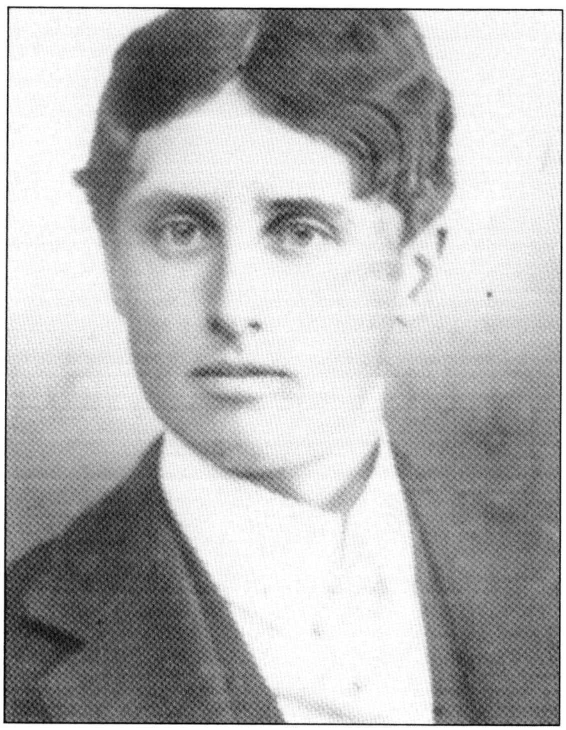

George Andrew Haupt was born March 10, 1877, and married Mary Rebecca Purnell on February 22, 1905. The Haupt family was in the real estate business and donated Haupt's Grove, now known as Frackville Memorial Park to the residents of our borough. Mr. Haupt died February 2, 1959, at the age of eighty-one.

Anna Wasielewski (left) is shown in her communion dress with her mother, Elizabeth, and her sisters Lottie (top), Alice (right), and Stella (front) in 1901. All ladies eventually married men who worked in the mines. Anna married Joseph Gibowicz and lived at 47 South Railroad Avenue from 1924 until her death in 1981.

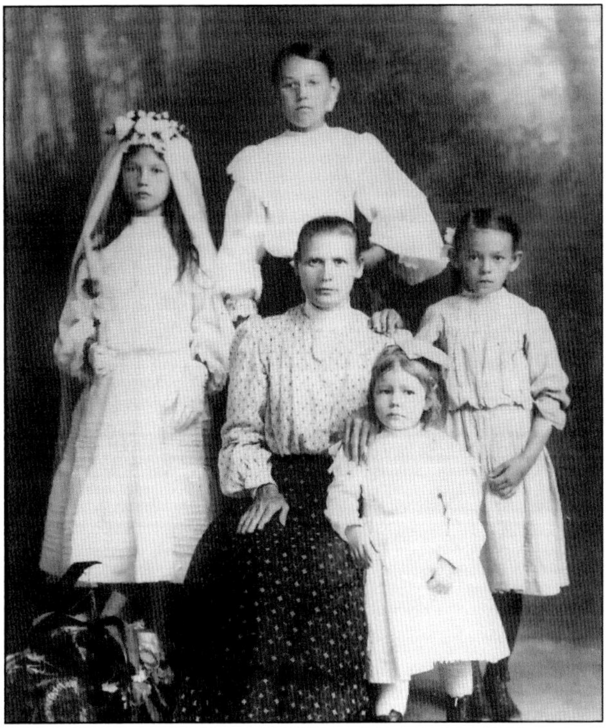

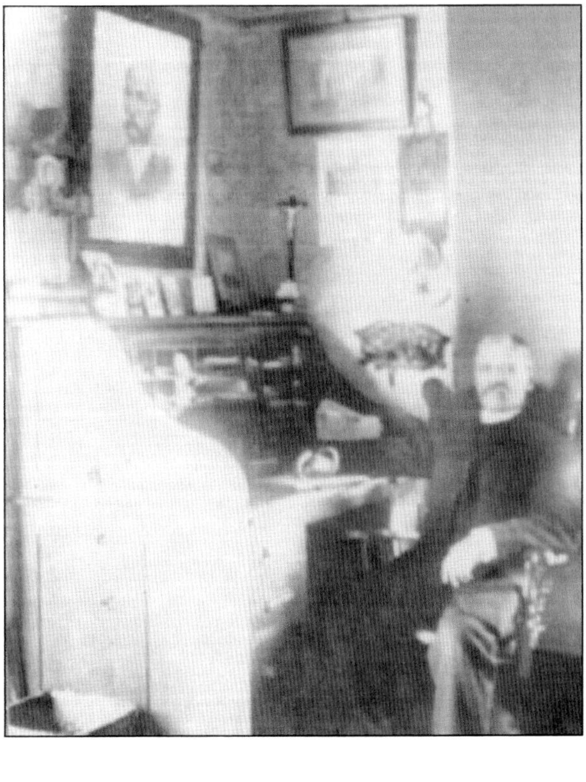

The Reverend Jonathan Miller began his priesthood on November 1, 1899, at Christ Church in Frackville and wrote a *History of Frackville* in 1934. He married Rebecca Breedon in 1885, and they were the parents of two daughters, Edna and Maud. Mrs. Miller died April 5, 1889, and the Reverend married his second wife, Cora Alice Etter, on June 19, 1890. He is pictured at his Christ Church desk in 1909.

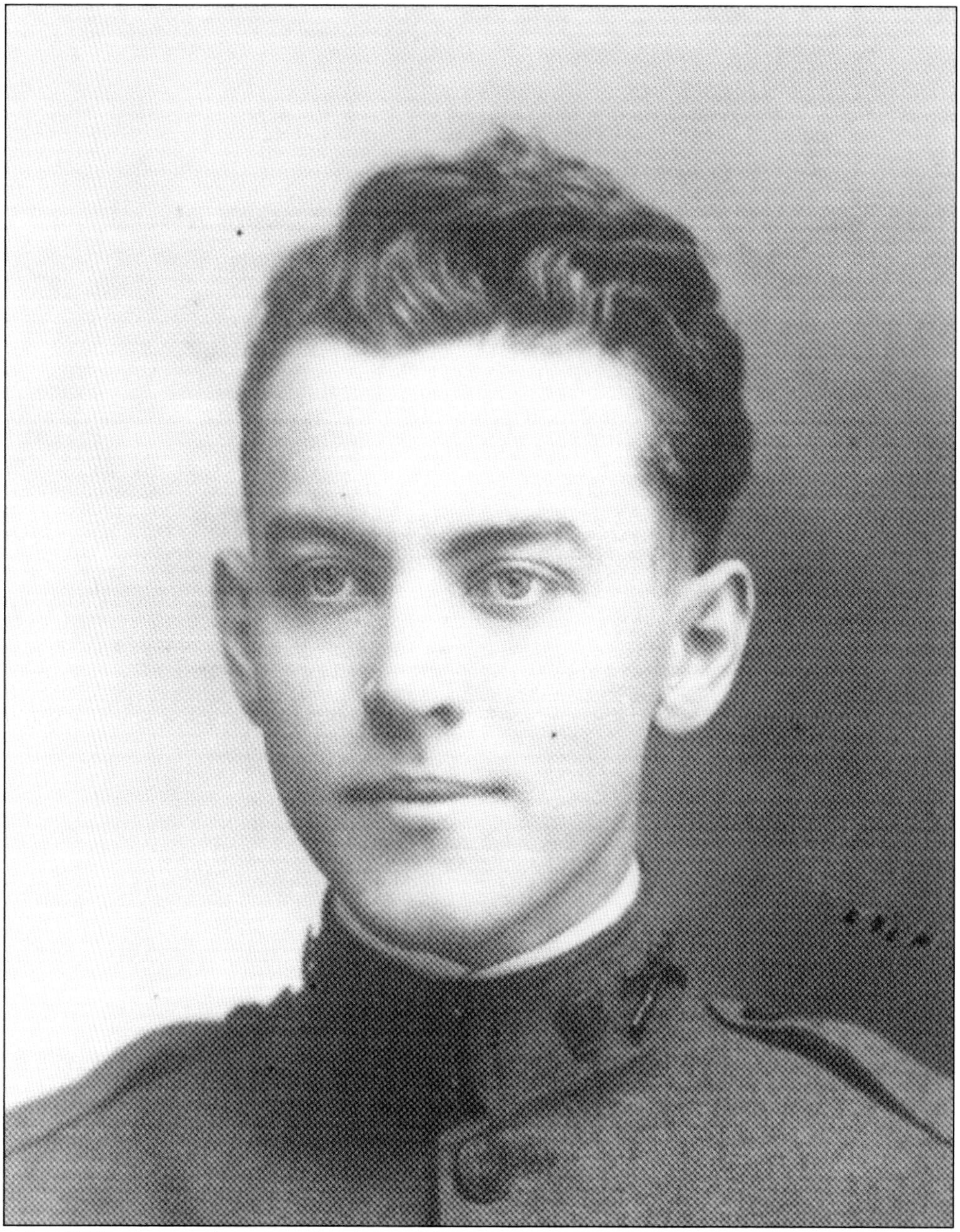

Schuylkill County's first casualty in World War I was a Frackville boy, Bernard J. McGinnis, who fell under an army motor bus at Camp Hancock, Georgia. A 1914 graduate of Frackville High School, he was a corporal in Co. C 103rd. Regr. Engineers, N.G.U.S. He and his brother, Clement, enlisted together, and a grand party toasted them before they left their home on North Nice Street. This portrait was presented by the FHS Class of 1917 for display in the Lincoln School Assembly Room. Clement was city editor of the *Tamaqua Courier*, worked for the *Pottsville Chronicle*, and was a correspondent for the *Evening Herald*. Their father, John C. McGinnis, was president of the First National Bank in 1917.

Joseph J. Kehler was born in Eldred Township, January 19, 1849, a son of George H. and Sarah (Fetterholf) Kehler. In 1872, he engaged in farming and operated a mill until 1887, when he moved to Frackville. In 1899 he established a clothing store on the corner of Balliet and Pine Streets and later had a general store on this location. He died December 25, 1922, and was buried at Greenwood Cemetery.

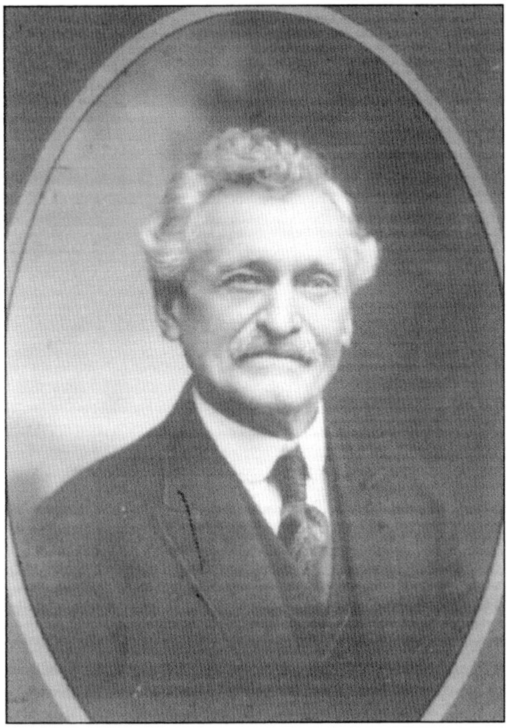

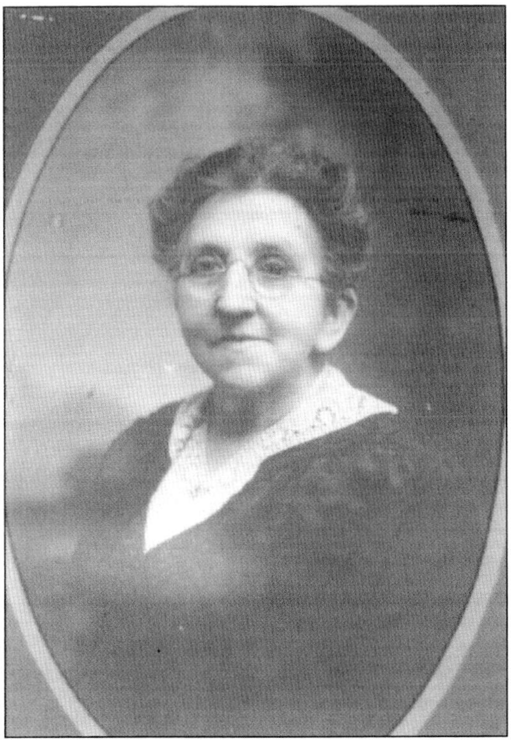

The daughter of Elias and Elizabeth (Fisher) Hepler, Mary Hepler Kehler married Joseph Kehler in 1871, and they had four children: T. Webster, Elizabeth A. (who married G.W. Hoppes), Jennie (who married John E. Dyer), and Joseph Jr. (who became principal of the Pottsville High School).

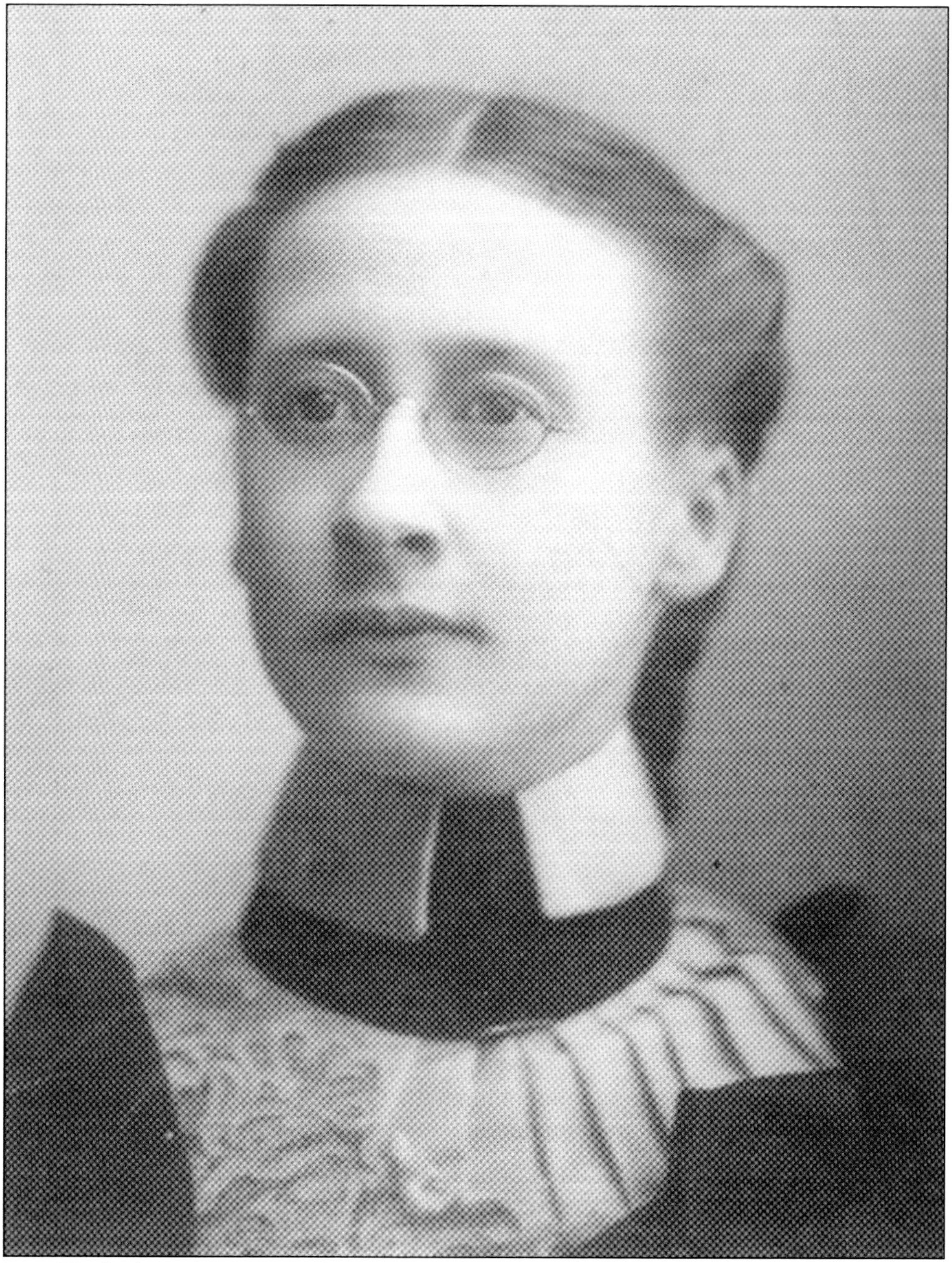

Mrs. Elizabeth Trautman was the daughter of Alexander and Elizabeth Ann Patten Scott, proprietors of Scott's General Store. Her father was the county sheriff from 1893 to 1896 and was the county Republican national delegate for three presidential nominations. He first moved to town in 1884 and was actively engaged in the civic advancement of our borough, serving as president of the school board for many years, as well as being the borough treasurer for a quarter of a century. Mrs. Trautman met her husband when they were both attending school. They married in 1911, and Prof. Trautman was the principal for many years. Mrs. Trautman graduated from FHS in 1900 and then attended the Pierce School of Business in Philadelphia.

Emma Gottschall Connelly was six years old when her family moved to Frackville. They lived at 61 North Balliet Street, and the house still remains in the family. Emma married Squire Michael J. Connelly, who had his office in the Wagner Building on West Frack Street. Their two daughters, Mary and Jean, were schoolteachers in the Frackville School System for many years.

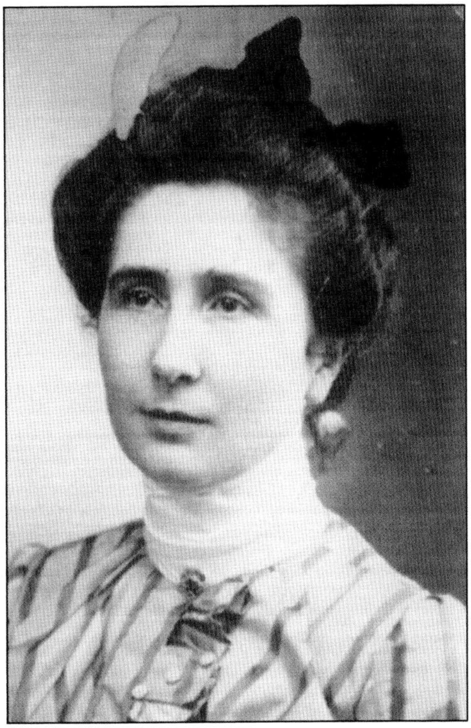

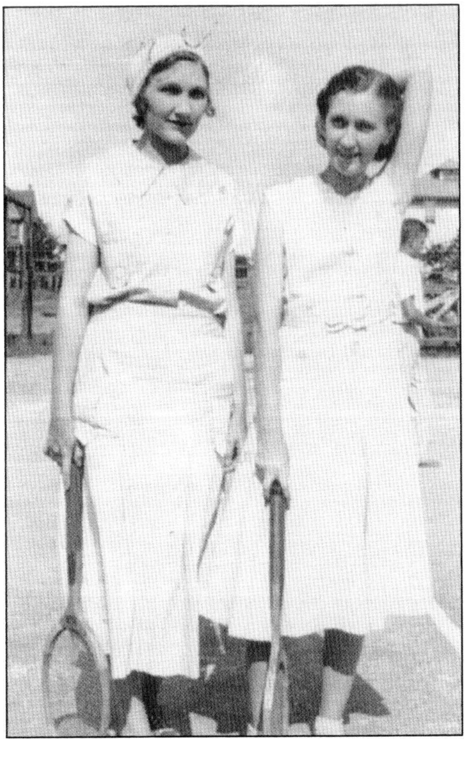

Mary (left) and Jean Connelly are pictured taking a brief rest before continuing their tennis game at the tennis court once located at Second and Chestnut Streets.

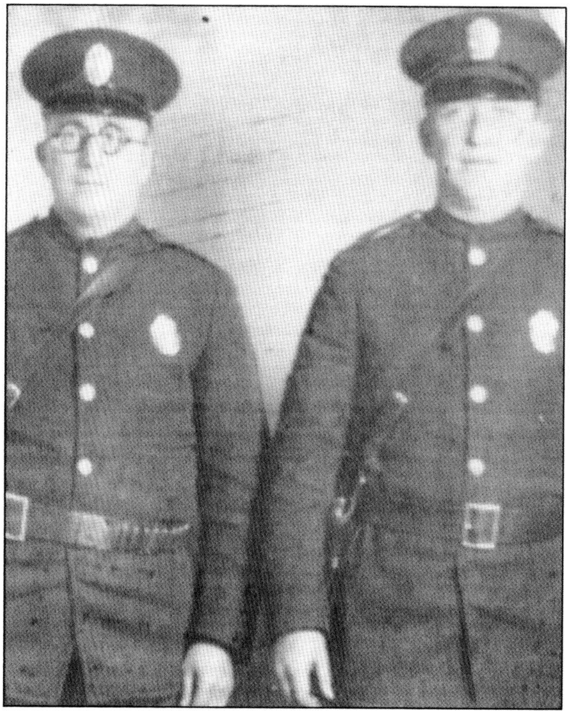

Do you remember the "Law" in Frackville in the Good Old Days? Chief William Hodgert was Frackville's first uniformed policeman. This picture was taken in March 1925; Chief Hodgert is on the left, and Miles Forney is on the right.

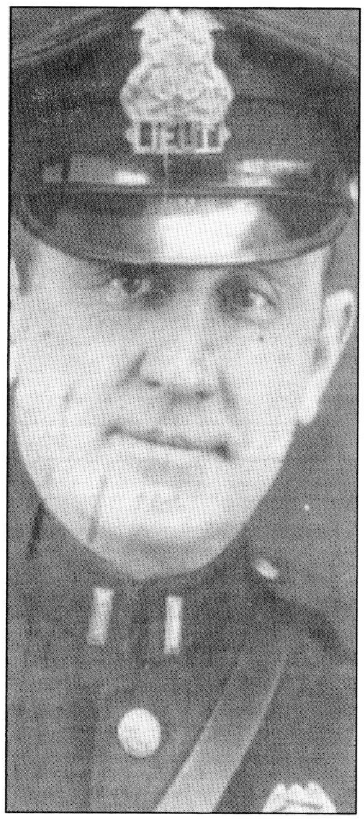

Another well-known law officer in town was Lt. Sam Walters, who served under Chief Hodgert for many years. This picture was taken in 1932.

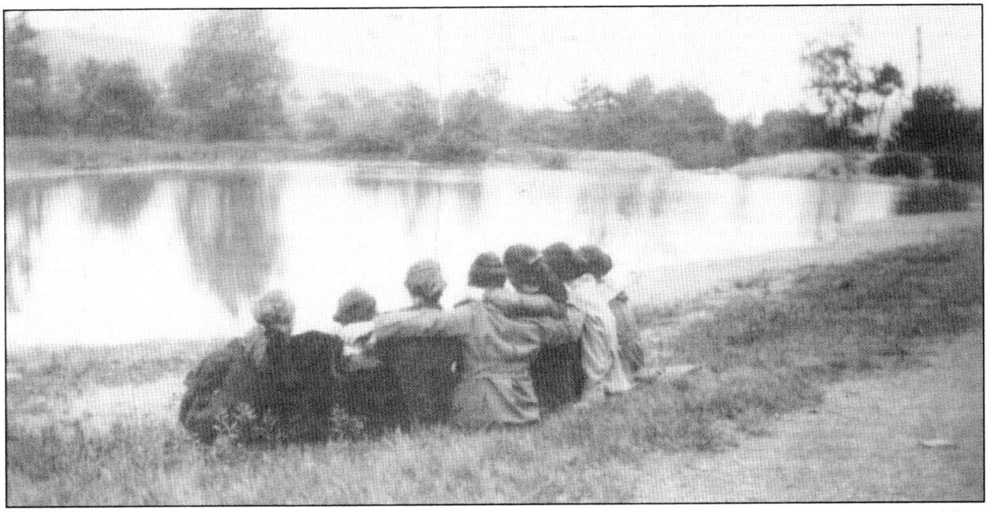

Grummies Dam, once located on the west side of town—the location of the West End Field—was the site of many picnics and fireworks displays. It was also the spot where all the boys went skinny-dipping as soon as the weather became warm. Many youngsters learned to swim there, and have fond boyhood memories of the "good old days" at Grummies.

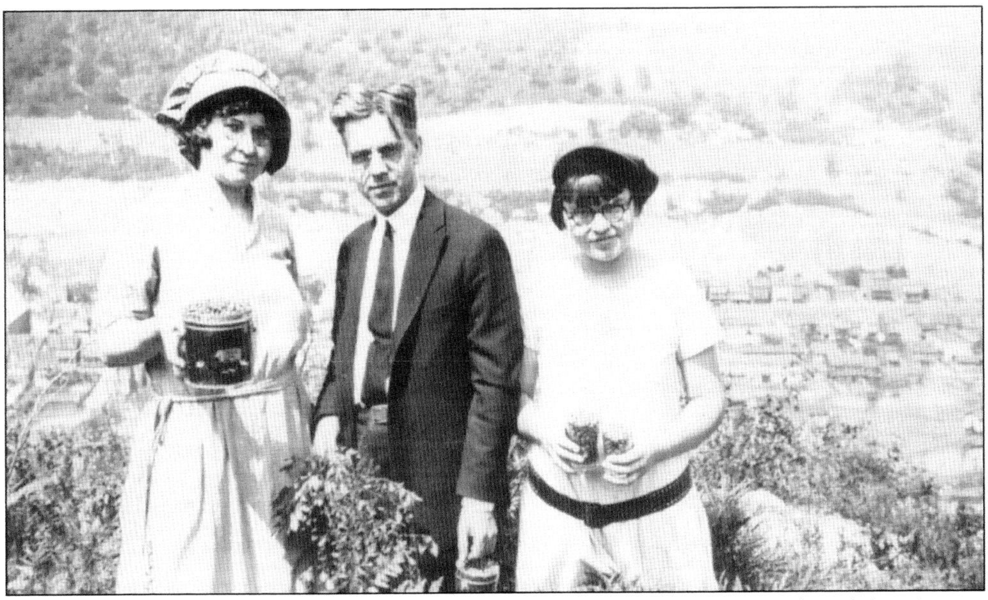

Remember picking huckleberries in the good old days? This Frackville trio gathered their berries on the north edge of Broad Mountain overlooking Mahanoy Plane. Pictured are Anna and Matilda Kowker with Tom Reese.

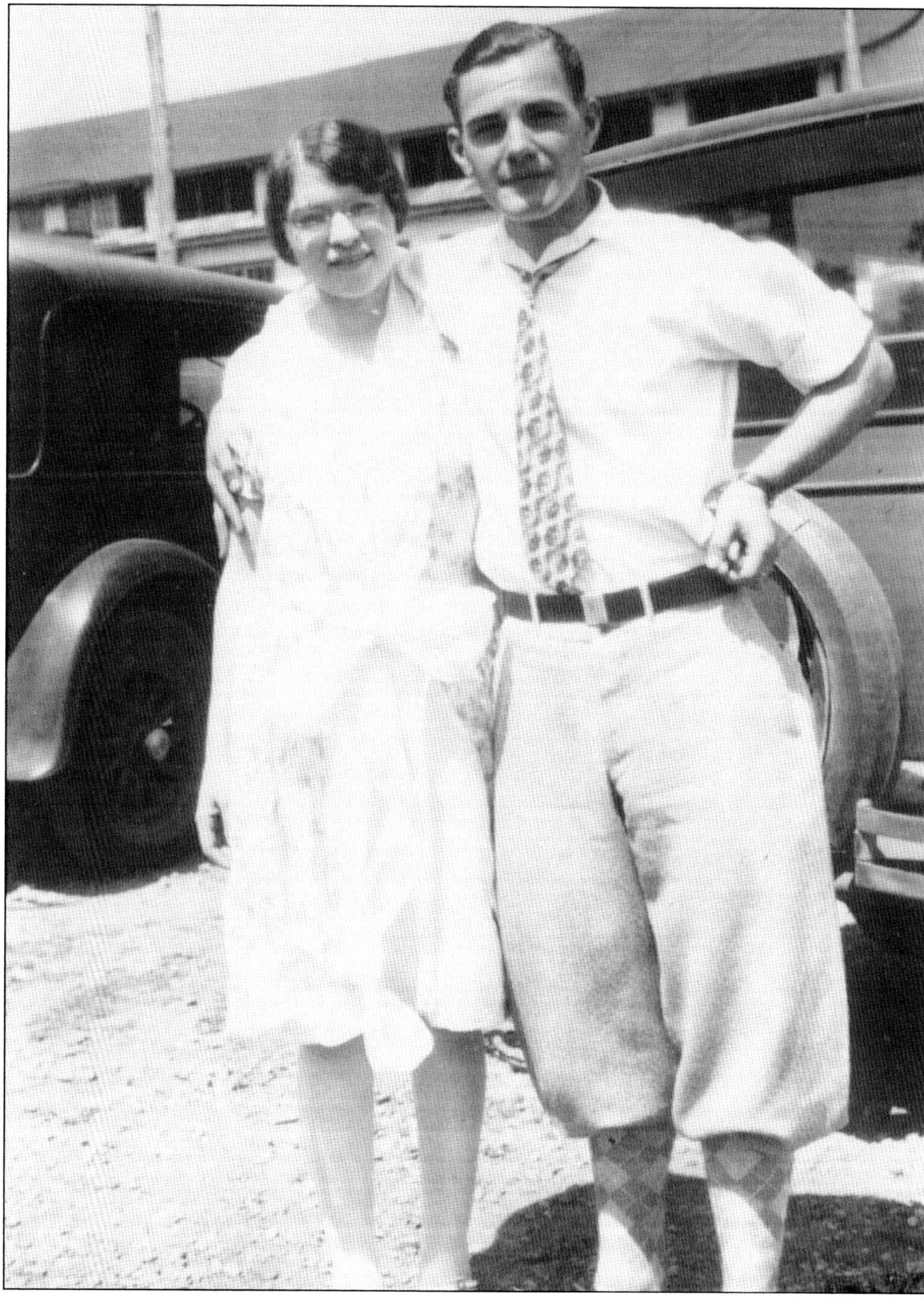

It was Lithuanian Day in 1928 at Lakewood Park when Pete Kowker snapped this photograph of his sister Matilda and Anthony Petrousky. The Lakewood ballroom had been dedicated as a brand new structure three years earlier on Memorial Day. The big band era was still ten years in the future, but the lively tunes of the flapper era kept the floor filled with couples going through the antics of such dances as the Turkey Trot and the Charleston. Tony is pictured in the fashion of the day—knickers and knee socks.

The Haupt family were early settlers of Frackville. Pictured are Samuel and Urzelia (Foltz) Haupt. Mrs. Haupt was born July 27, 1850, and died March 25, 1932. Mr. Haupt was born May 12, 1847, and died April 23, 1918. This picture was taken at their home at 64 North Nice Street. The elder Samuel Haupt was born January 11, 1804, and moved to Frackville in 1854. He was the owner of 500 acres on the west side of town. The family established the waterworks and many other utilities and had the largest real estate company in town. In 1862 Mr. Haupt presented a lot on the east side of North Nice Street to the school board for the erection of the first public school.

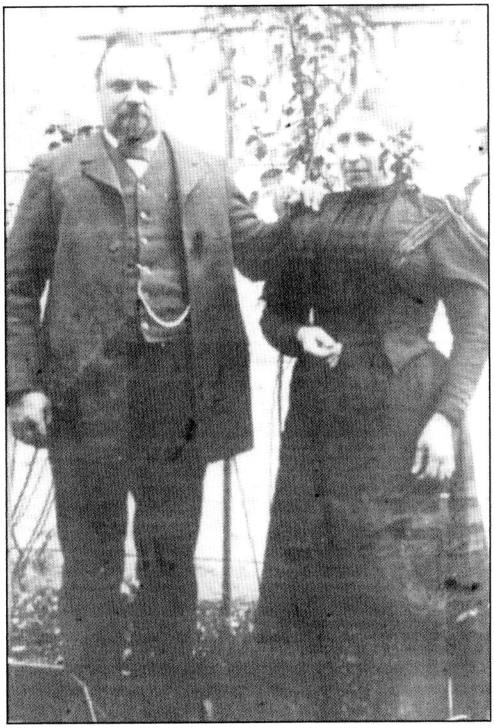

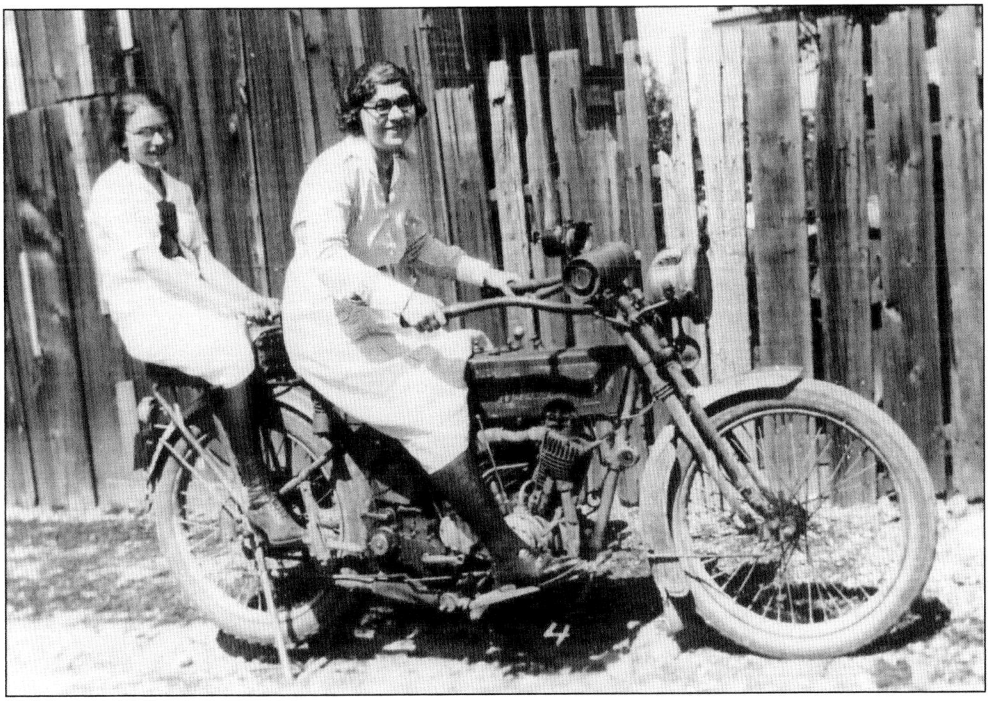

"Excuse my dust," said Matilda and Helen Kowker as they prepared to ride their cousin's motorcycle on the dirt streets of Frackville in 1922.

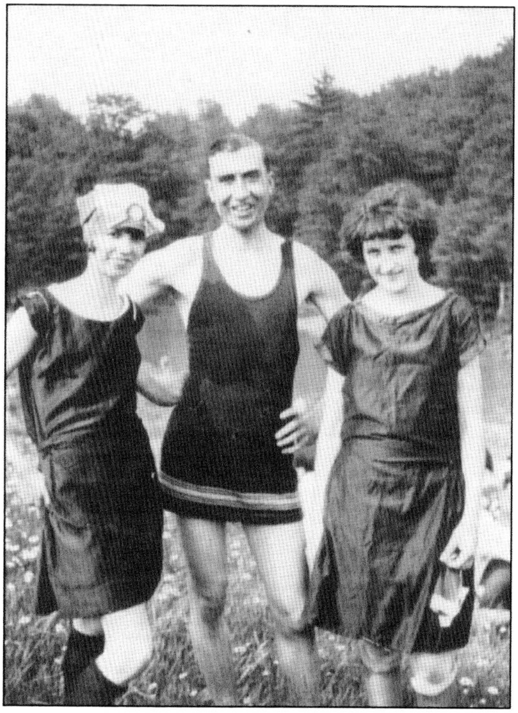

Fashionable ladies and gents wore clothes like these while enjoying the great outdoors years ago. The dapper gent in the swimsuit is Pete Kowker, pictured with his two lady friends at Marlin Park.

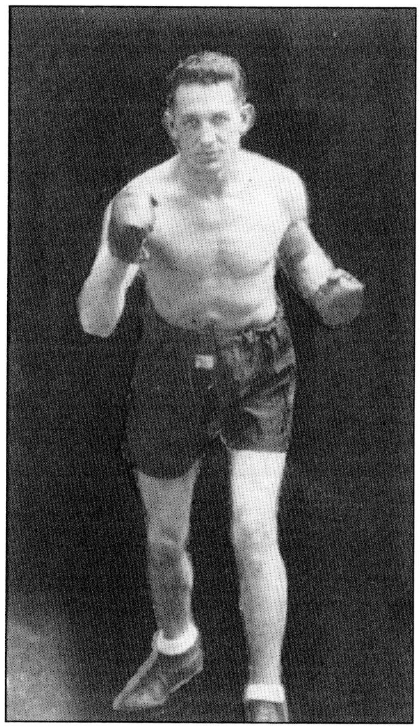

Do you remember Iron Mike Kushwara, one of the most prominent prizefighters in Schuylkill County during the 1930s? His record read thirty-nine knockouts in forty-one bouts.

Richard L. Fennelly began his career with the Philadelphia and Reading Railroad while he was very young and remained a "railroader" for many years. He was very punctual and was known to sit at his engine with one hand on the brake and the other holding his watch so that he could release the brake and start out "on the second" scheduled.

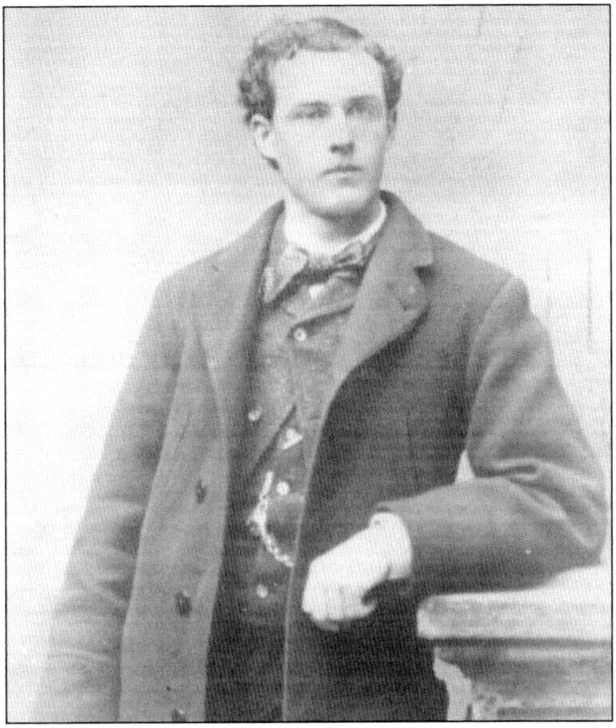

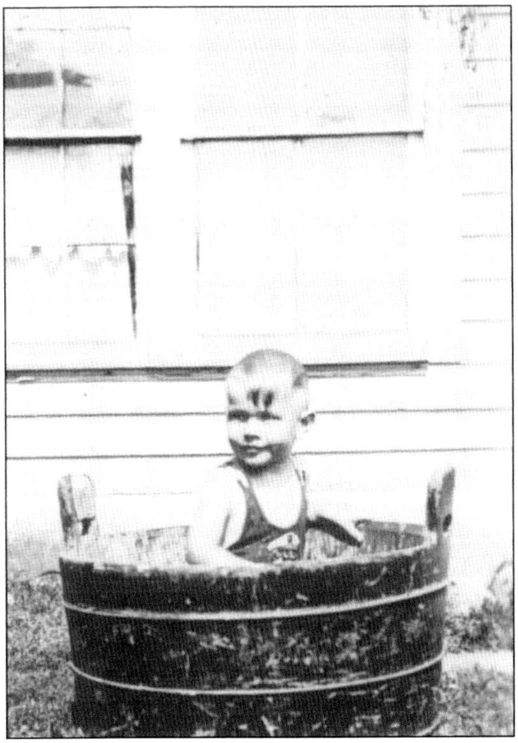

The old wooden washtub was used for several reasons: mashing grapes for wine, washing clothes, and washing kids one at a time until all had their bath with no change of water—with the dirtiest kid going last. The tub was next to the old coal stove in the kitchen, and Octagon soap was used to remove the grime. Pictured is Don Petrosky at 262 North Balliet Street in the year 1933.

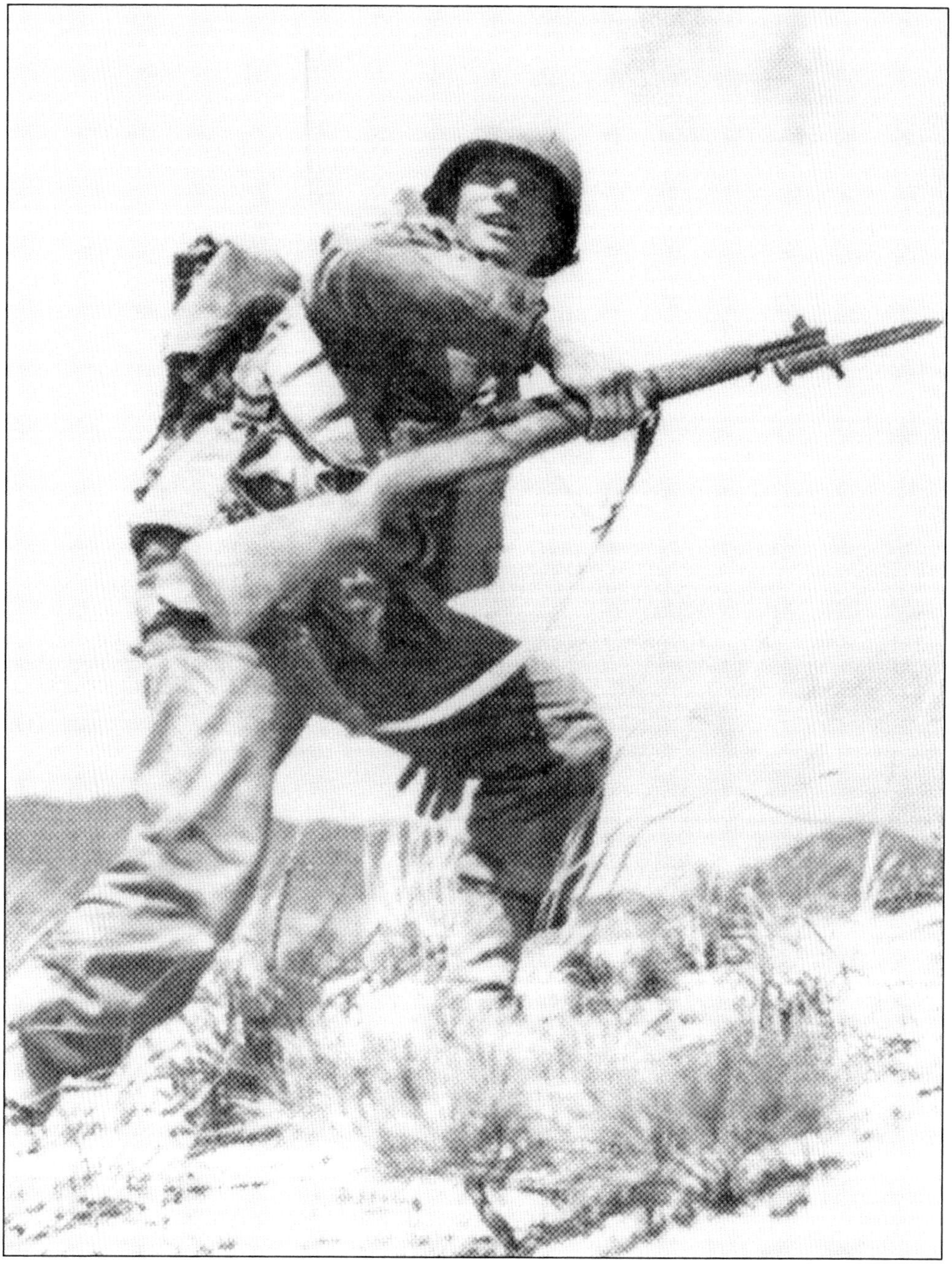

The 1951 *New York Times Magazine* featured Infantryman John J. Allen in battle regalia, climbing a rocky ridge on the dividing line between North and South Korea. The photograph, entitled "the 38th Parallel" and honored as a Picture of the Year, is the property of the Defense Department and is filed with other photographs, such as those titled "Spirit of Seventy-Six" and "Raising the Flag on Iwo Jima." Jack and his parents lived at 9 East Frack Street for many years. He graduated from FHS in 1947 and was awarded the Bronze Star for heroism in ground combat north of Seoul, Korea, May 20, 1951, at a ceremony held at Indiantown Gap Military Reservation on August 27, 1951.

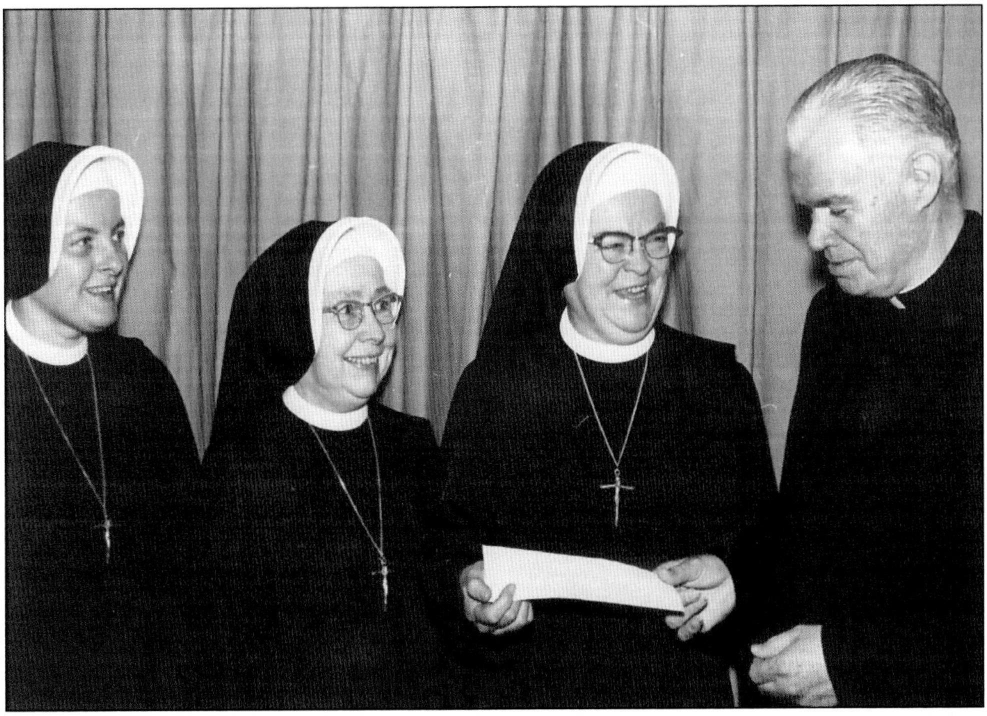

Pictured leaving St. Joseph's Church with its pastor, Fr. William H. Conley are Immaculate Heart of Mary Sisters Sr. Maureen Ann, Sr. Alma Dolores, and Sr. M. Marguerite (from left to right).

The Frackville Library purchased its new library building at 56 North Lehigh Avenue in 1972 after the Borough Council approved a donation of $5,000 to be used as a down payment on the building. Students pictured helping with the move are as follows: Eugene Alshon, Mari Ann Becker, Joe Charsick, Theresa Sippie, Barry Brecker, Joe Andrews, and Bob Kaledas.

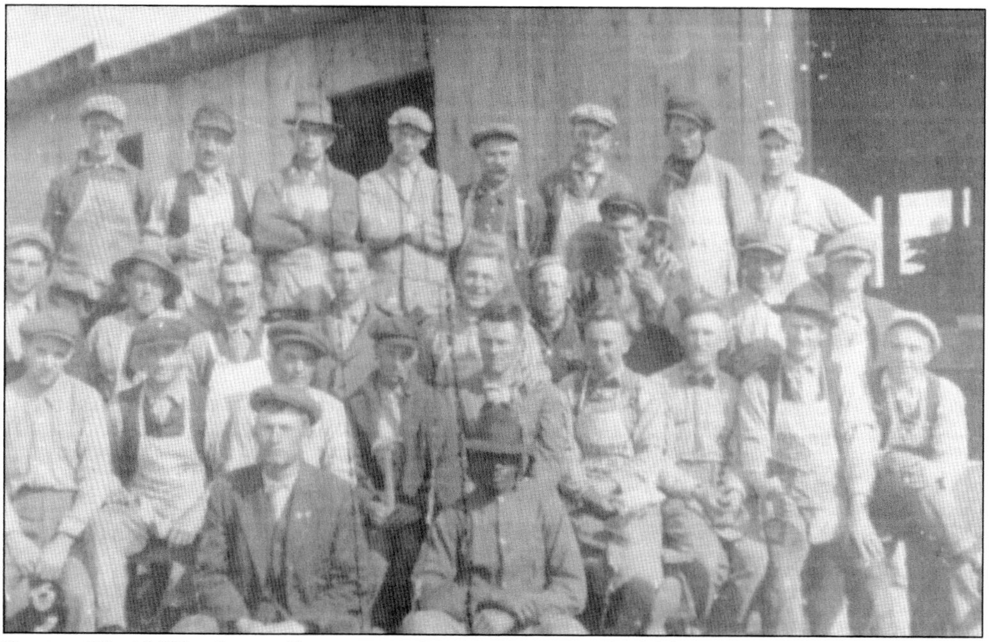

During World War I, a call went out for carpenters to build barracks for the thousands of doughboys reporting for training at Camp Dix. Pictured are: Ike Moyer, Henry Foulk, Maurice Rubright, Maurice Burchill, Charles Houser, Joe Walsh, Fred Wagner, Floyd Kaup, George Rubright, Jim Coon, Gus Heine, Larry Kiefer, Bill Williams, Ellsworth Hay, Jack Kiensle, Bill Prynn, Edward Heine, Jim Williams, and Jack Harris.

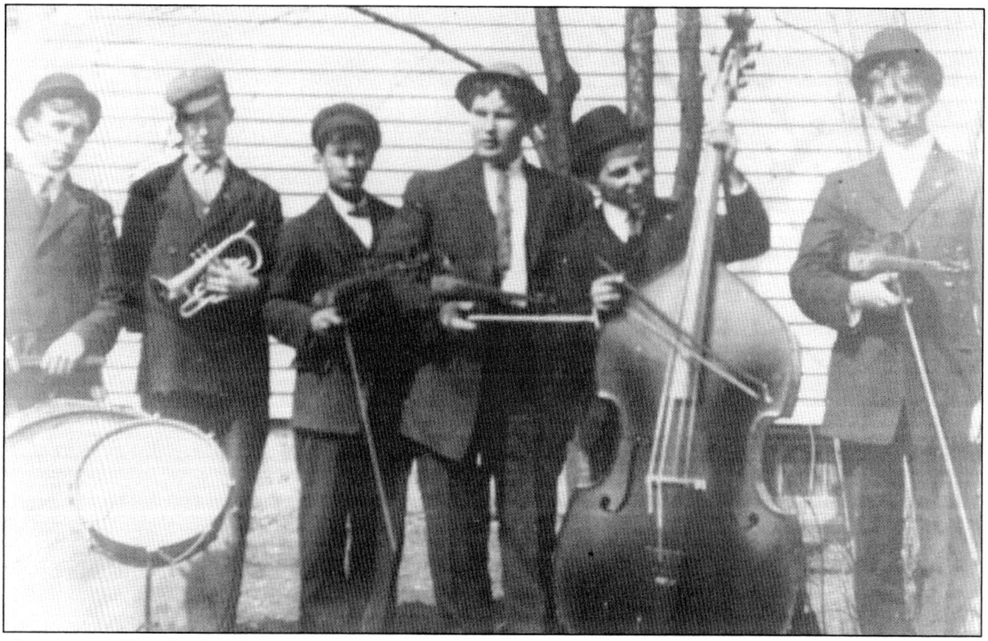

Players in Fat Richard's Band in 1912, from left to right, were as follows: Lance Pierce (trombone), George Kessler (2nd trumpet), Ollie Kreitzer (violin and piano), Fat Richards (piano and violin), Tom Kreitzer (guitar, bass, and violin), and Fred Hoffman (1st trumpet). Many residents remember hearing this band at the Hildebrand Hotel on North Balliet Street.

Six

Pleasant Memories

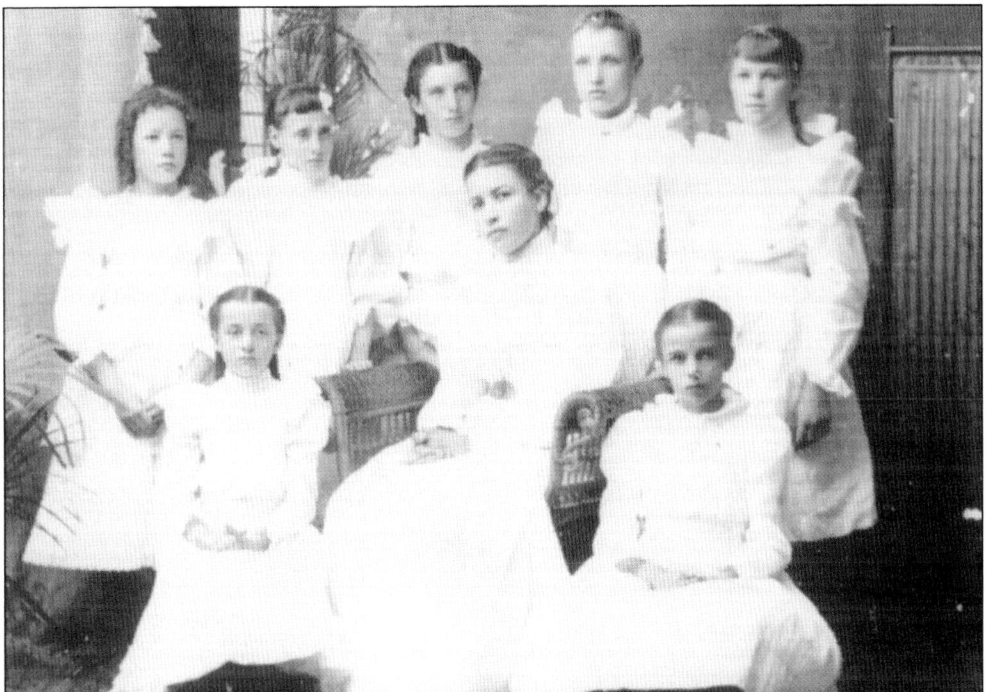

This is the first communion class at St. Joseph's Church on Broad Mountain Avenue. The parish had no priest assigned at the time and the sacrament was administered by the pastor from Mahanoy Plane. Class members, from left to right, were as follows: (first row) Mary Nash, teacher Mary Huth, and Bertha Huth; (second row) Marion Fennelly, Elizabeth Schaeffer, Mary Murphy, Gertrude Fennessy, and Mary Minahan.

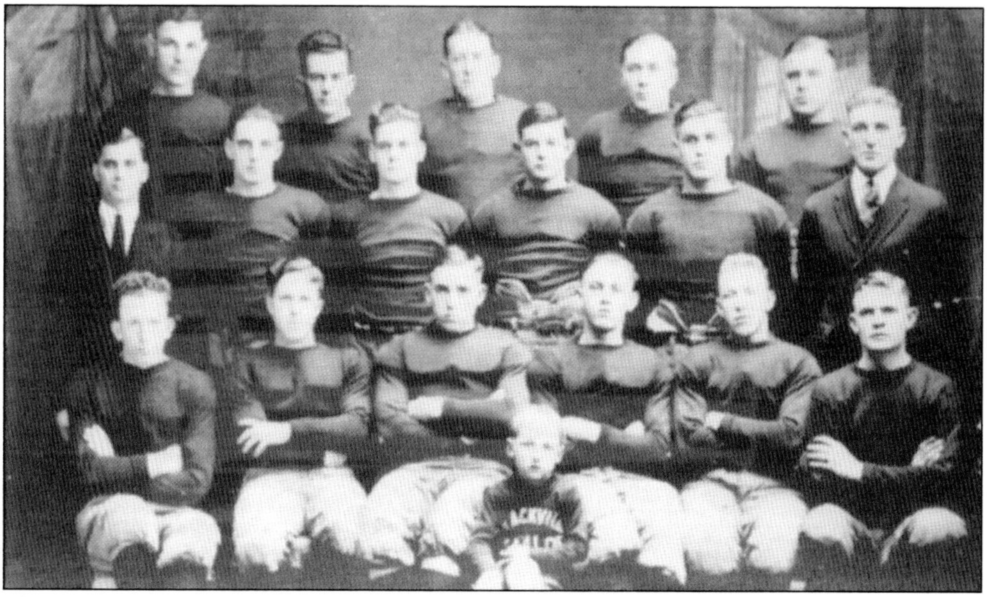

The Frackville Buffaloes won sixty-seven straight football games before losing 3–0 to the Queen City AA from Allentown during a seven-year span. They held a reunion on November 9, 1963, at the Ace Banquet Hall with Rex Roberts as master of ceremonies. The Buffaloes, who boasted some of the finest talent in the coal region during their existence, were beaten only three times: by the Queen City AA, Glovers Hill, and Lykens. Pictured are, as listed on the back on the original photograph: Charles Murphy (mascot); (bottom row) Alan Edwards, Earl Owens, Emerson Diebert, William Purcell, Adam Caton, and Alfred Phillips; (second row) Tommy Goodis (manager), Bertram Roeder, Charles Tregembo, Harold Robbins, Ralph Tregembo, and Harry Murphy (manager); (top row) Jack Foltz, William Miller, Arthur Wagner, and Victor Drasdis. Some members of the team were not present for this picture.

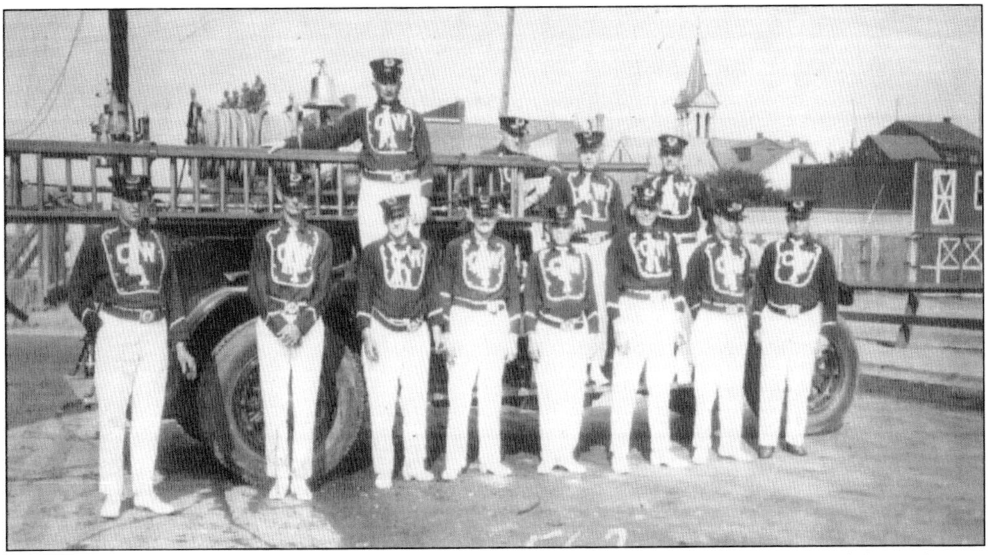

The Goodwill Hose Company was incorporated November 15, 1910, and received their charter on December 19, 1910. There were sixteen charter members: James Gray, John Pauley, John Kotz, Jacob Timmins, Harry Timmins, Harry Kraemer, Daniel Frack Jr., Thomas Guinther, Harvey Steigerwalt, George Eiler, Edward Griffiths, Roy Richards, Henry Hahn, Alfred Thomas, Oscar Morgan, and William Wagner.

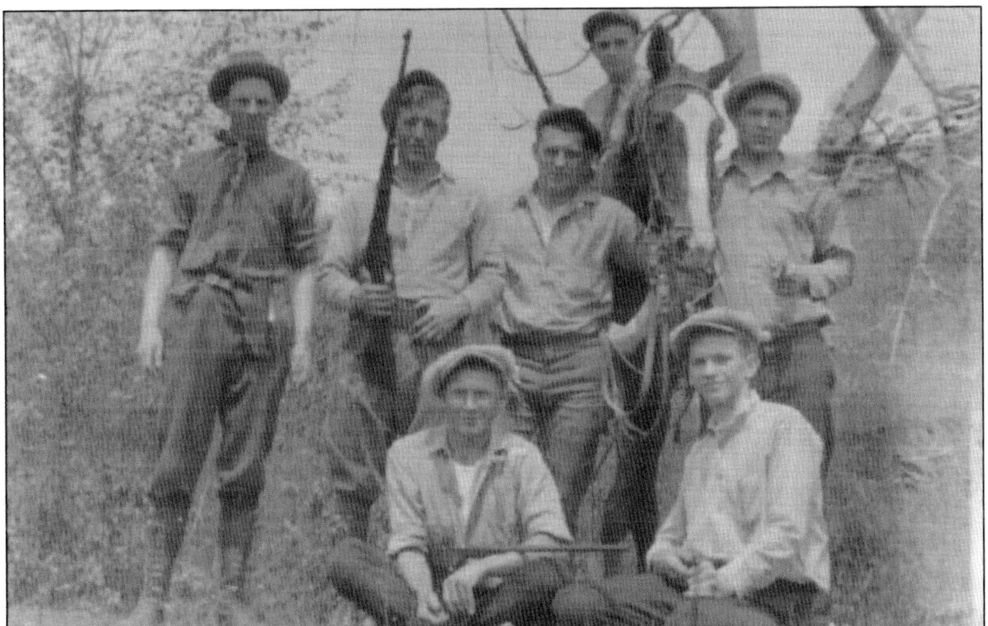

Do you remember the Frackville Rifle Club? Pictured here on May 30, 1924, are, from left to right, as follows: (sitting) Bert Domaleski and Mickey Krushana; (standing) Bill Minahan, Harold Derr, Harry Mauger, and Henny Houser; and (on horse) Harvey Dillman.

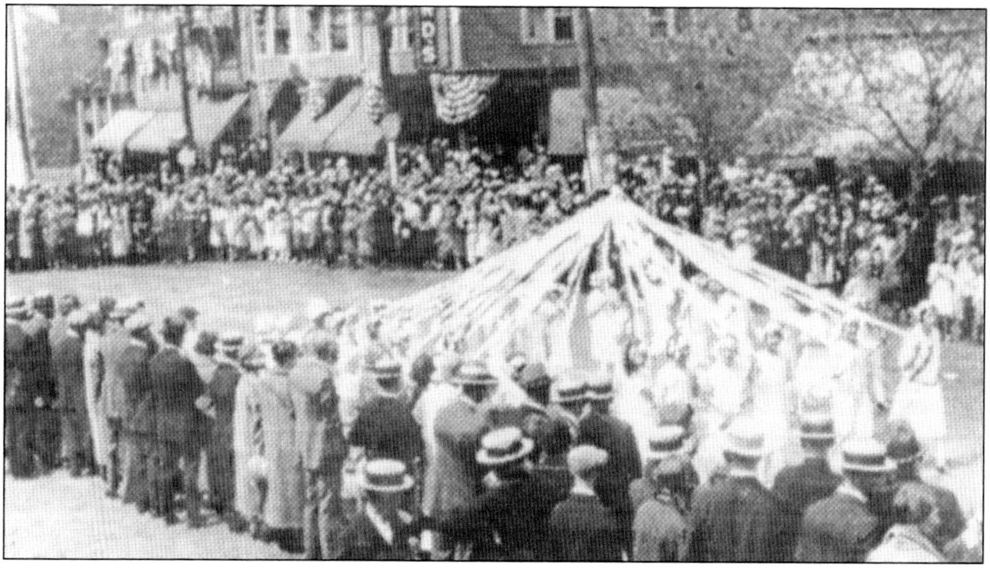

Hundreds of people marched in the 1925 Washington School dedication parade. Thousands of people from all over the county came by train to watch the festivities. This picture was taken on Lehigh Avenue at the intersection at Frack Street.

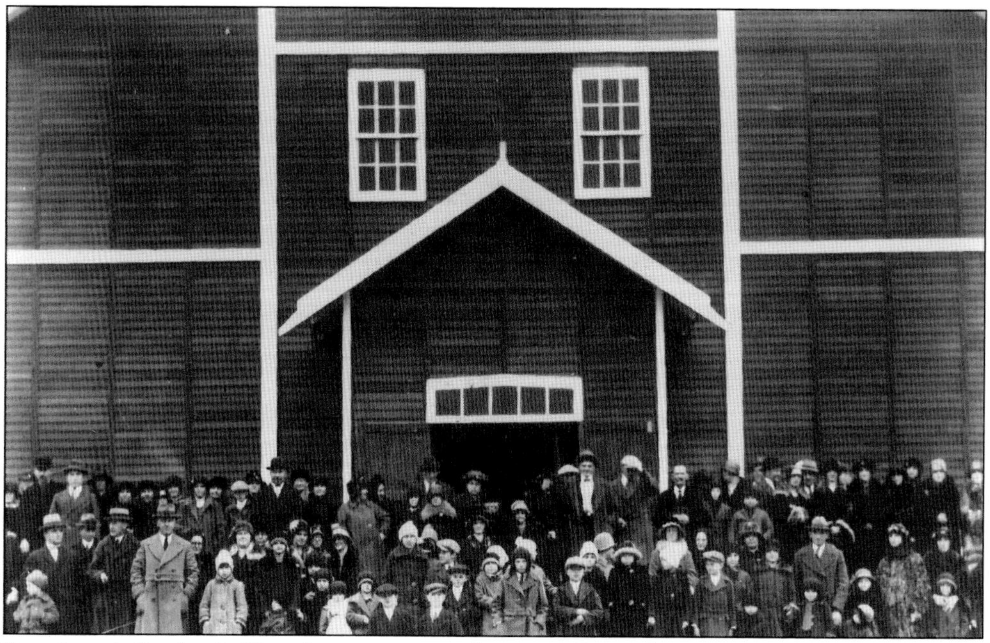

Seen here is St. Ann's Church upon its completion on December 21, 1925. One of the longest strikes in the history of anthracite mining took place that year. The miners, all Polish immigrants, had come to Schuylkill County and wanted to build a church of their own, which proved to be an economic burden due to the five-month strike. After much thought, the congregation bought a Circle A Portable and Sectional Building, one of the first "pre-fab" buildings built in our town.

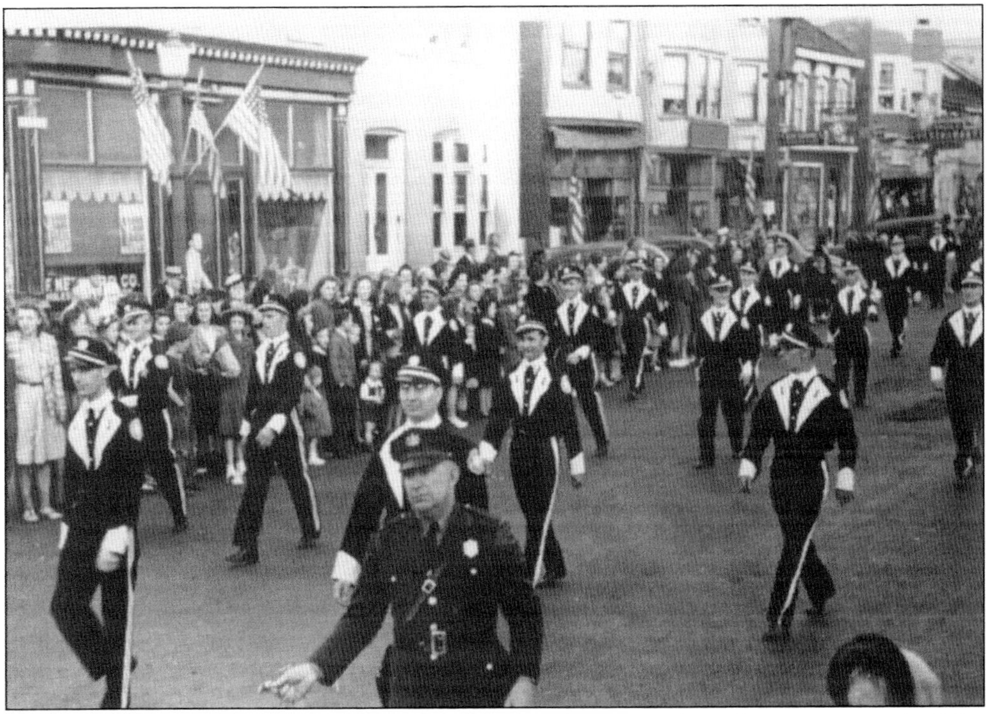

Remember the fine appearance the Goodwill Hose Company made at the various parades? The scene at Frack Street and Lehigh Avenue shows the police chief, Miles Forney, keeping the parade route clear.

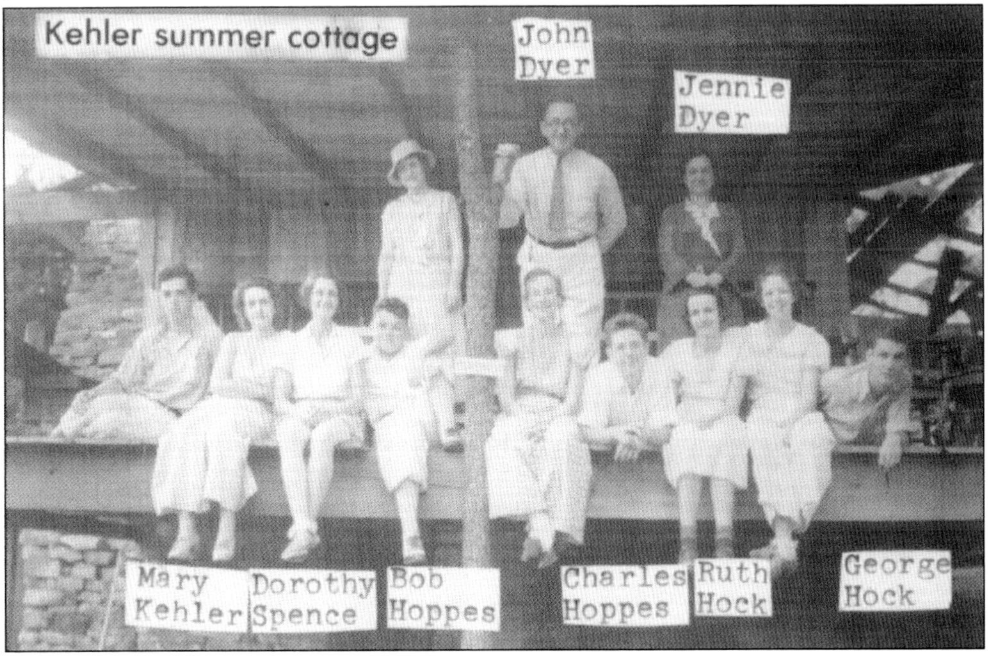

The Kehler family first came to Frackville in 1887. Mr. Kehler was a stockbroker and director of the First National Bank, as well as one of its original organizers. He also served one term on the Borough Council. Pictured are family and friends of the Kehler family.

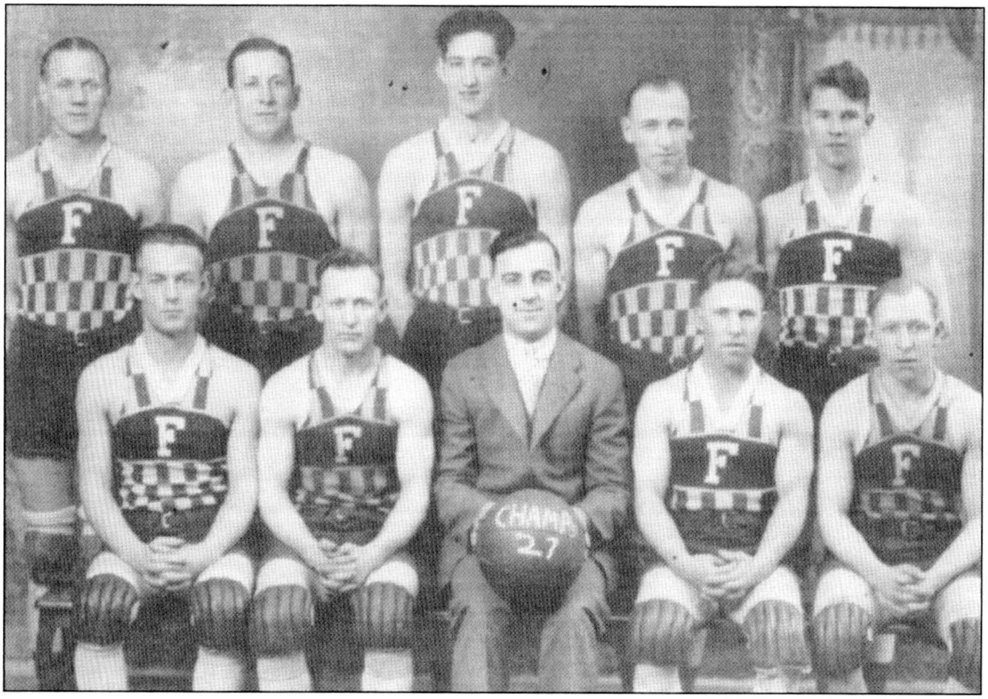

Frackville's 1927/28 Anthracite League Champions were as follows: (front) Jerry Foulk, Vernon Caton, Elmer Evans, Mickey Owens, and Adam Caton; (rear) Mike Hodgert, Bill Miller, Bob Copeland, Bill Caton, and Charlie Herb.

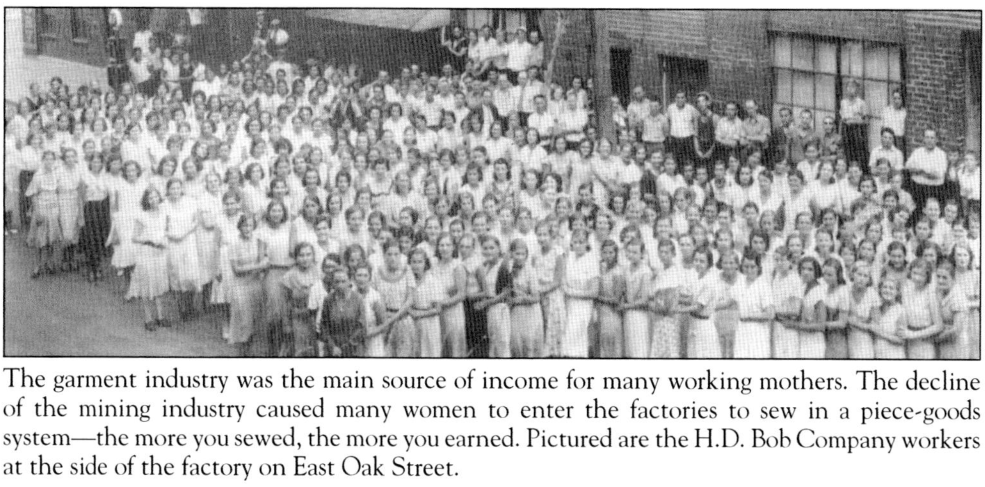

The garment industry was the main source of income for many working mothers. The decline of the mining industry caused many women to enter the factories to sew in a piece-goods system—the more you sewed, the more you earned. Pictured are the H.D. Bob Company workers at the side of the factory on East Oak Street.

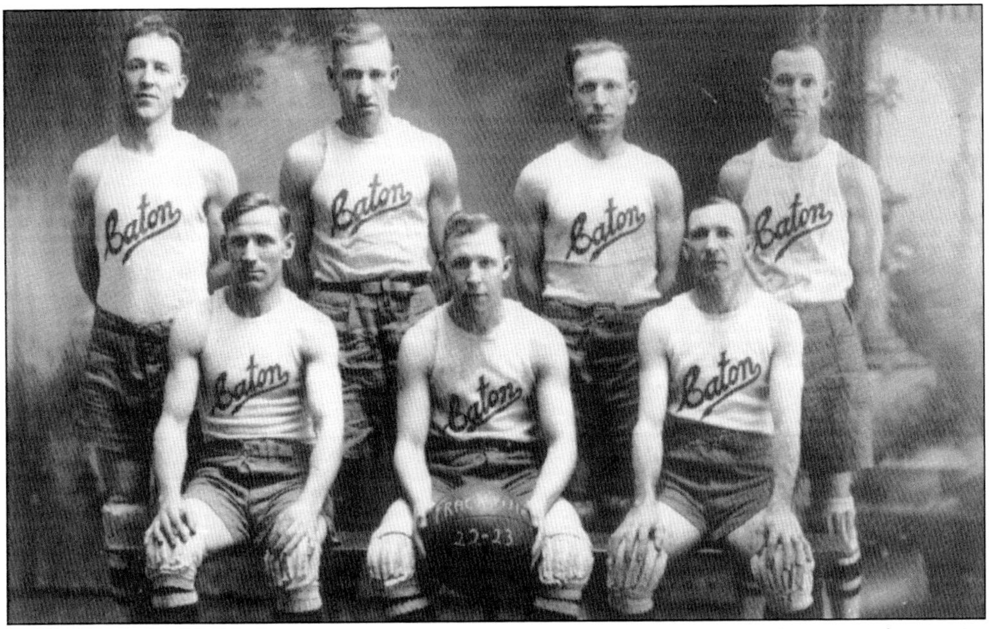

Here are the famed Caton Brothers, who put Frackville on the basketball map in the 1920s. From left to right are: (seated) Vertal, Adam, and Charlie; (standing) George, Bill, Vernon, and Bob.

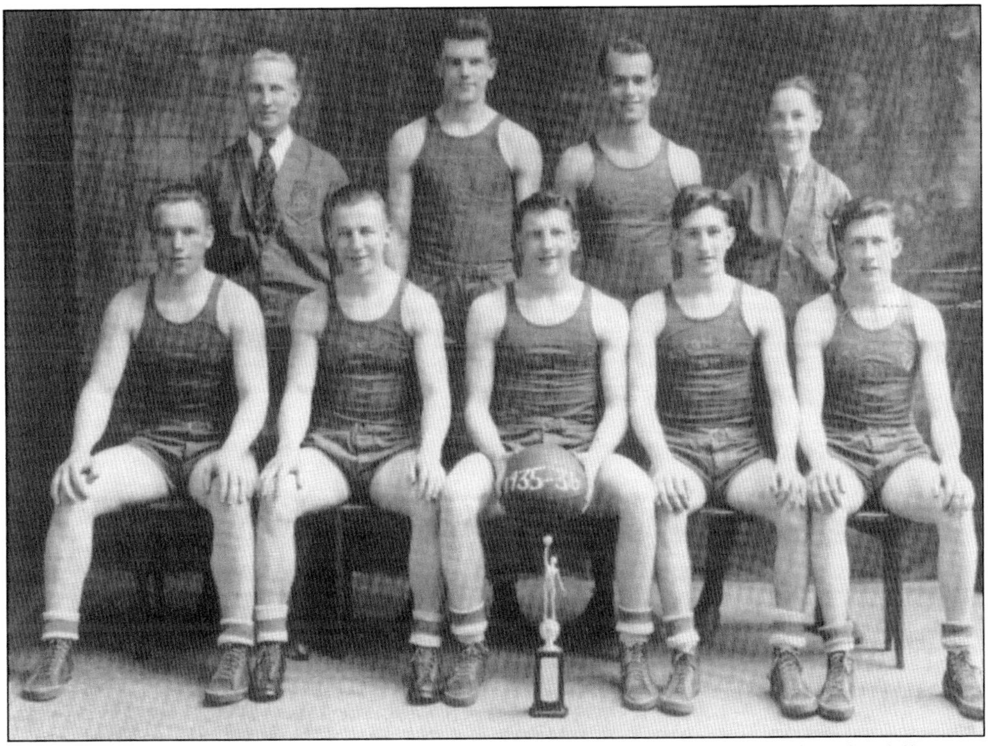

Members of the Frackville Stegmeiers basketball team of the 1930s included the following: (front row) Stanley Slovak, John Pilconis, George Povailitis, Cyril Copeland, and Charlie Caton; (rear) Bill Kirelawich (manager), Bill Savitsky, Walter Heim, and John Kociusko.

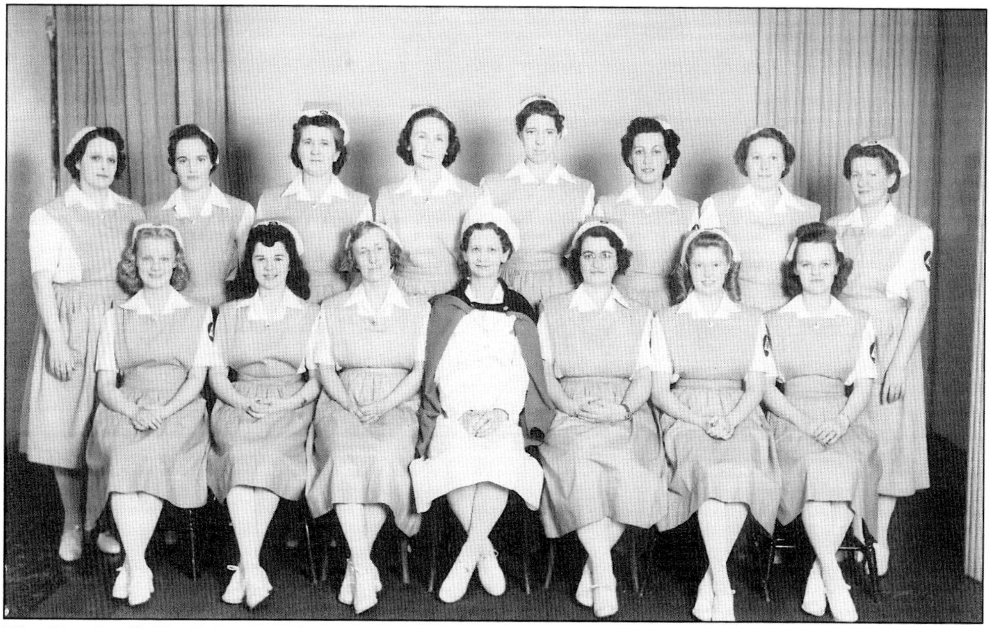

The Frackville Red Cross Volunteer Nurses Aides in 1941 were as follows: (front row) unknown, Bernadette Birster, Mia Frew, Mrs. Placida Grant (instructor), Erdie Bardorf, Grace Bevan Best, and unknown; (back row) Maude Eyster, Jennie Fellows, Catherine Williams, Mary Connelly, Bertha Houser, Ruth Swartz, Helen Polli, and unknown.

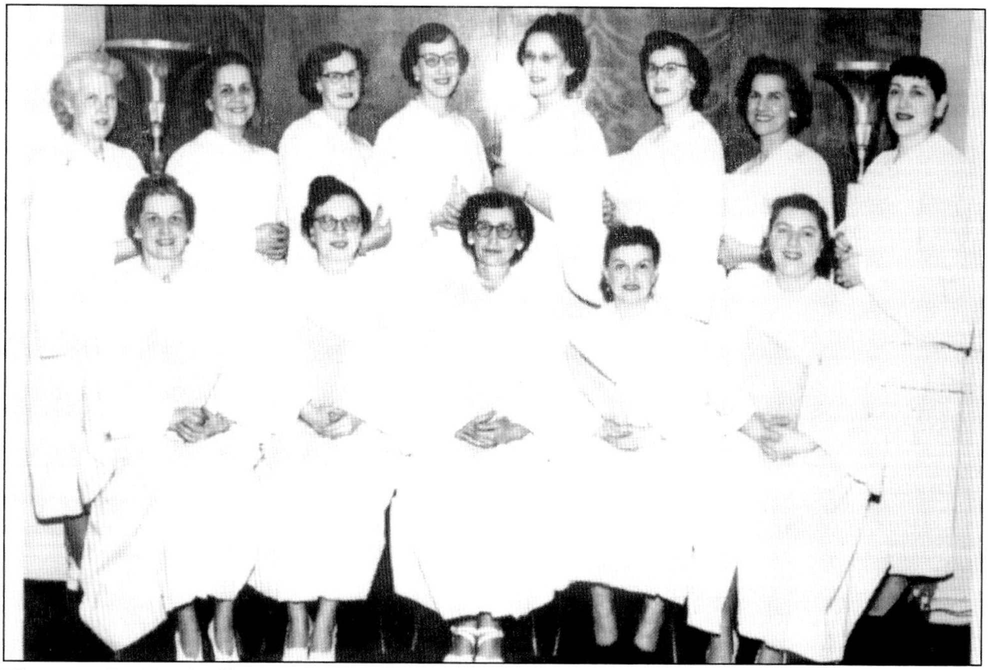

This was the Frackville Woman's Club Chorus. Singers included: (front row) Harriet Dalton, Jeanette Niel, Dorothy Spence, Gertrude Tenenholz, and Elizabeth Foulk; (back row) Edna Bowe, Madlyn Kistler, Elsie Hughes, Audrey Hinkle, Miriam Brienich, Charlotte Smith, Betty Runkle, and Frances Supowit.

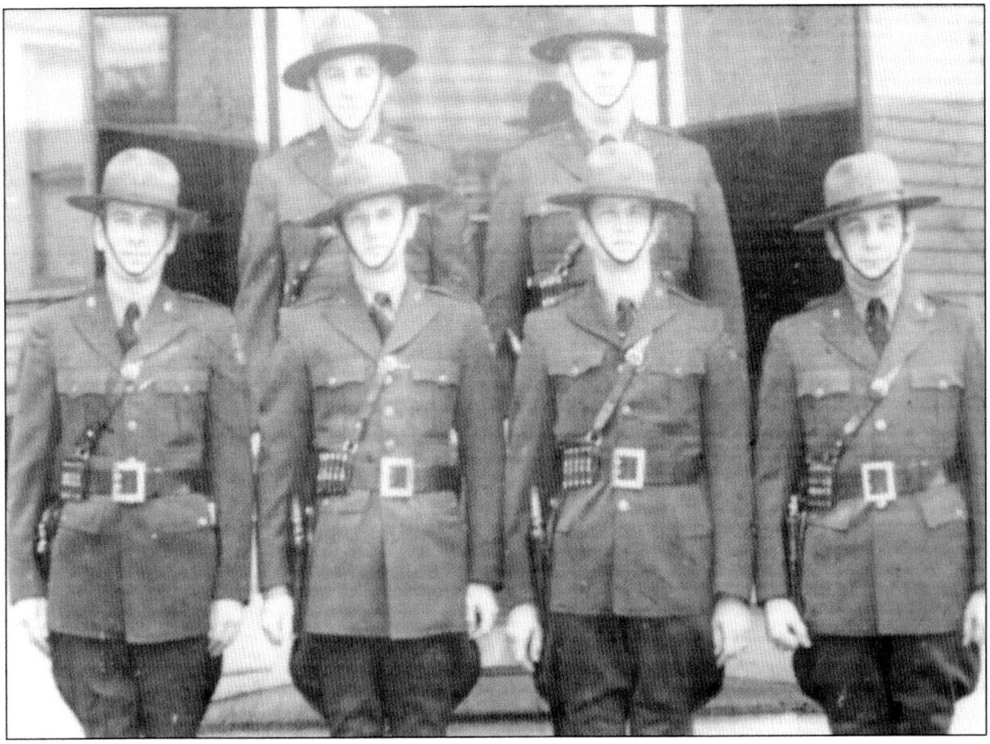

State troopers stationed at the Frackville Barracks in October 1948 were: (front) Pvt. George Fisher, Pvt. James Meginnis, Pvt. Stanley Petzak, and Pvt. Donald Ravina; (back) Cpl. Frank Evans and Pvt. James McGrew. First located in the Barker House on East Oak Street, the barracks was later moved to West Oak Street and is now located on the Morea Road.

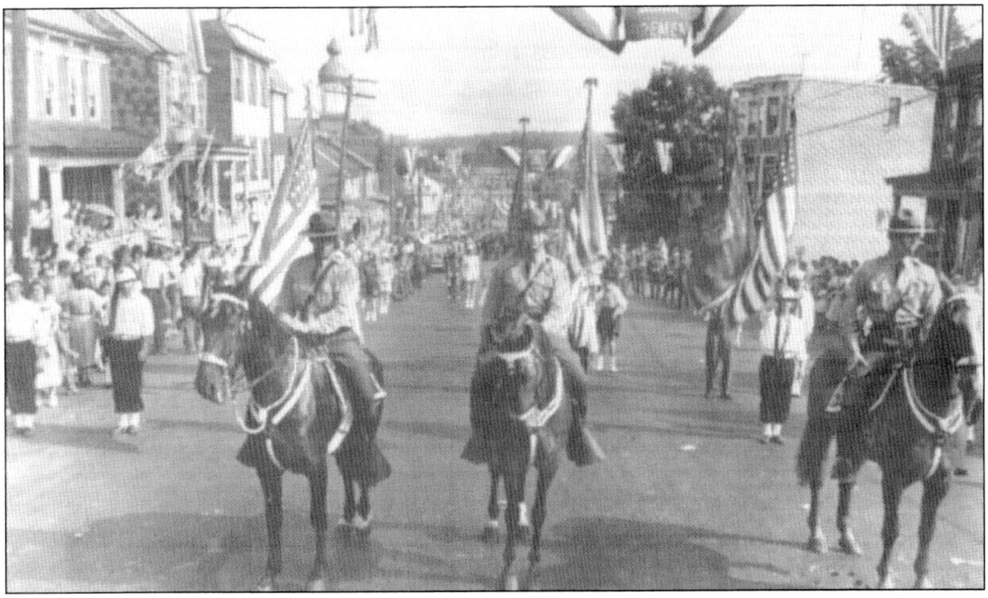

This scene is from the 1957 Schuylkill County Firemen's Convention and shows the State Police mounted colorguard leading the marchers up South Lehigh Avenue. The home at the left was later razed, and the post office is now located there.

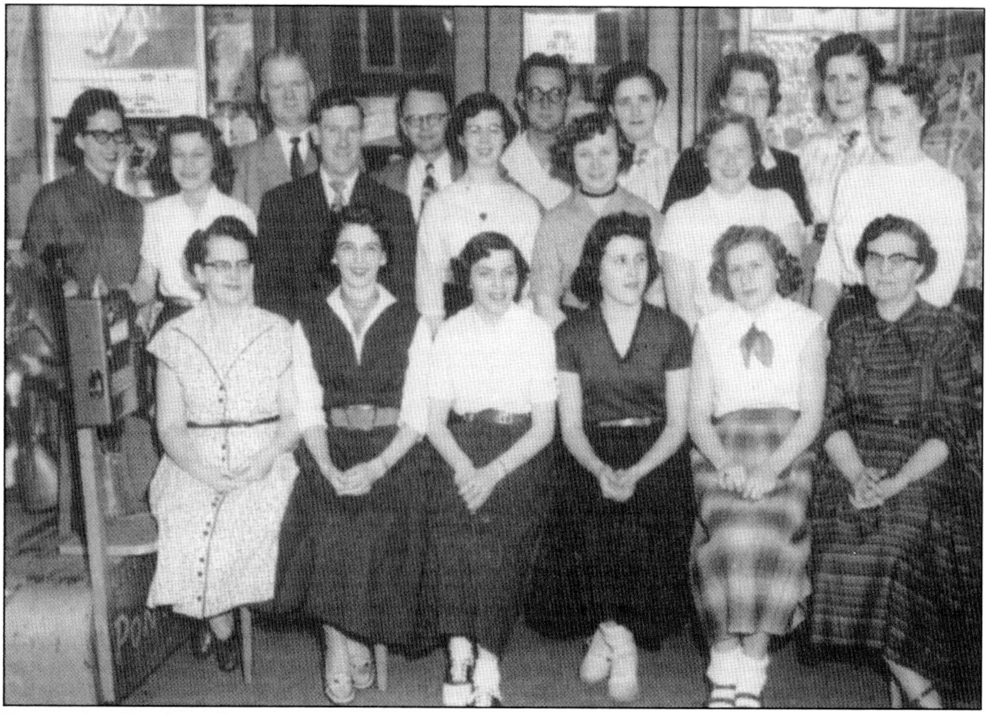

Remember Brady Atkin's 5 & 10 at 44 South Lehigh Avenue? This 1955 photograph shows, from left to right, the clerks who worked there at that time: (front row) Elva Soult, Fay Lore, June Sherry, Kathryn Tregelias, Ruth Powis, and Blanche James; (second row) Alice Rice, Eva Semanchick, Sam Morgan, Lois Evans, Helen Slovick, Sally Bajejiam, and Mabel Hinkel; (top row) Brady Atkins (owner), George Manderlick (manager), Kenny Knittle, Shirley Klimko, Dorothy Dellock, and Dorothy Klimko.

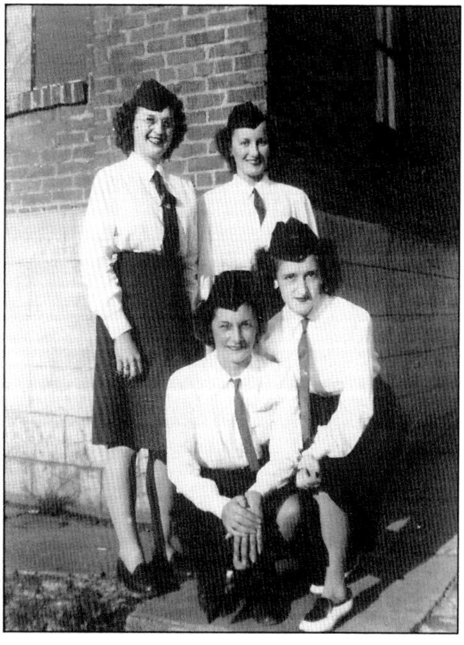

The Frackville Victory Parade was held September 26, 1945. The ladies who worked for the Charles Rabin Company stayed after work hours to help make the Botany blue skirts and hats so that all workers could march in uniform in this parade. Pictured are, from left to right: (standing) Lorraine Gibowicz and Pauline Cheryaka; (kneeling) Rose Wilinsky and Olga Koropchak.

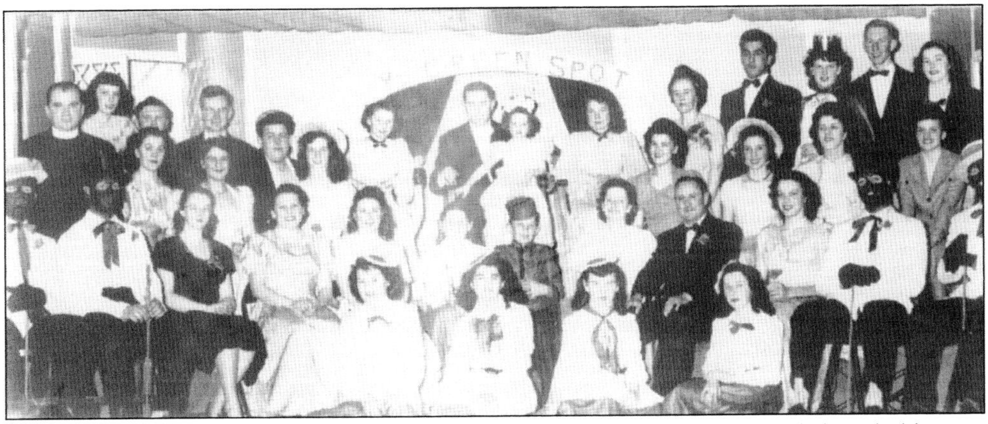

Here are members of the cast of *Ye Green Spot In Kilarney*, the first minstrel show held at St. Joseph's Church in March 1948. Players were: (front row) Patricia Smith, Theresa Canto, Joan Scully, and Jean Carroll; (second row) Francis Heine, Russell Pleva, Mary Carroll, Harriet Lawrence, Phyllis Fennelly, Margaret Chapman, James Haley, Bernice Neary, Jacob Kleman, Mary Huth, James Curry, and Joseph Purcell; (third row) Father Forgotch, Dorothy Oleksick, Alice Ellis, Pat DiRomulda, Priscilla Gray, Marguerite Green, James Dougherty, Ellen Noonan, Alice English, Rose DiJinio, Mercedes Escudera, Marie Elias, and Kathryn Kelly; (back row) Arlene Pulaski, Fred Dengler, Bernard Hartz, Pauline Fennelly (director), Thomas Anthony, Catherine Kiefer, John Allen, and Nonie Moran.

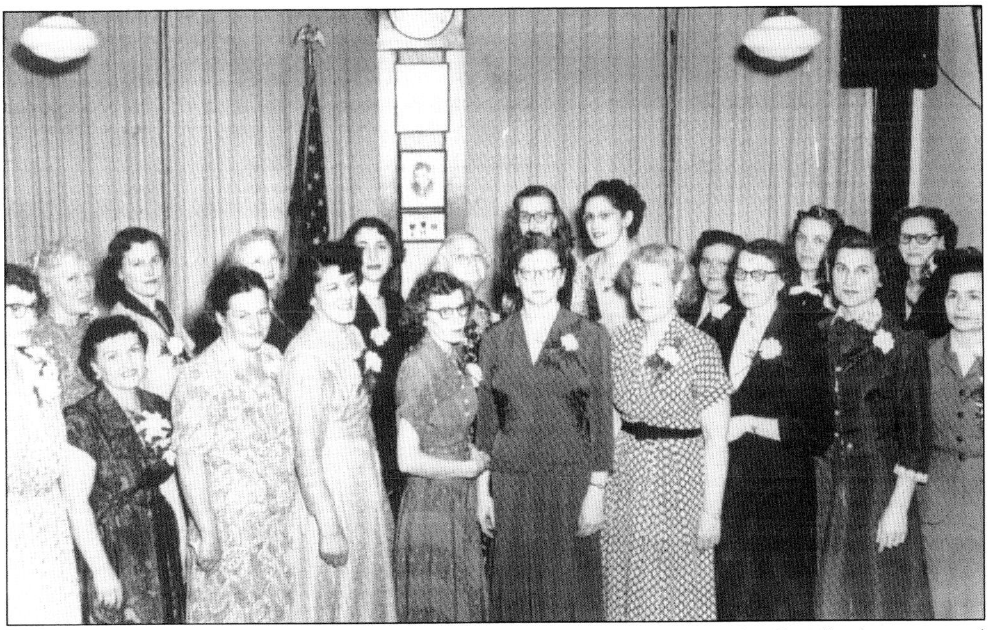

This group got together for a Mother's Day program in 1951 at the Frackville Elks for a musical tribute to mothers. Pictured are: (front) Dorothy Spence (chorus director), Gertrude Tenenholz (pianist), Marie Zaylskus, Marie Elias, Elizabeth Kellet, Marion Fiske, Edna Bowe, Clara Kellet, Betty Runkle, and Mrs. Henninger (guest soloist); (second row) Anna Schinkel, Anne Mirocke, Mary Noonan, Fran Supowit, Mary Hentz, Audrey Hinkle, Miriam Breinich, Melva Thomas, Gertrude Heim, and Elsie Hughes.

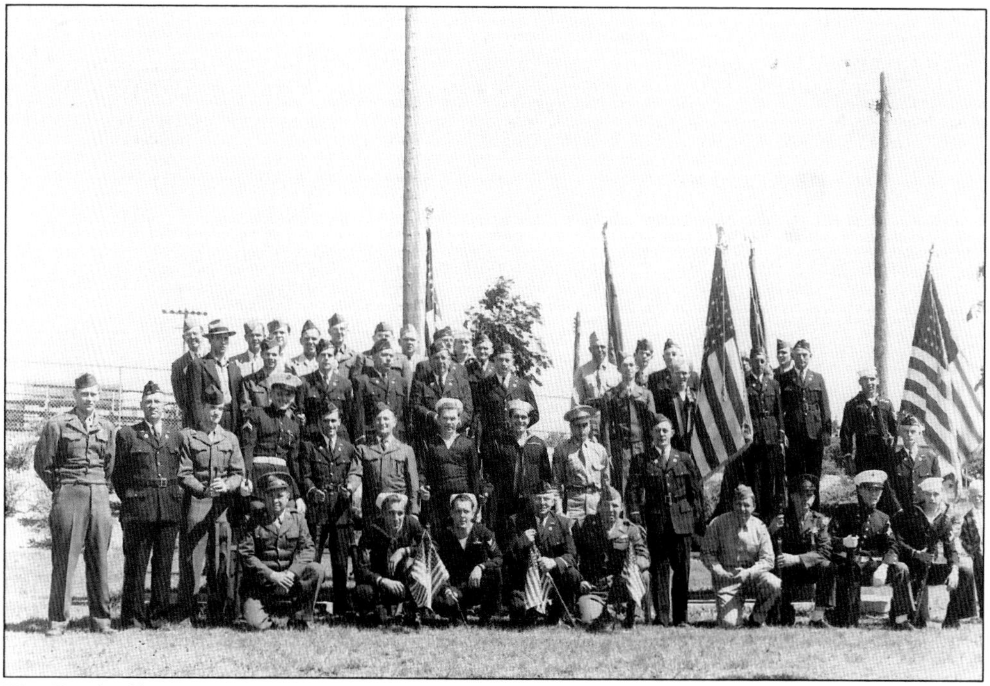

The Frackville American Legion Post was formed in 1919 in the Garden Theater Building and received its charter in 1920 with the following officers: Joseph Batdorf (commander), George Pauly (first vice commander), John Kessler (second vice commander), Joseph Anty (adjutant), Wm. Davis (finance officer), Alex Shelcuskie (chaplain), and Wm. Roberts, Al Pasker, and Henry Leck (trustees). This picture was taken at a parade in 1955.

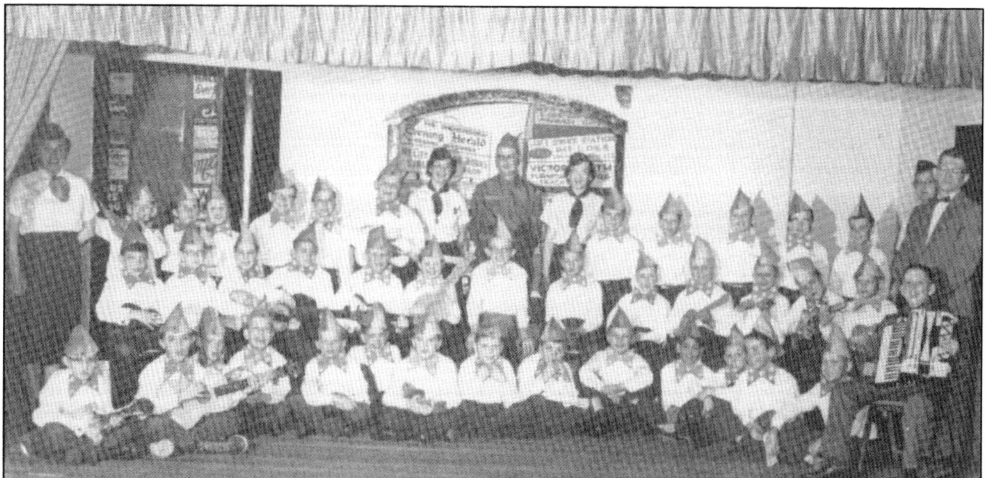

Cub Pack 92 of St. Joseph's Church held a minstrel for their parents at a monthly pack meeting. Pictured are: W. Curran, T. Curry, J. Becker, L. Farrone, R. Hall, J. Arcuri, D. Stanton, L. Rader, J. Marhon, M. Kokinda, Mrs. F. Rogers, C. Tomalavage, J. Neary, S. Zamonski, K. Schott, G. Petronko, R. Stanton, W. Schappell, J. Shearn, G. Kost, J. Dombrosky, C. Sienkiewicz, J. Baran, A. Baran, D. Fennelly, C. Miller, R. Ansbach, W. Rogers, Mrs. K. Schappell (Cubmaster), W. Schappell, Mrs. L. Stanton, J. Purcell, J. Seipp, G. Wolfe, W. Wolfe, Mrs. Benesky, and P. Becker.

Seven

Sights and Scenes

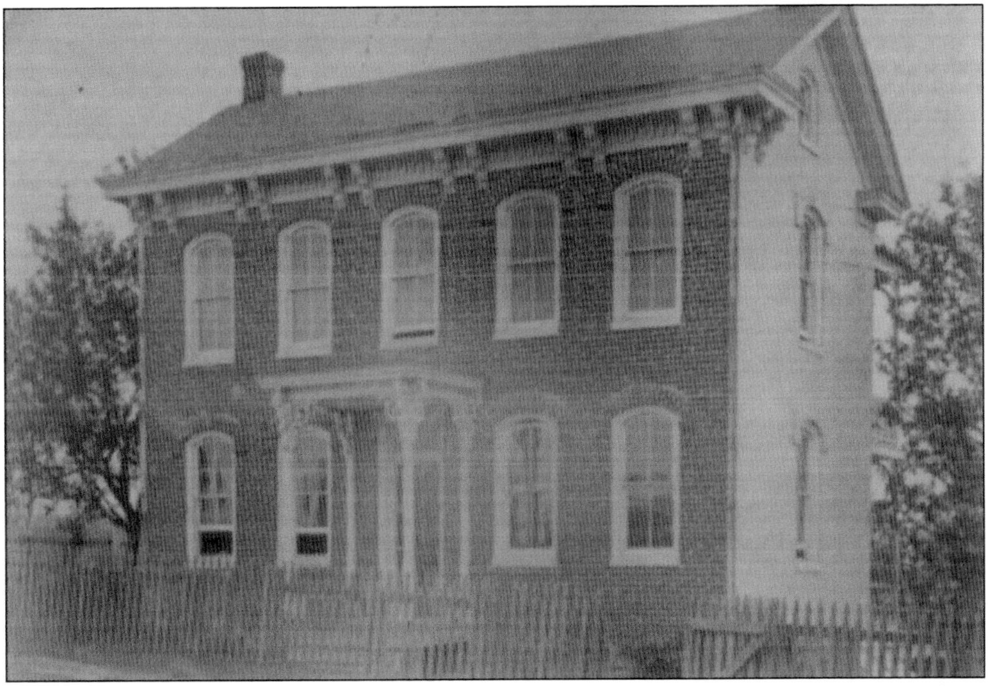

Built in 1877 by Alfred Wilson, the Miller residence at 62 East Pine Street was one of the earliest houses built in Frackville. It was built of "10,000 bricks delivered on a freight train from Reading to Frackville at a cost of $167.31." A coal stove was used for heat, and a kerosene lamp was used for light. Mr. Wilson was a miner and lived here only three years when he passed away in 1881. His widow, Maria Wilson, and her five children lived here, and to supplement her income she rented rooms to teachers in the school system. East Pine Street was a busy street in the early days. Funerals from Mahanoy Plane came up over the tracks and up Pine Street to the cemeteries. Most often only two carriages were used, and the mourners walked up the hill behind the hearse.

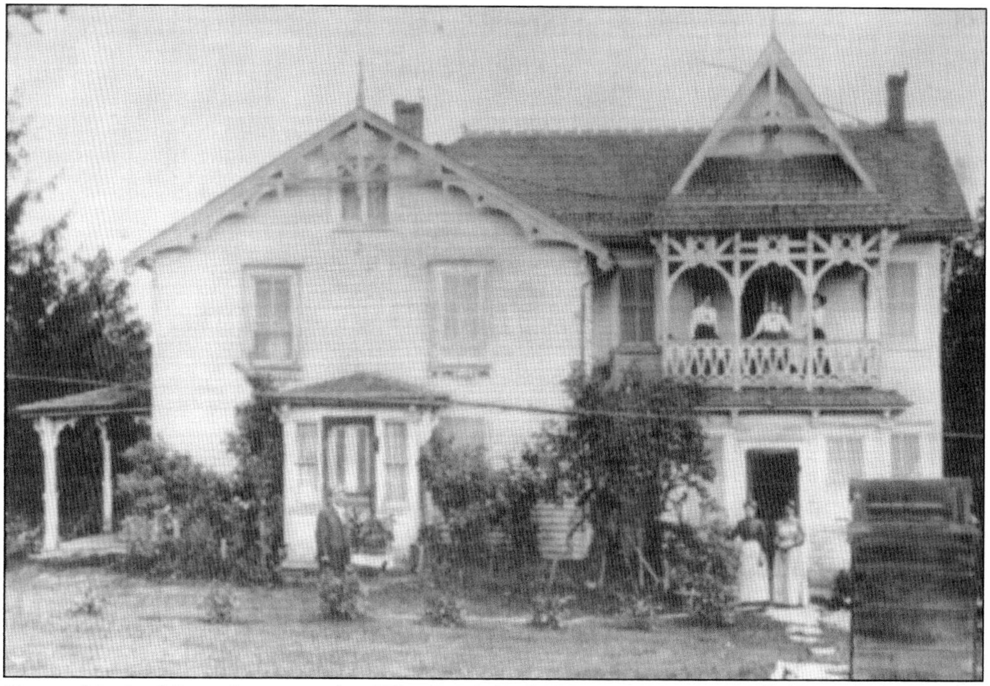

Pictured is the Haupt homestead at Third and Arch Streets as it appeared in 1901. The Haupt family moved to Frackville in 1854 and owned 500 acres of land on the west side of town. The G.A. Haupt Jr. Lumber Company began business on March 1, 1924. An entry in their business journal indicated that they built, sold, and, in many cases, financed 828 houses in town.

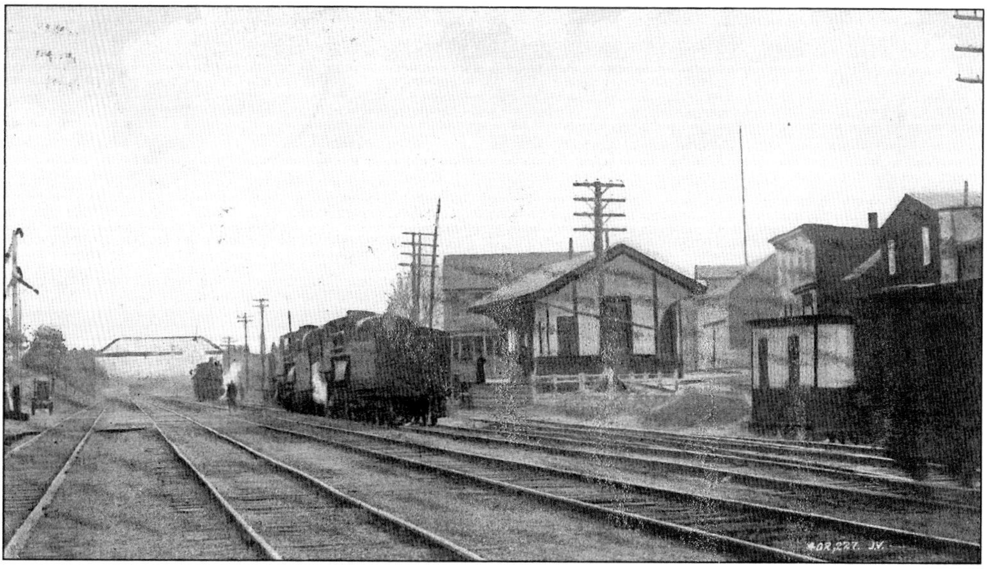

Do you remember the many trains that passed through Frackville in the early days? Many people traveled via train to Niagara Falls on a honeymoon, on excursions to basketball and football games, and on vacations to the shore, which were "quite the thing." This is a 1912 picture of the Pennsylvania and Reading Depot in our town.

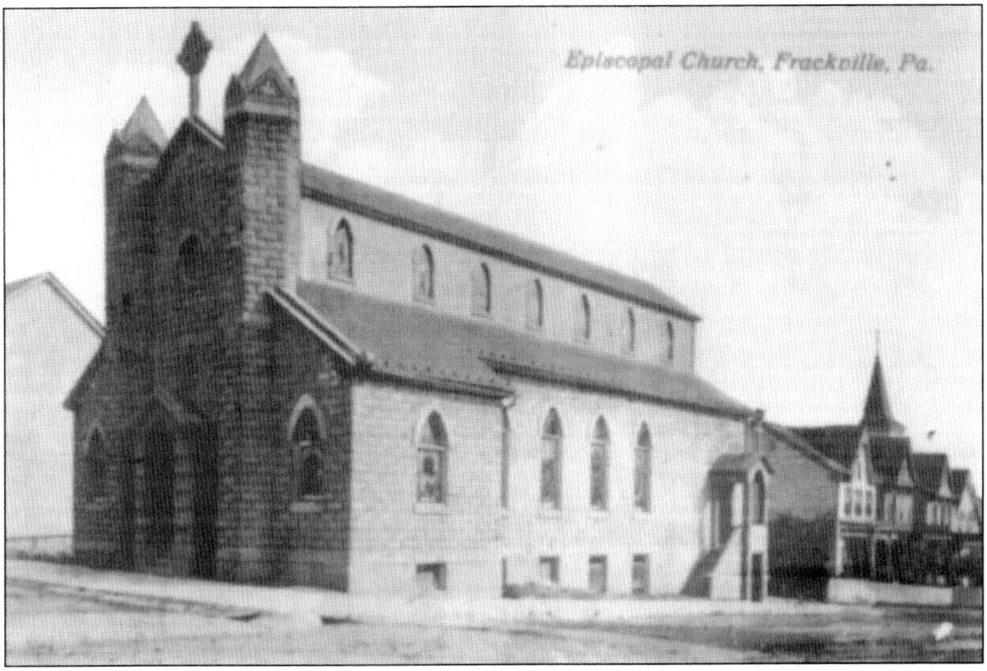

The Christ Episcopal Church was built in 1910 on a lot donated by Daniel Frack. While the church was being built, services were held in the home of Robert Hunt and Mrs. William Sanner. The church pictured was built in 1908.

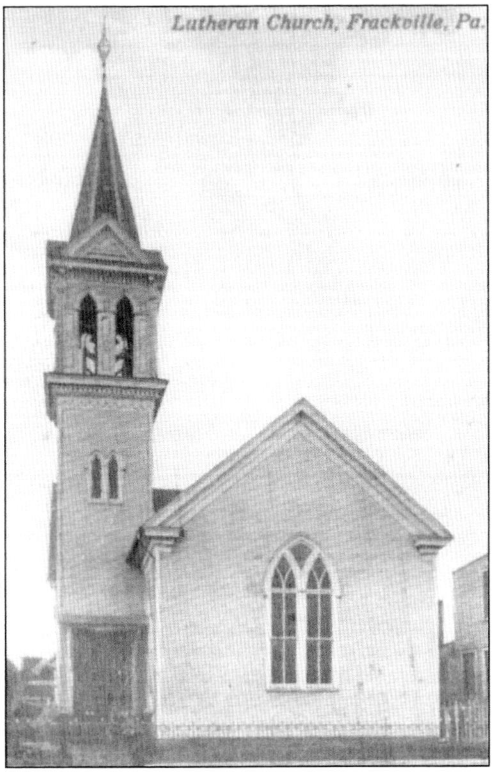

The Lutheran church was dedicated on October 20, 1895. It was the second Zion's church on this site, the first being razed in 1894. Built at a cost of $5,000 on property donated by Daniel Frack, it was used until 1925, when the third church was built at Oak and Nice Streets.

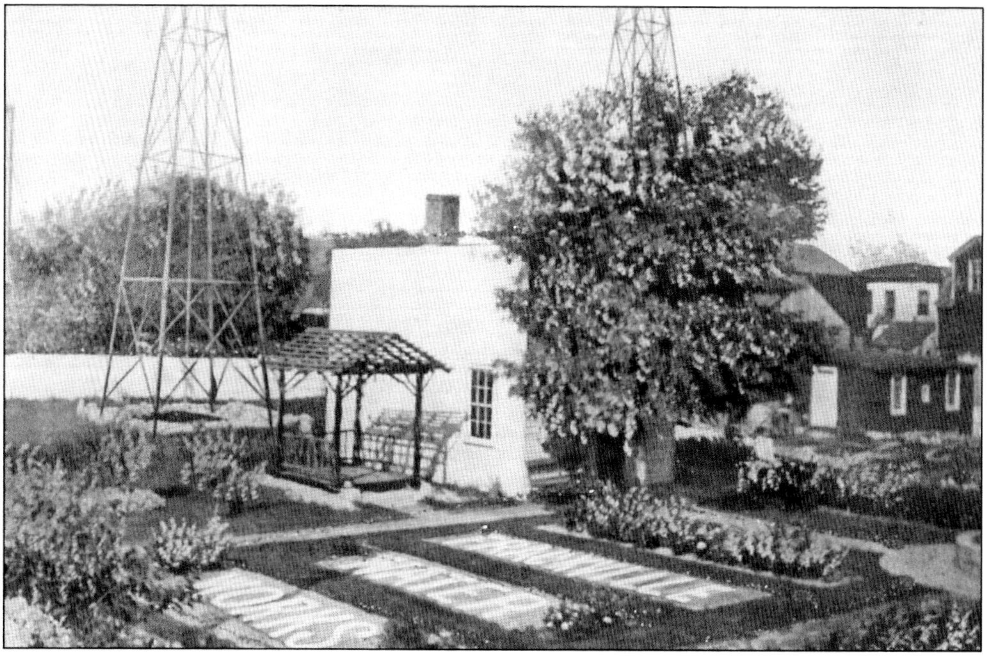

This postcard of the Frackville Water Works on Nice Street was purchased for 1¢ in 1906 by Mr. Frank Kiefer, who paid 1¢ to mail it to a friend in California. I bought it back sixty-eight years later at a flea market in Lancaster and paid 50¢ for it!

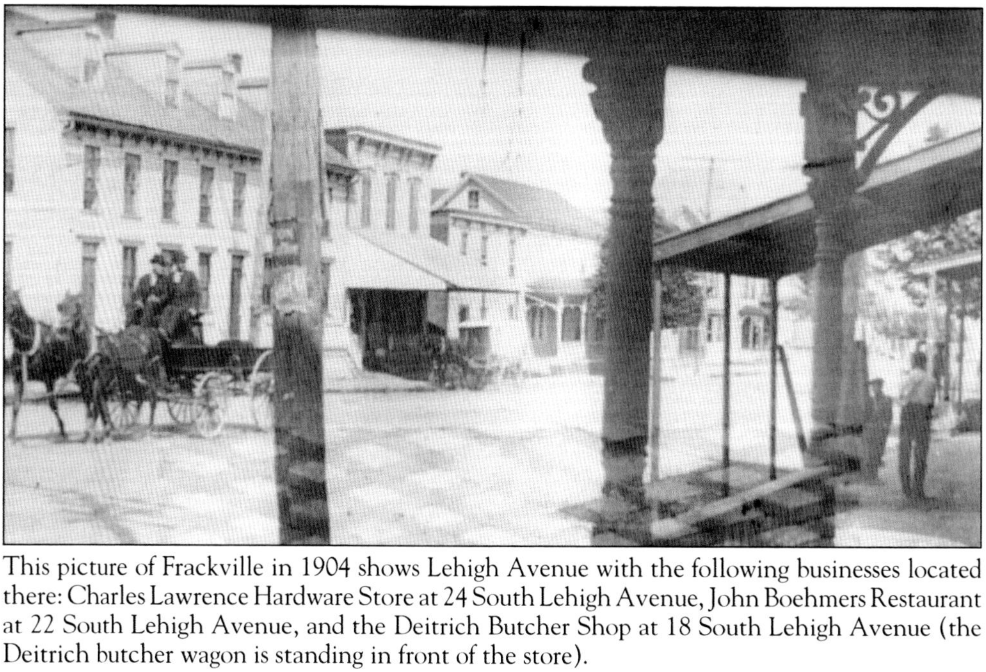

This picture of Frackville in 1904 shows Lehigh Avenue with the following businesses located there: Charles Lawrence Hardware Store at 24 South Lehigh Avenue, John Boehmers Restaurant at 22 South Lehigh Avenue, and the Deitrich Butcher Shop at 18 South Lehigh Avenue (the Deitrich butcher wagon is standing in front of the store).

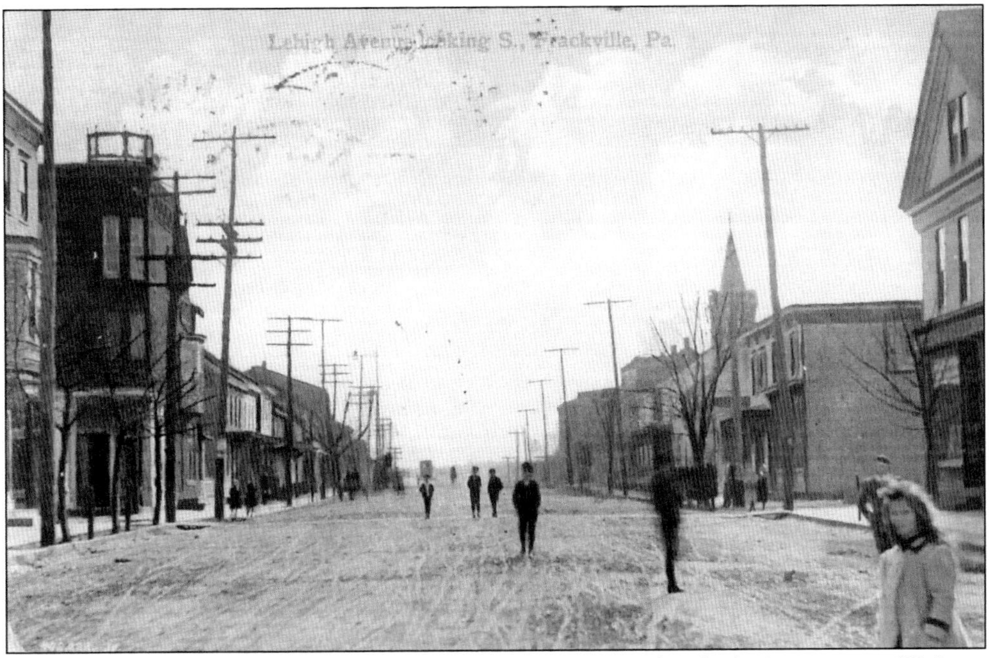

The four businesses at the intersection of Frack Street and Lehigh Avenue are Webster Kehler's Clothing Store and the Seaman's Store (on the left), and Sanner's Store and the Scott General Store (on the right), which was moved to the rear of the lot and is now the sight of CoreStates Bank.

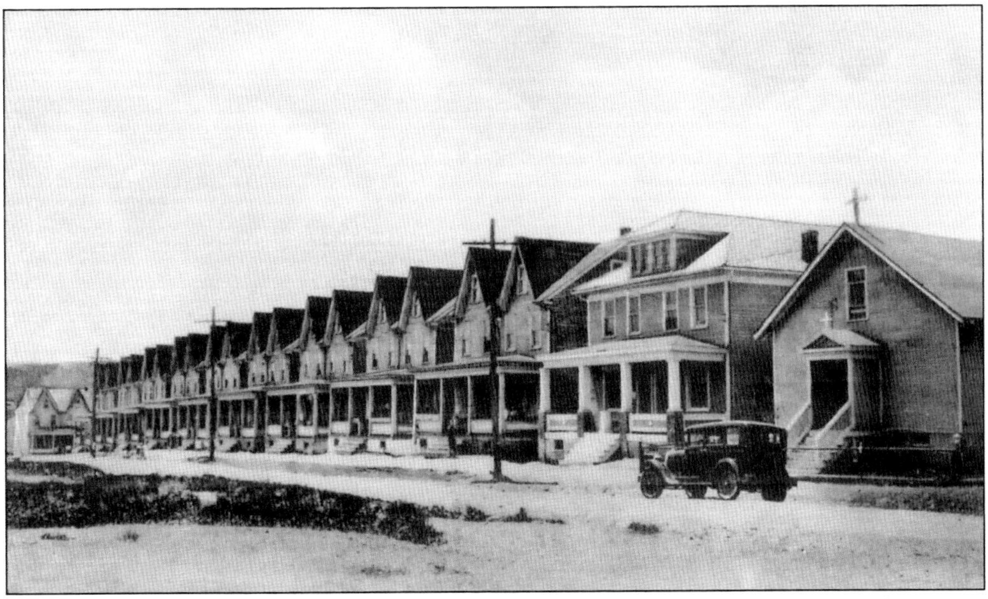

These houses on South Second Street were built in the early 1920s and were once known as Haupt Square. St. John's Polish National Church is on the right. Mr. George Haupt was a contractor and had a lumberyard at the south end of Middle Street.

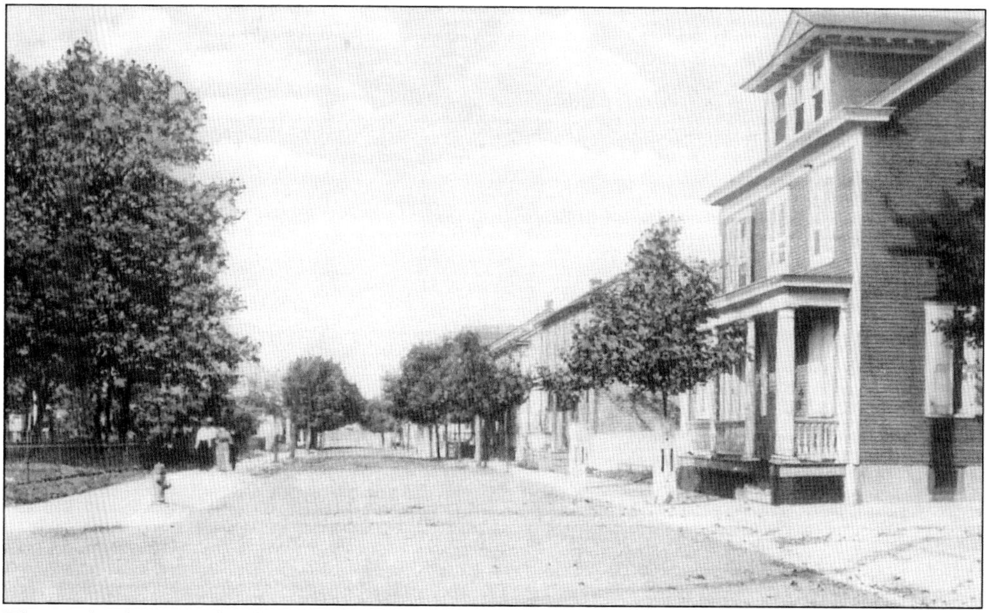

This early photograph of South Nice Street shows the chestnut grove in St. Joseph's garden (at left), although a blight in 1917 destroyed most of these trees. Dr. Berk lived in the house on the right, and the Meyers family now resides there.

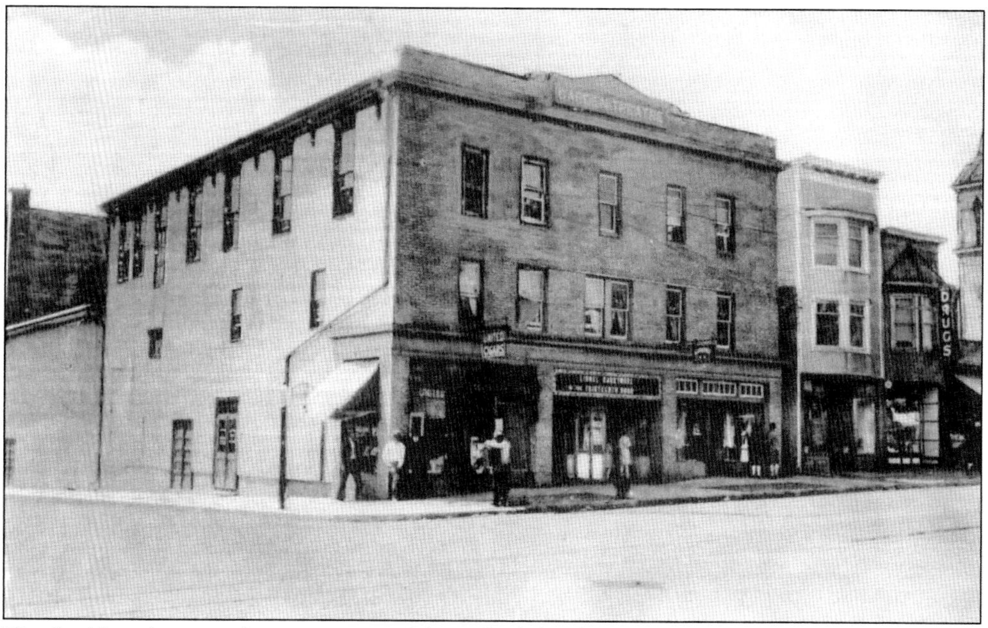

This building (previously seen on page 61) was built by the Frackville Patriotic Sons of America about 1870. It was operated as several theaters. There was also a bowling alley in the basement, and the upper rooms were used as lodge rooms.

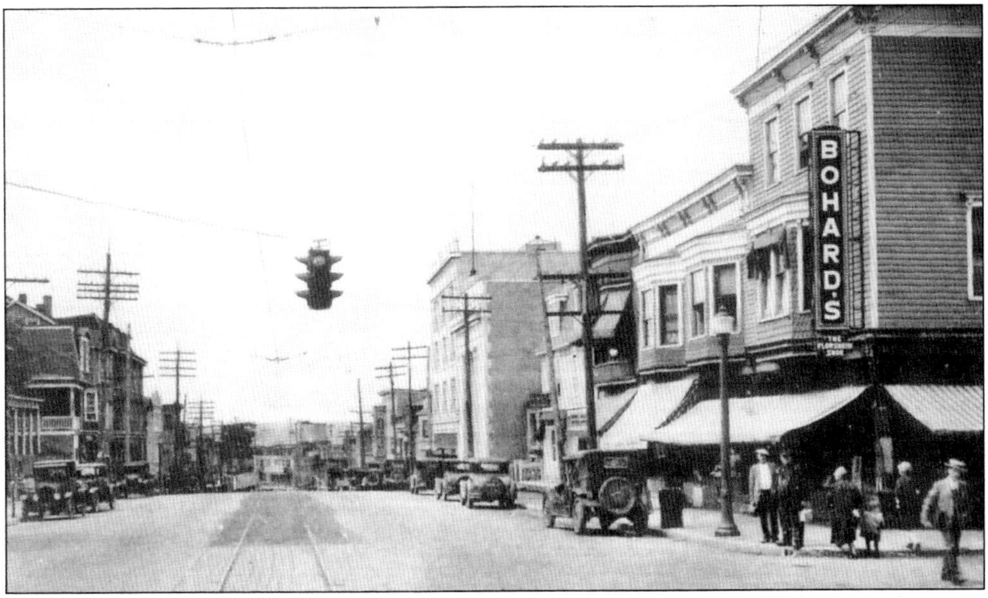

Pictured is a view of Lehigh Avenue looking north in 1929. Some businesses here at that time were Webster Kehler Clothing Store (later Bohard's), Mrs. Allen Hat Shoppe, Charles Seaman Cobbler Shop, Holt Drug Store, Nice Funeral Home, Purnell's Barber Shop, People's Trust Bank, and the Zetusky Building. Trolley tracks can be seen in the center of the picture, but the rest of the street was unpaved. A Maxwell touring car and a Model A Ford are also pictured.

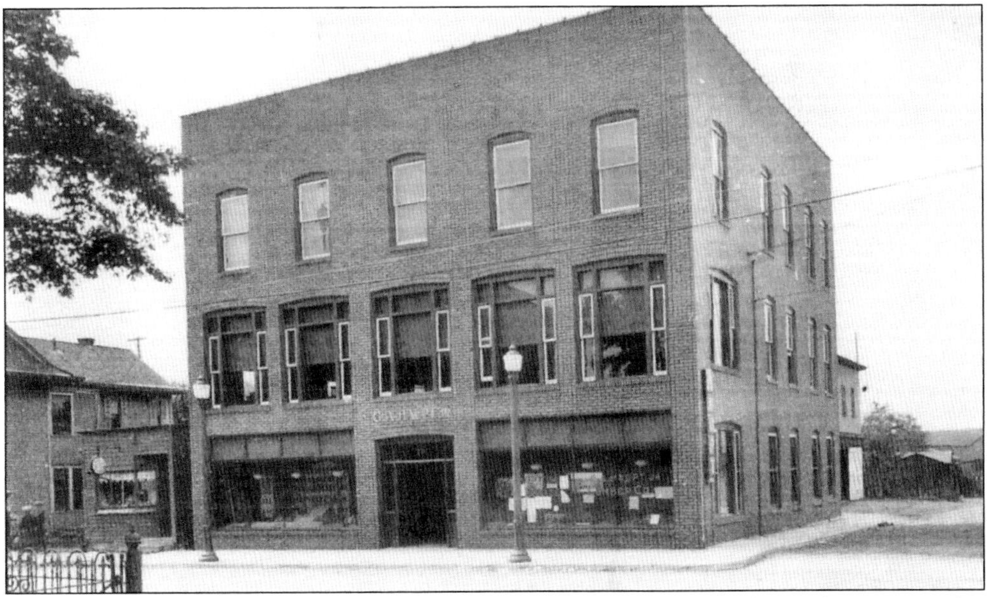

A model of a courthouse was built by Clarence Brosius and Caspar Arder in the 1920s and is pictured in the left window of the G.A. Haupt Jr. building at 25 West Frack Street. Mr. Haupt predicted that someday the courthouse would be located in town, but, as we all know, this never occurred; the model remained at the Haupt mill for many years.

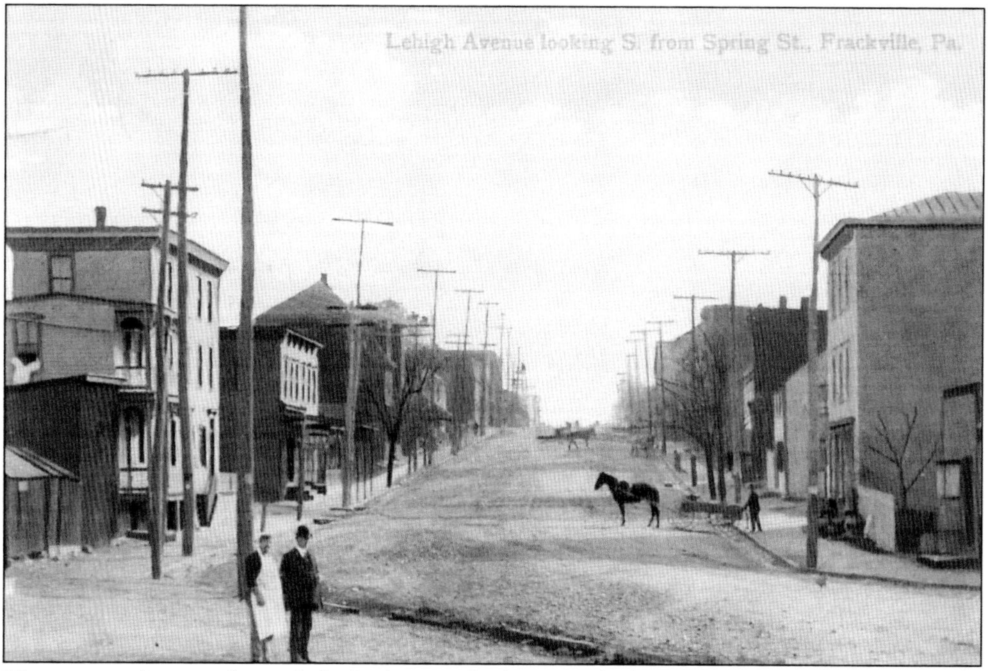

This postcard scene shows Lehigh Avenue looking south down Spring Street. Some of the businesses in town at that time were Barrett Butcher Shop (Mr. Barret is the man in the white apron), Palsgrove Hardware Store, Blue Star Diner, Darby Foulk Tavern, Charles Kirelawich Tavern, and Westminster Hotel.

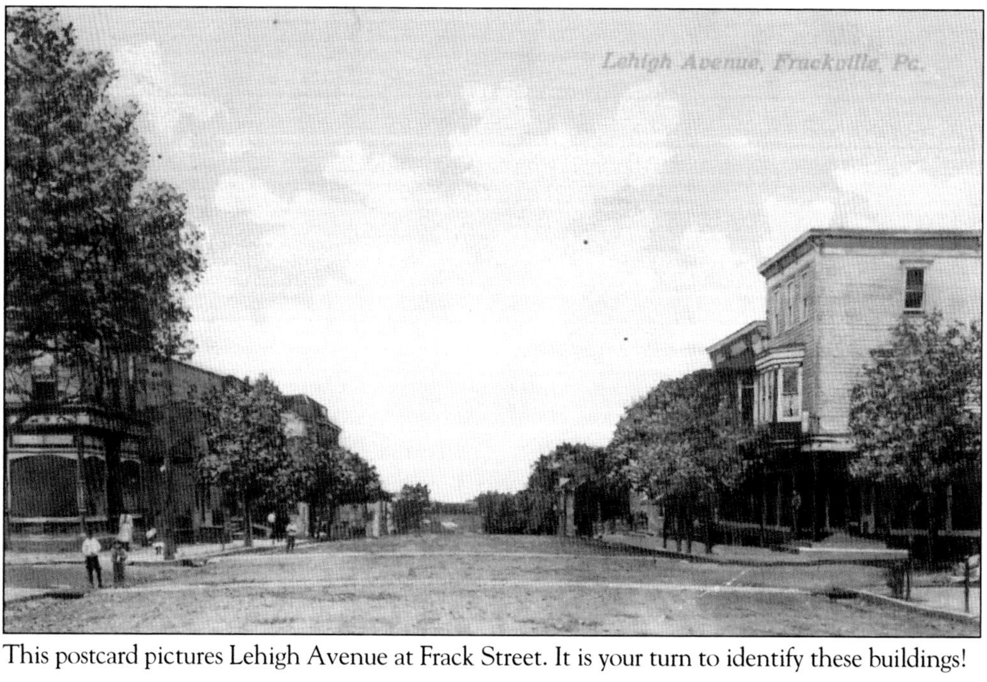

This postcard pictures Lehigh Avenue at Frack Street. It is your turn to identify these buildings!

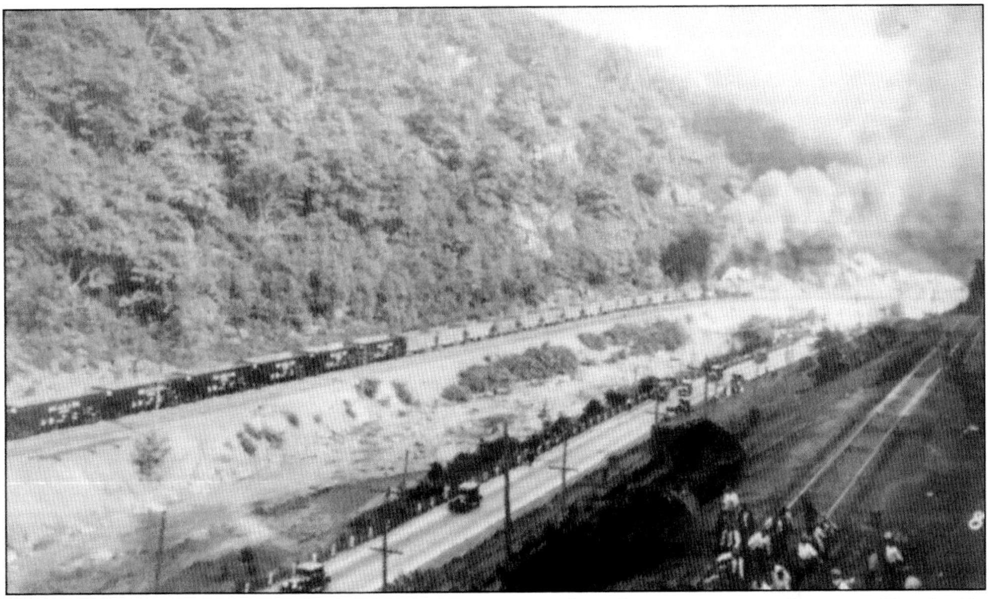

This scene from yesteryear shows the three main modes of transportation between Frackville and St. Clair: railroad, highway, and trolley line. Only the highway remains in use. The trolleys went out of business in 1927, and the railroad was never repaired after the June 1972 washouts caused by Tropical Storm Agnes.

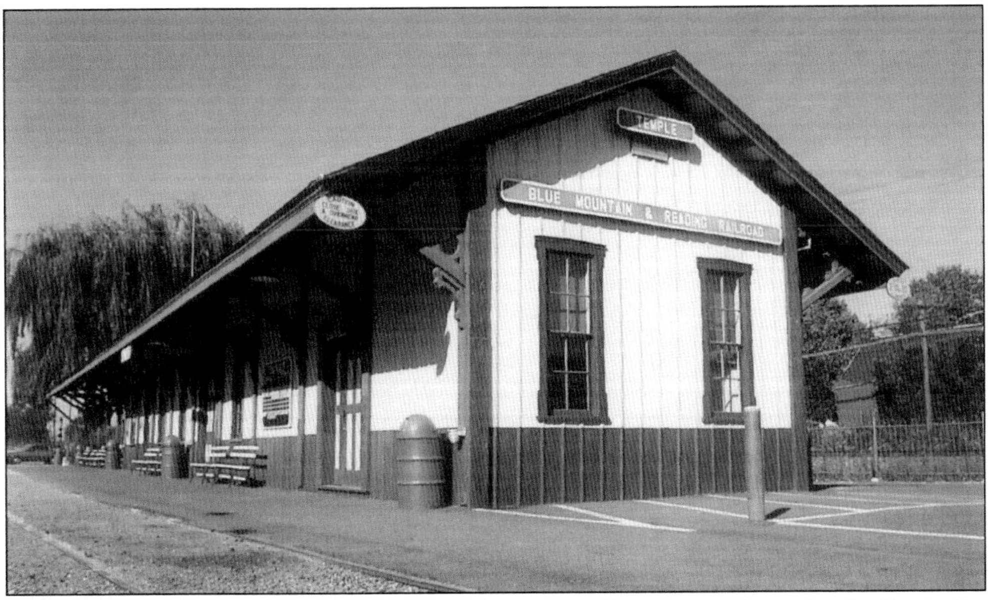

The Blue Mountain and Reading Railroad located at Temple was formerly the Frackville Reading Railroad Station, which was built in 1885. The Blue Mountain and Reading Railroad purchased this station in 1985 and completely disassembled and reassembled it at its current location in Temple.

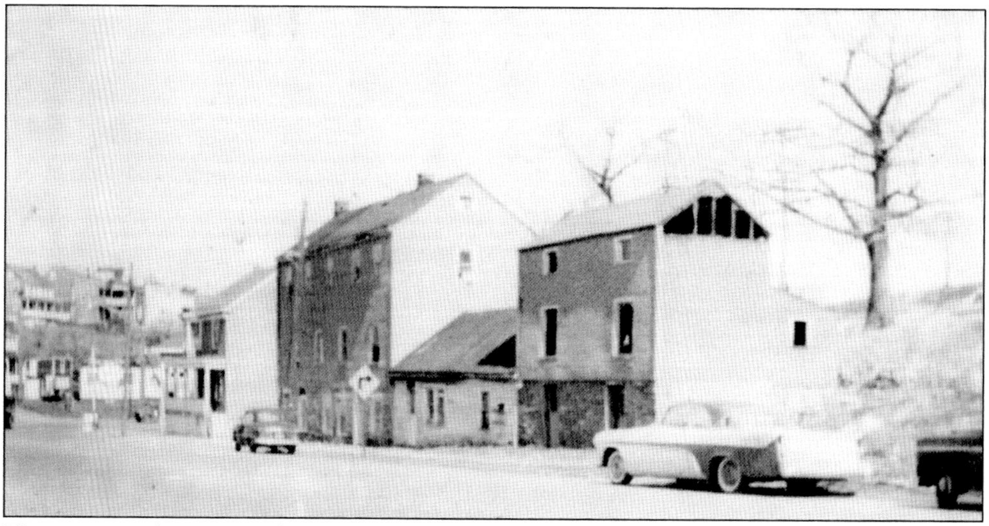

This picture taken in April 1958 was the last of the old Stone Hotel on North Lehigh Avenue. It was built in the 1860s and was owned by George Ernst in 1889. The Miller Service Station is now located on this site. These houses were demolished in June 1958.

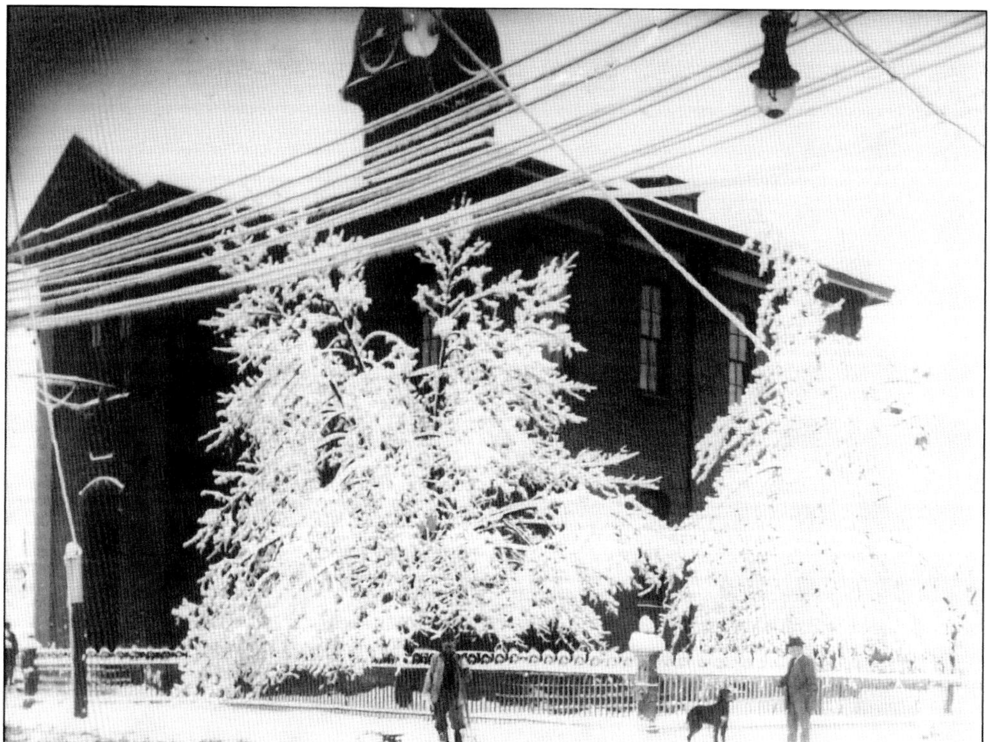

This beautiful winter scene shows the Town Clock Building on West Frack Street in the 1920s. While some townspeople were looking forward to the completion of a new medical complex, others weren't so happy that a century-old building was being razed to make way for it. The wrecker's ball took its first swipe in May 1986 on a building destined to be a state historical site.

The property on which St. Peter's Reformed Church was built was bought from William Haupt in the spring of 1892. The church was built at a cost of $4,200 and was dedicated October 30, 1892. Reverend Bower was pastor of the church and lived at 33 South Nice Street.

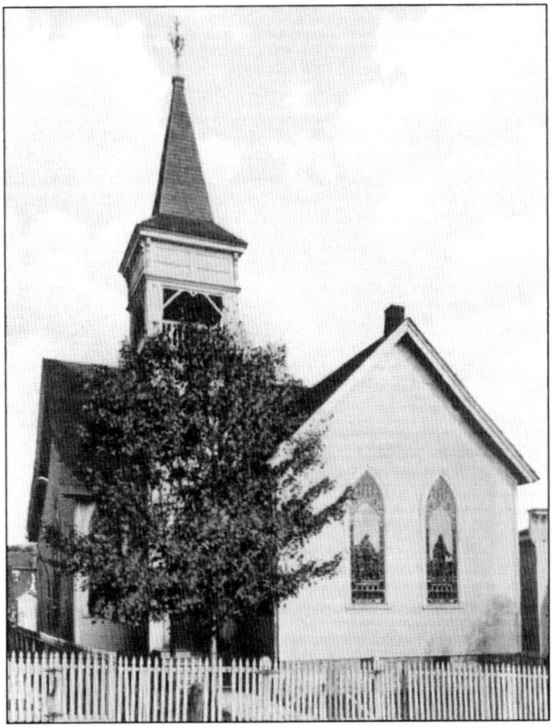

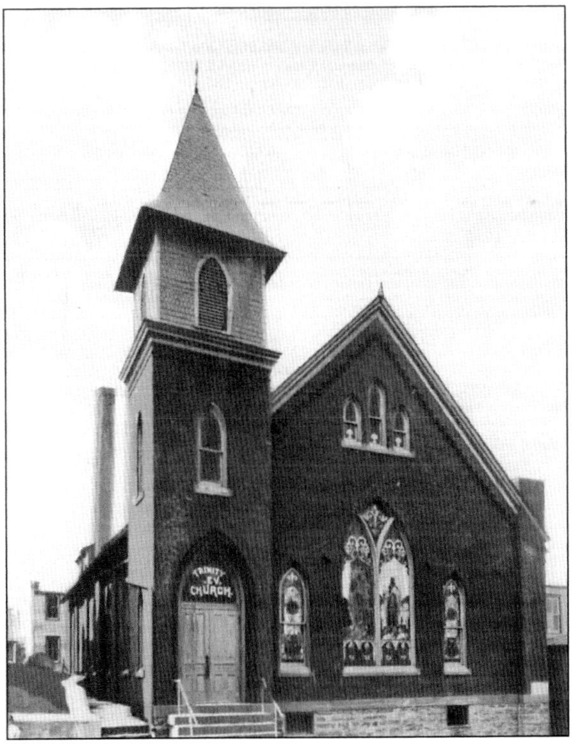

The Trinity E.V. Church was dedicated on February 9, 1902, at 56 North Balliet Street. The building committee consisted of F.S. Herb, G. Sebold, Harry Speidel, J.J. Kehler, Albert Kurtz, Harry Berkheiser, Charles Berger, and Reverend William J. Scheifley.

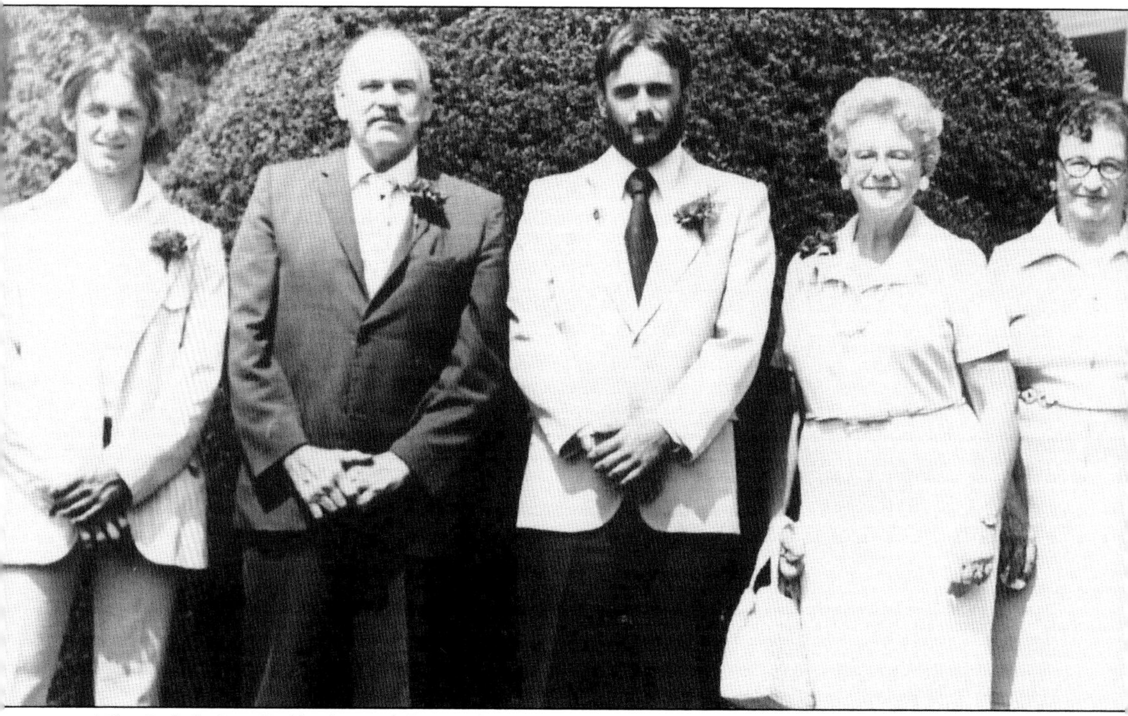

The Polish Star Belles hosted descendants of the Frack family at a garden party held at St. Ann's Church on August 22, 1976. Present were, from left to right, Jesse Frack Jr., Jesse Frack Sr., Daniel Frack, Mildred Orf, and Blanche Dewey. Jesse Sr. and Mrs. Orf were great grandchildren of the founder of Frackville. Jesse Jr. and Daniel were great-great grandchildren of Mr. Frack, and Mrs. Dewey was a friend of the family. Mrs. Orf was also the granddaughter of Lenora Meredith, the first postmistress of Frackville.

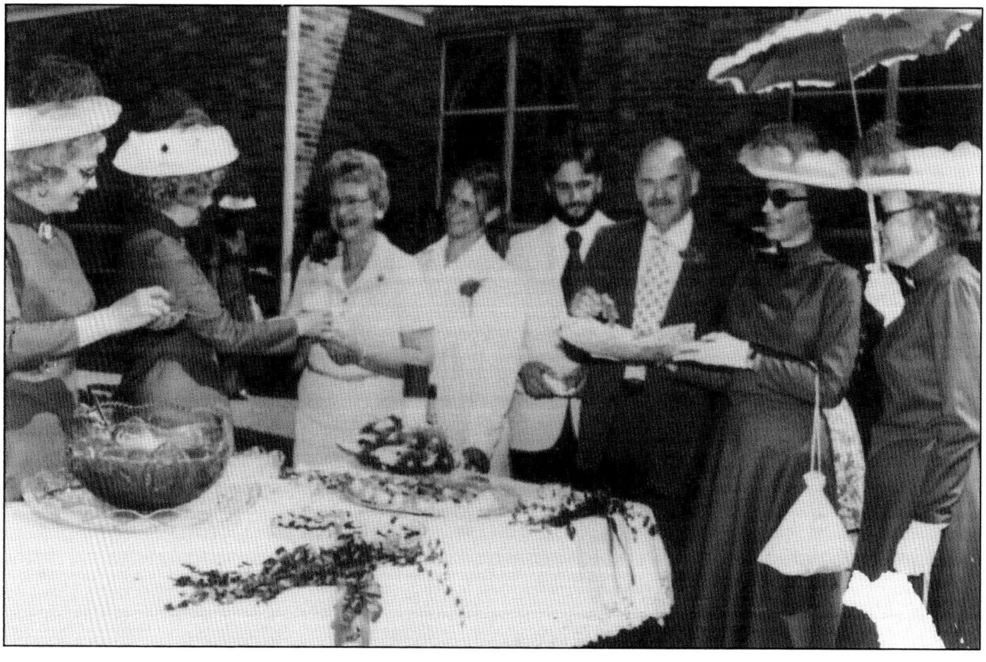

Eight

Centennial Celebration

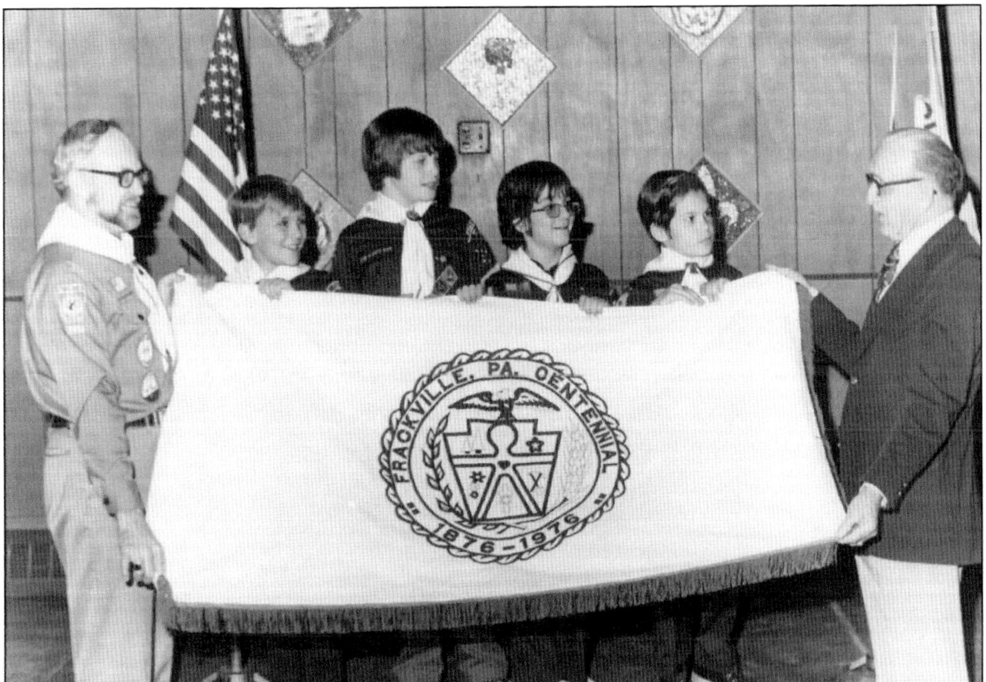

Highlights of the sixth annual Blue and Gold Awards banquet of Cub Pack 790 of Zion Lutheran Church in February 1976 included a presentation of the official Frackville Centennial Flag to Centennial Chairman James Hahn. The flag, which was used in all centennial functions, was purchased from proceeds earned by the Cubs in fund-raising campaigns. The emblem was designed by Attorney John Fields for the borough's 100th anniversary celebration. Pictured are, from left to right: Bob Berg (cubmaster), Joseph Bolinsky, Duane Dean, Wade Brosius, Roger Lane, and James Hahn.

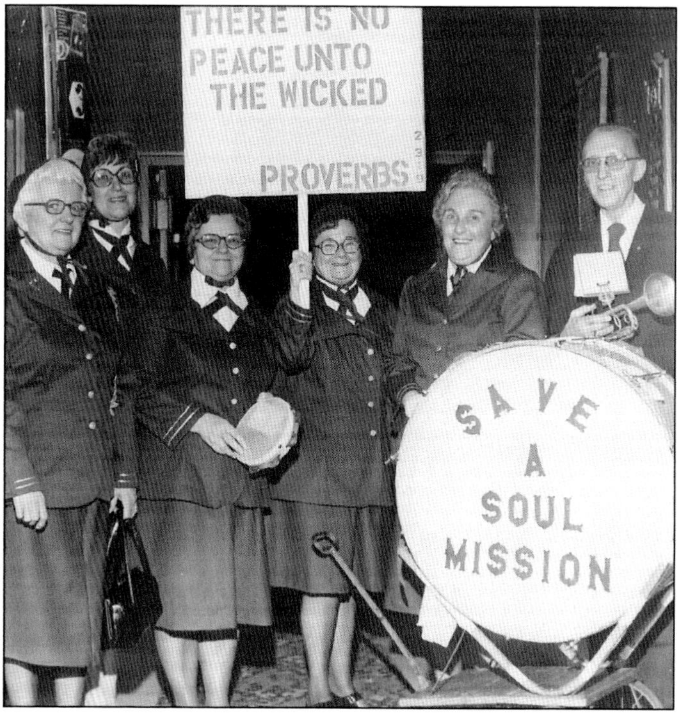

Members of the Frackville Elks 1533 Players put on a show at the lodge in 1976 as part of the annual Elks ladies' installation night. Pictured from left to right are: Barbara Grabey, Audrey Hinkle, Melva and Ruth Thomas, Florence Rogers, and Wilfred Thomas.

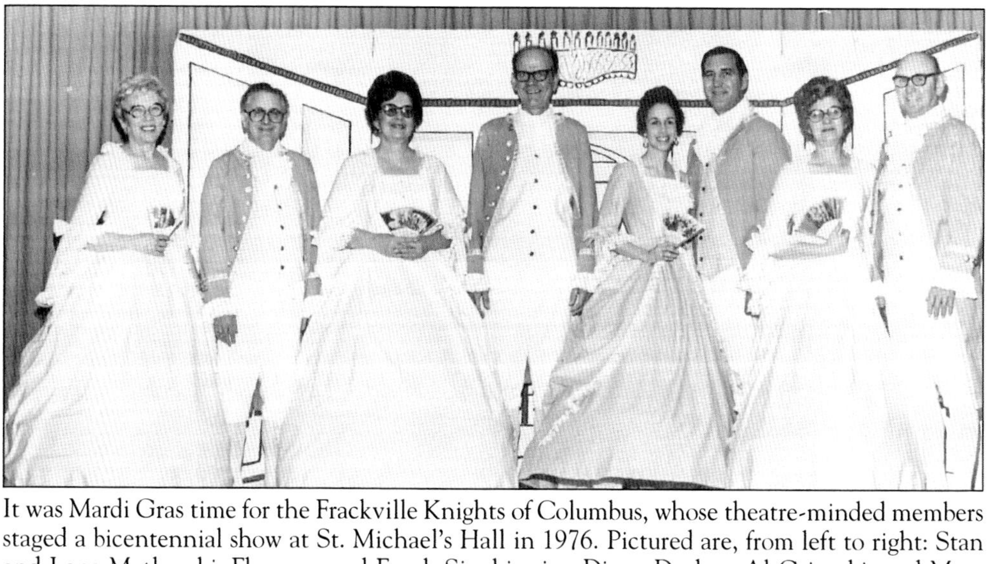

It was Mardi Gras time for the Frackville Knights of Columbus, whose theatre-minded members staged a bicentennial show at St. Michael's Hall in 1976. Pictured are, from left to right: Stan and Lena Matlowski, Florence and Frank Sienkiewicz, Diane Decker, Al Gricoski, and Mary and Andrew Humetsky.

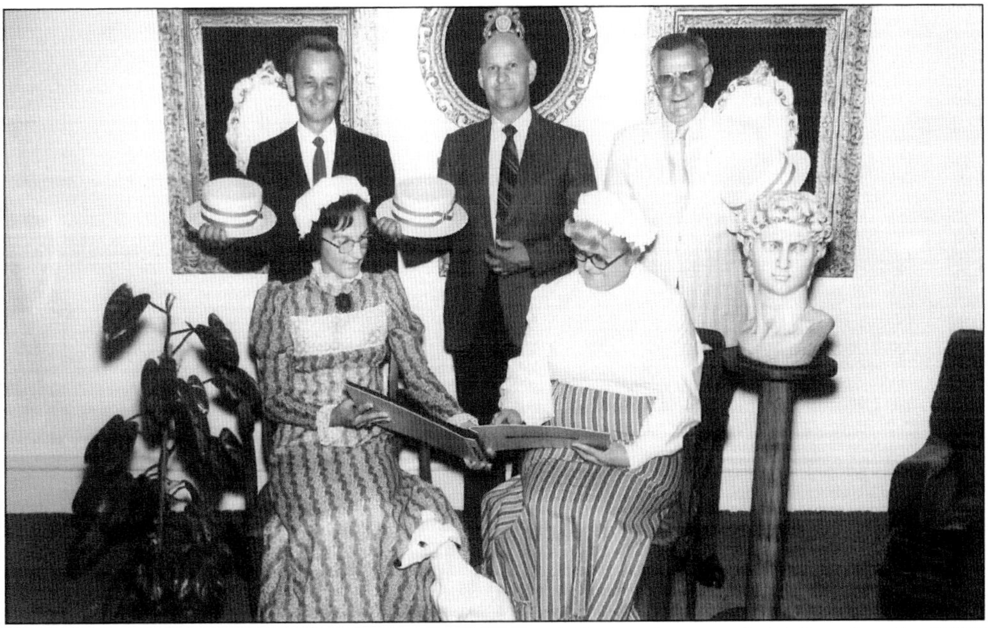

Do you remember the Old Tymers Nite of Fun and Frolic that was held October 6, 1973? A night of old-fashioned singing and dancing was held with old and young residents joining in. Committee members were, from left to right: (seated) Lorraine Stanton, Ann Dougherty; (standing) Joseph Olshalsky, Russell Pleva, and Woods Etherington.

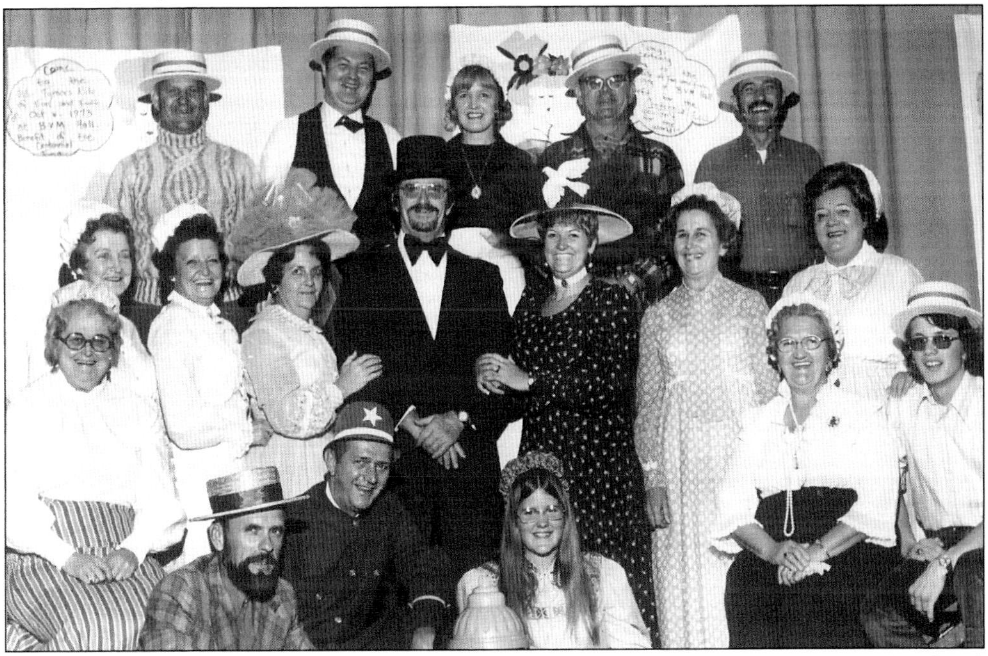

The cast for the Old Tymers Nite of Fun and Frolic were, from left to right, as follows: (on floor) Francis Sapp, Maurice Heim, and Janine Pleva; (sitting on right) Sallie Starkey and Ellen Sapp; (second row) Ann Dougherty, Ann Amber, Mary Cickavage, Marion Holden, Joseph Maley, Winnie Etherington, Grace Heim, and Jenny Leim; (top row) Russell Pleva, Bill Davis, Mary Theresa Mucha, Francis Heine, and George Guldin.

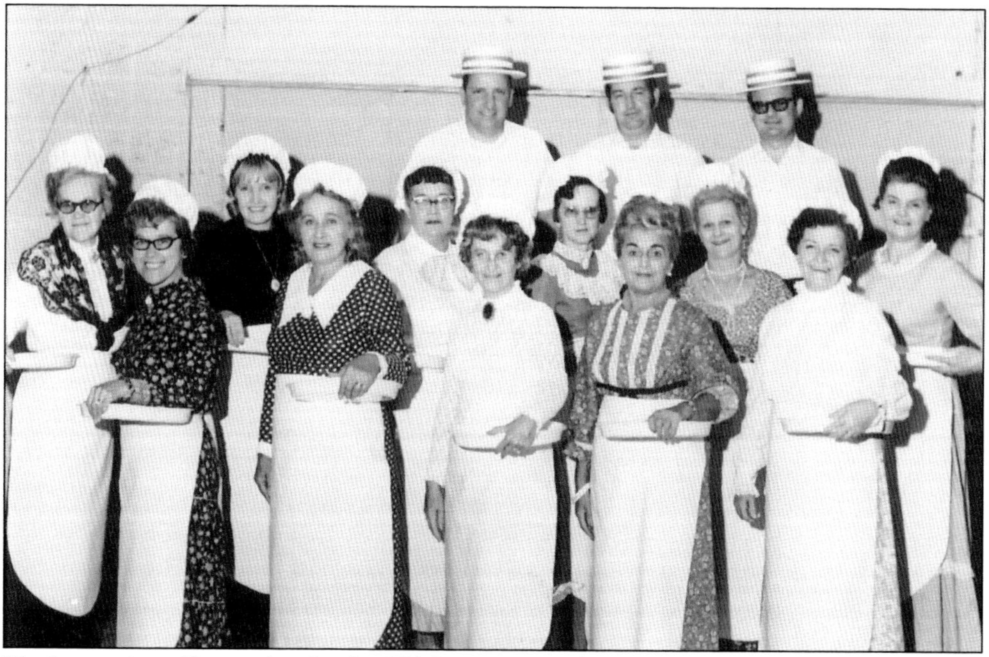

The barmaids and bartenders for the Old Tymers Nite of Fun and Frolic were, from left to right, as follows: (first row) Verna Petschul, Helen Kost, Dottie Stoudt, Eleanor Yancofsky, and Mary Cickavage; (second row) Dorothy Wabo, Mary Theresa Mucha, Jennie Leim, Eugenia Scanlan, Ann Brennan, and Ann Bendrick; (top) Arlan Swade, George Thomas, and Robert Kuchta.

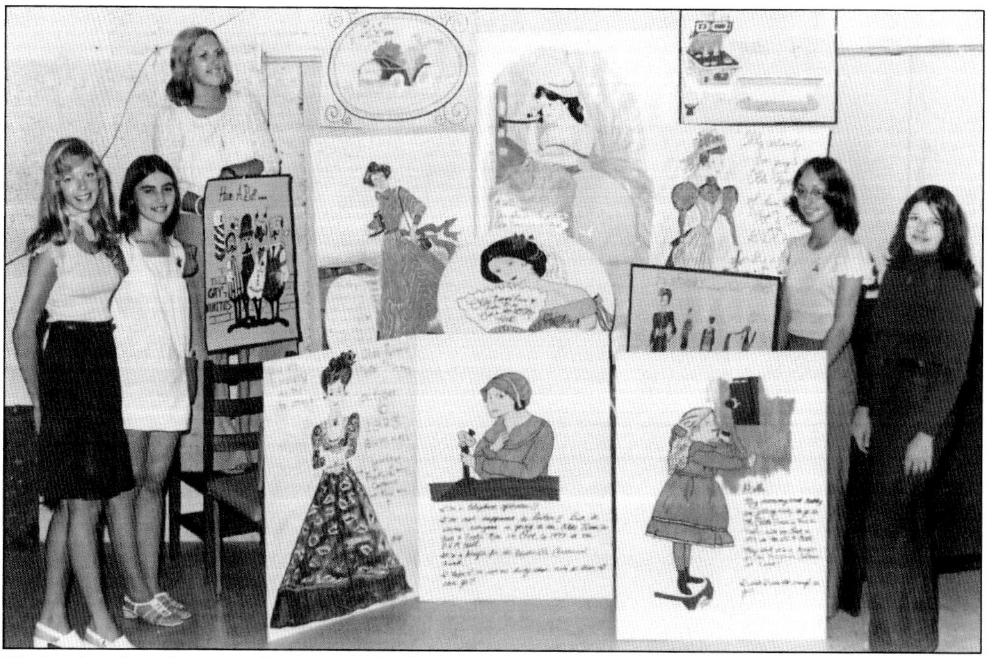

High school students made posters which were placed in all stores to publicize Old Tymers Nite. The students were, from left to right: Elaine Kasmer, Cynthia Stoppi, Hally Pascavage, Debi Tatusko, and Mary Ann Field.

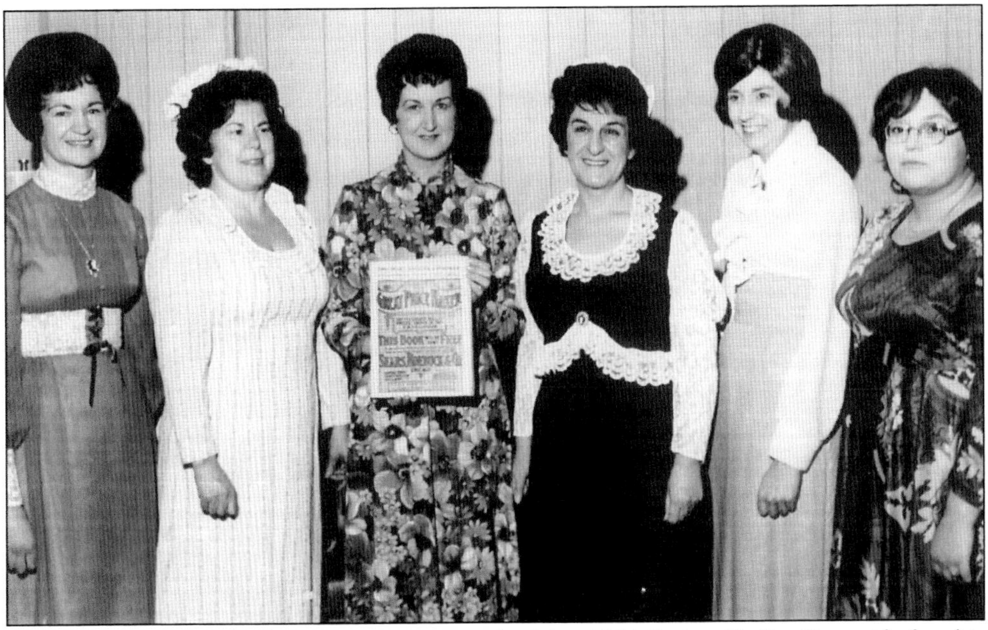

Another centennial fund-raising project was the May 1974 Spring Frolic. Barmaids for this occasion were, from left to right, as follows: Marie Costa, June Anthony, Dolores Medvetz (holding a 1902 Sears catalog), Lenore Yashin, Barbara Roper, and Brenda Bennett.

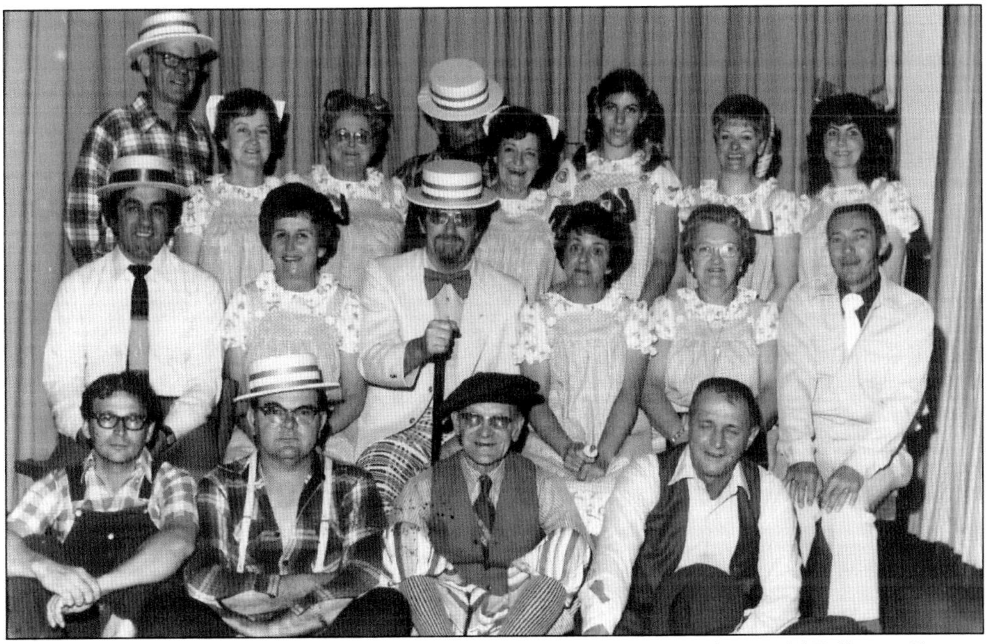

Cast members for the Spring Frolic were, from left to right: (first row) Donald Dillman, Francis Heine, William Stank, and Maurice Heim; (second row) Thomas Anthony, Grace Heim, Joseph Maley, Marion Holden, Sally Starkey, and George Guldin; (third row) Frank Sienkiewicz, Anna Amber, Ann Dougherty, Francis Sapp, Mary Cickavage, Helen Gricoski, Winnie Etherington, and Ann Ploxa.

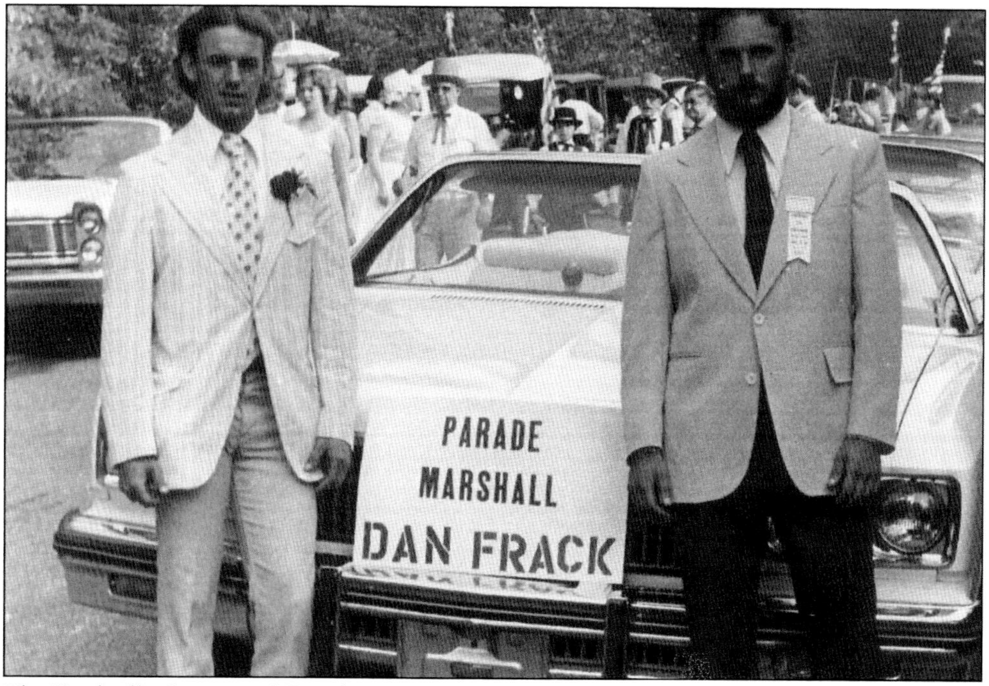

The Frackville Centennial Parade in August 1976 started promptly at 1 pm with church bells ringing and whistles blowing, and the parade was led by Chief of Police Michael Petronko, along with the American Legion Color Guard. Daniel Frack (on the right), the parade marshall, was the great-great grandson of Frackville's founder, and he is pictured here with his brother, Jesse Jr. (on the left).

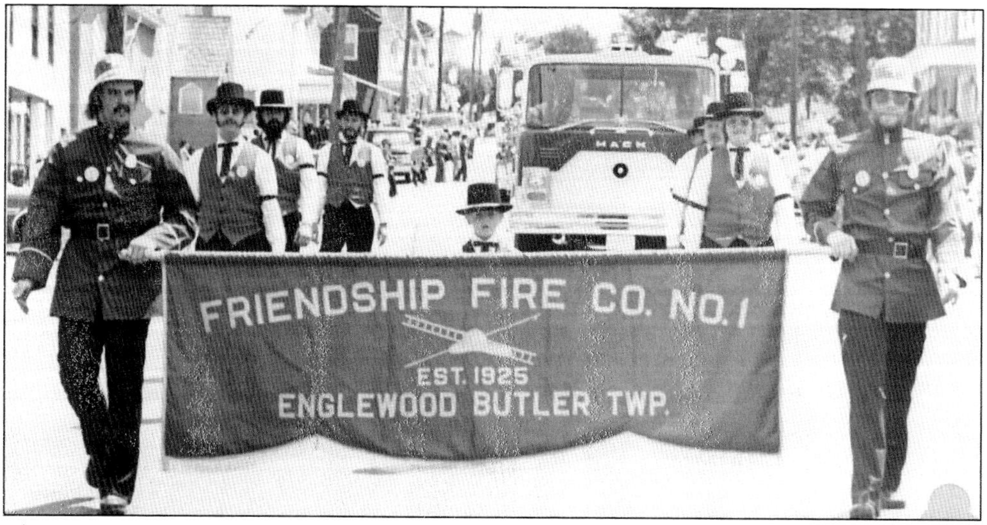

The Centennial Kickoff Parade on April 10, 1976, brought out all the fire companies, scouts, centennial "Belles," bands, Brownies, and "Keystone Kops" to march along the parade route. Pictured is the Friendship Fire Company #1 of Englewood, Butler Township.

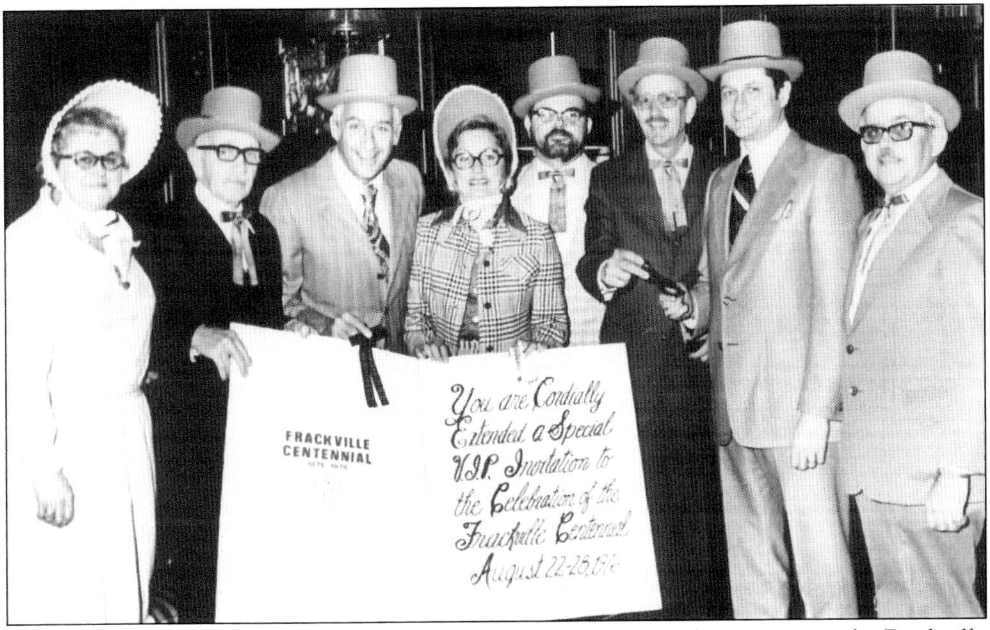

Committee members and guests shown here are holding the official invitation to the Frackville Centennial. Pictured are: Ann Dougherty, James Hahn, Lt. Governor and Mrs. Kline, Francis Heine, Bruce Hinkle, Rep. James Goodman, and Paul Malinchock.

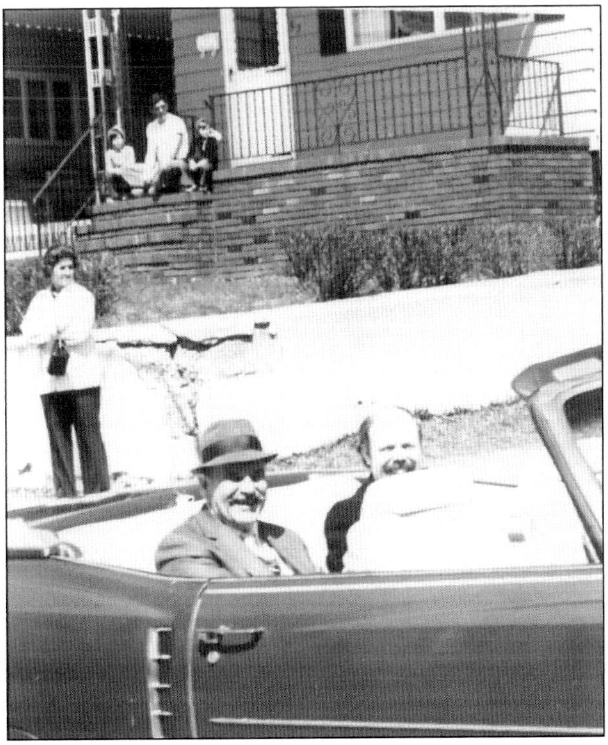

Jesse Frack was the grand marshall for the Frackville Centennial Kickoff Parade held April 10, 1976. Frack, the great-grandson of Frackville's founder, is pictured riding in the lead car with Reverend R. Kehrli.

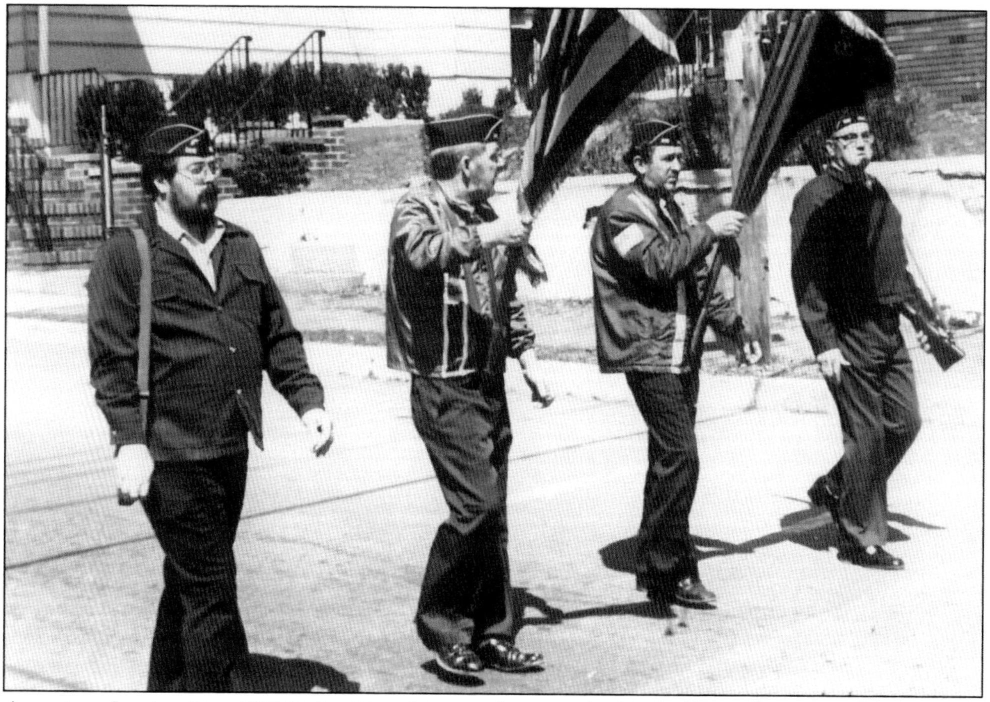

American Legion Post 398 Color Guard is marching in the Kickoff Parade on April 10, 1976.

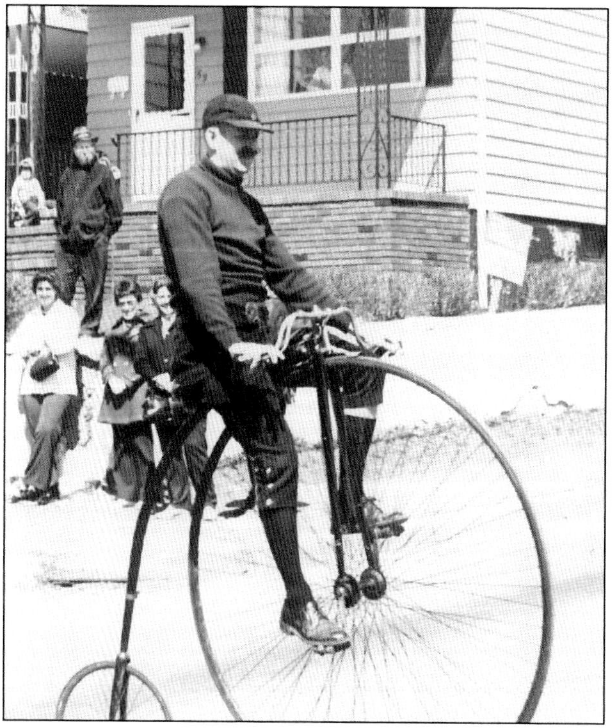

Riding in the style of yesteryear is Folsom resident Bob Shadel, formerly of Frackville, in the Kickoff Parade.

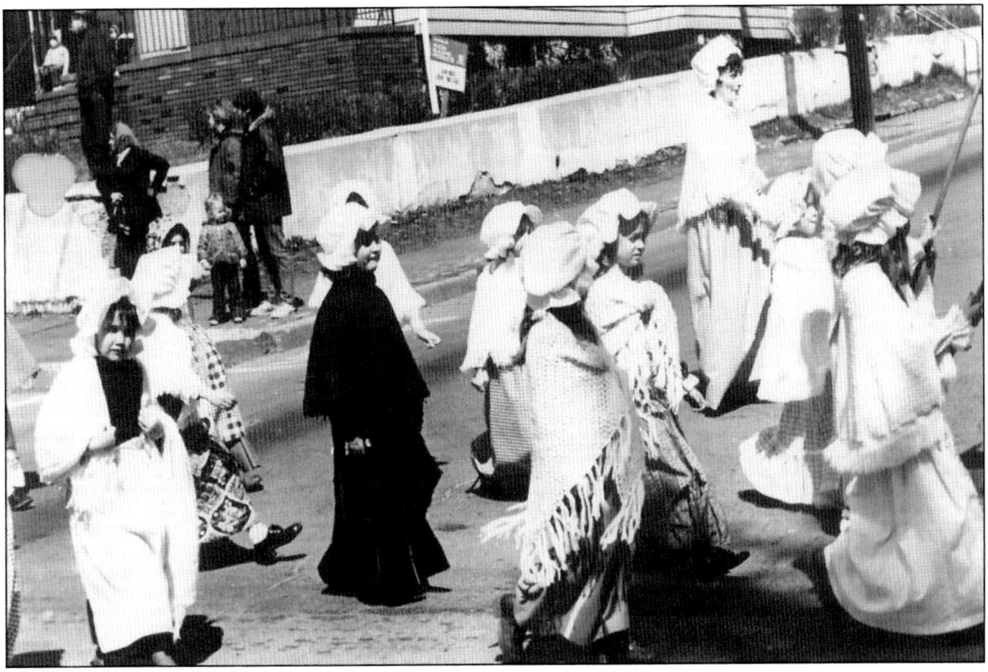

Brownie Troop 136 is pictured marching in the Centennial Parade at the corner of Balliet and Oak Streets.

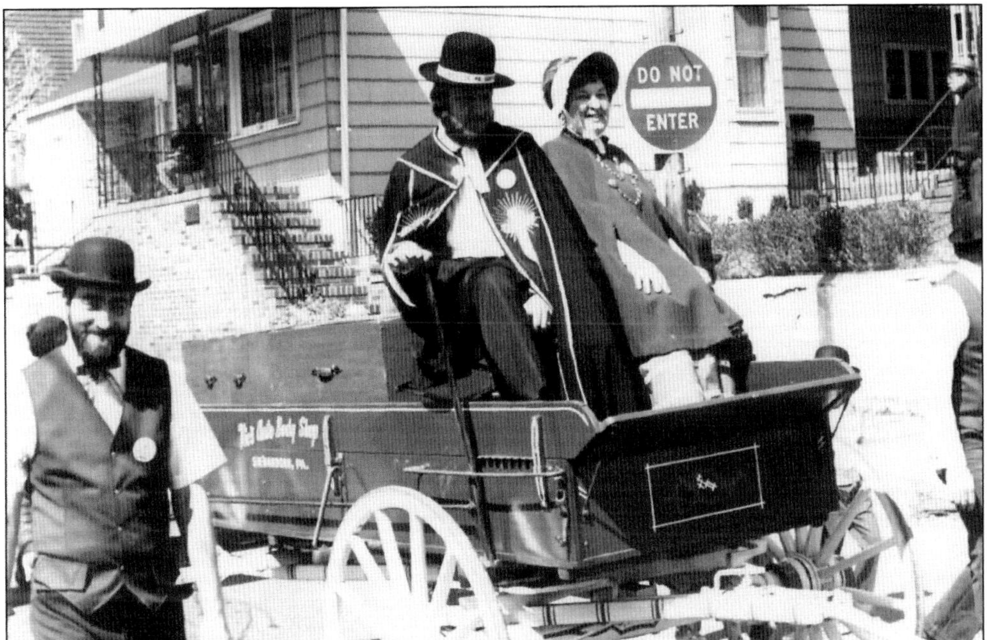

A wagon with Ted Souchak (chairman of the Brothers of the Brush) and Peg Zamonsky (chairwoman for the Belles) carries a black coffin in which was placed all shaving equipment and female cosmetics. The rules were: "No man shall shave before the centennial festivities unless a shaving permit was purchased, and no woman shall use cosmetics without buying a cosmetic permit."

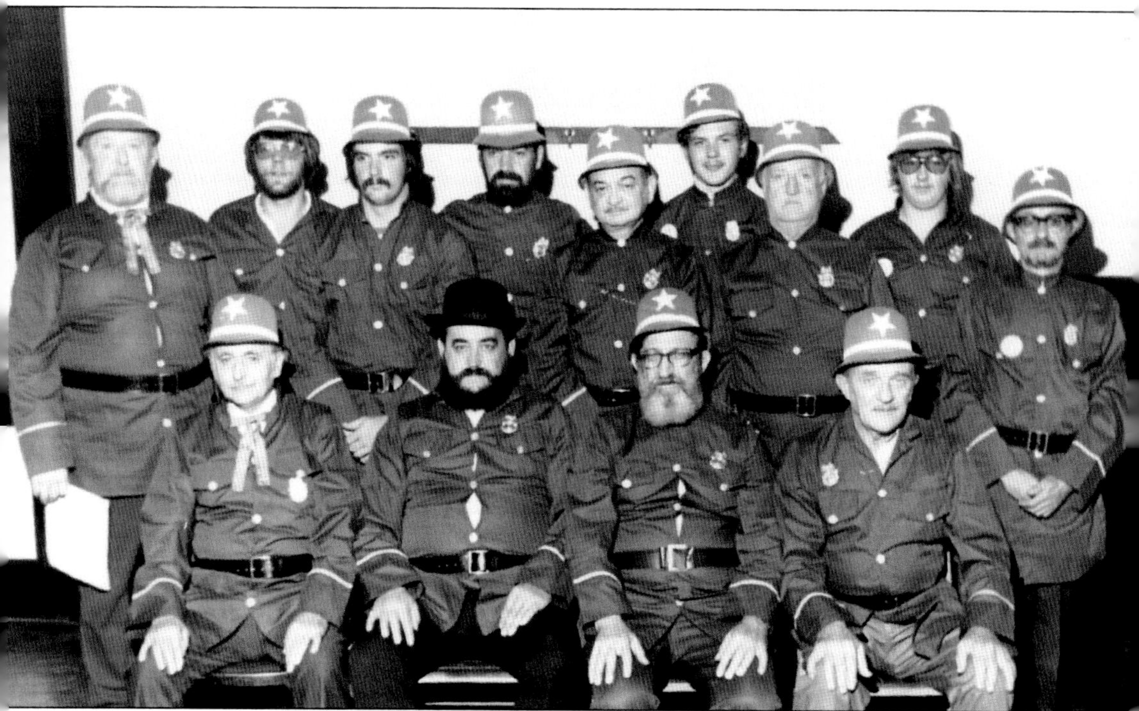

It was the duty of the Keystone Kops to ride around town and look for people who violated the rules of the Centennial. Violations included failure to wear some visible centennial apparel (such as hats, ties, or centennial buttons). Under the rules, men were not allowed to shave and women had to wear the official garter. These "Kops" had a lot of fun looking for violators, often placing them in the centennial "jail." Pictured are, from left to right: (first row) Stanley Matlowski, Donald Heckler, Eric Petschul, and Clem Kosmisky; (back row) Bill Kaledas, Joe Prock, Wayne Frantz, Ray Andershonis, Steve Harvest, Bob Becker, Gerard Rubright, Bob Niewzwiecki, and Harry Budwash.

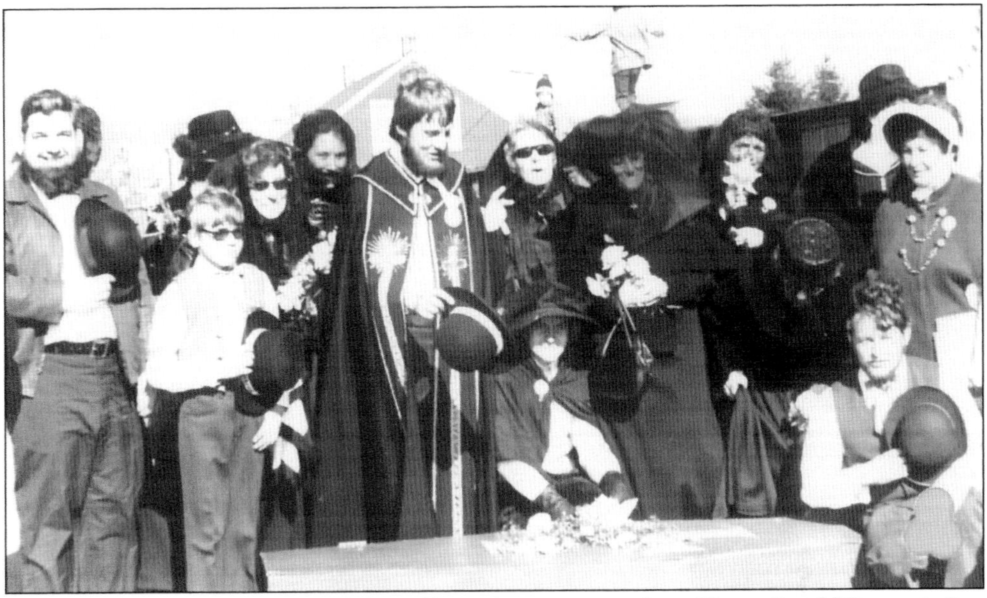

Several "mourners" gather around the coffin as they prepare to bury "Razors" and "Cosmetics" so that beards and old-time attire might flourish for the remainder of the Frackville Centennial.

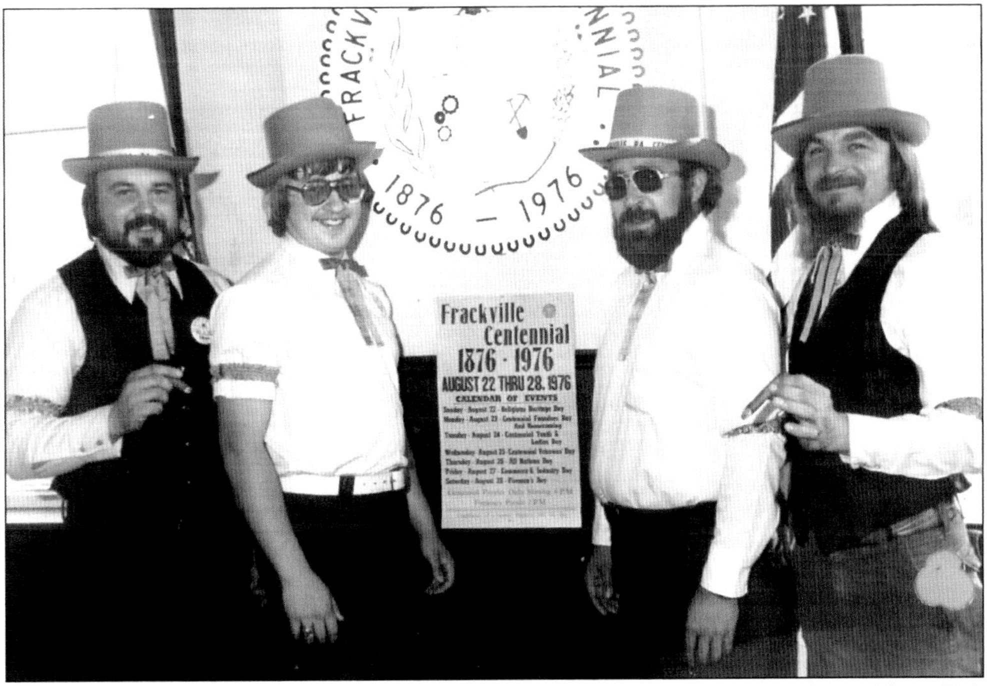

Jaycee Brothers of the Brush members included, from left to right, Jack Zaylskus, Bob Niedzwiecki, Geary Anthony, and Ray Kostic.

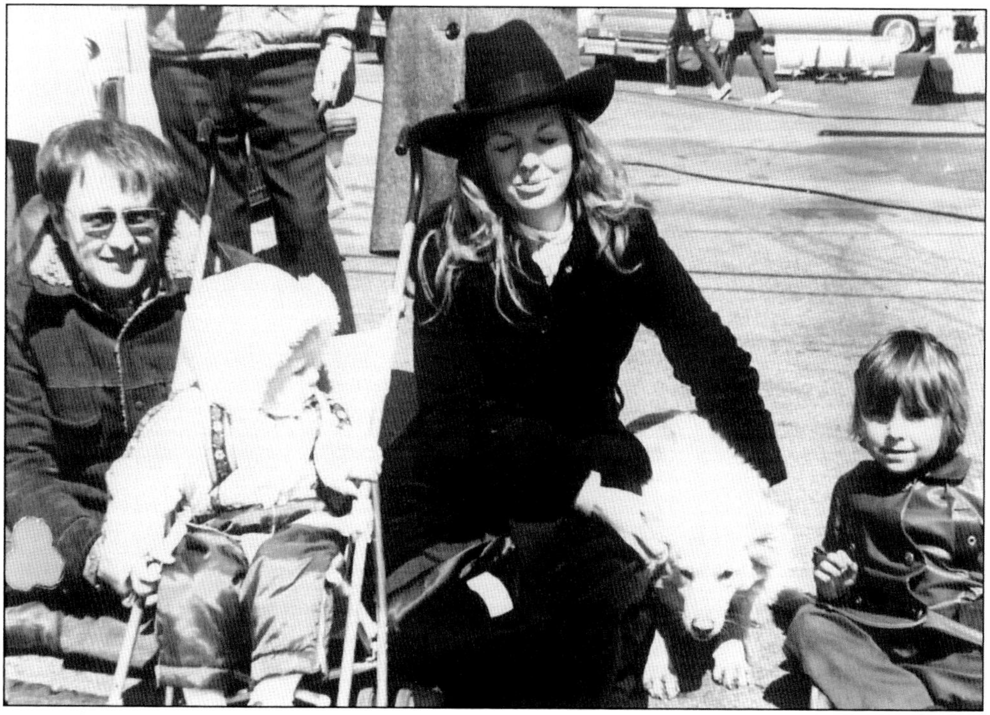
Mr. and Mrs. Victor Prep Jr. are pictured watching the centennial parade on April 10, 1976.

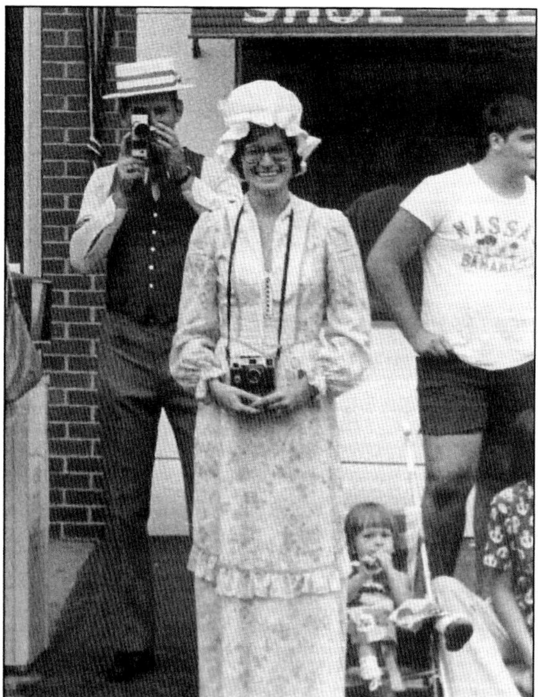
Barry, Debi, and Jessica Janov are taking a picture of Jesse Frack across the street (who was also taking their picture) during Centennial Week.

Miss Nancy Cicioni was named "Miss Community Spirit" by her fellow contestants and received a special trophy at the Coronation Ball and Pageant, which was held June 12, 1976. The contest was run on a monetary basis with the girl earning the most money for the Centennial Fund being chosen the Queen.

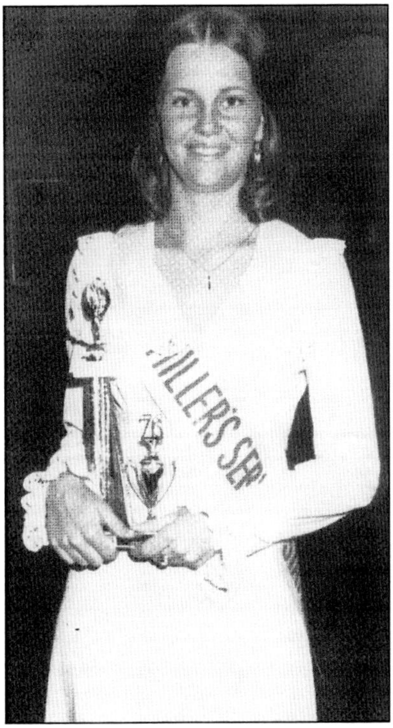

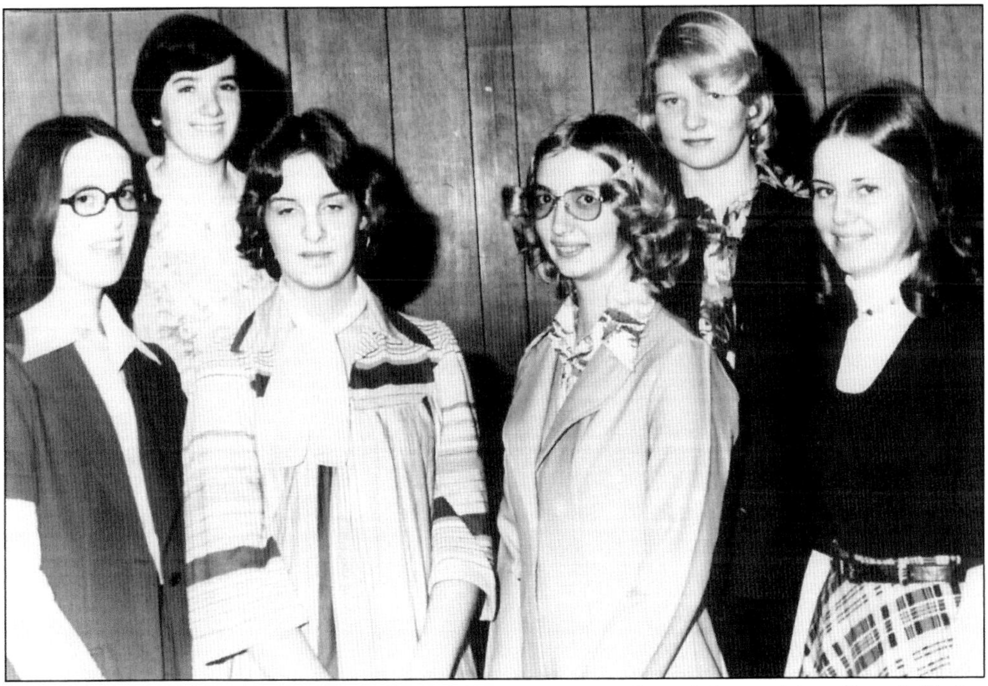

Contestants for the Coronation Ball and Pageant were, from left to right: (front) Kathy Woodring, Karen Cameron, Dorothy Truskowski, and Nancy Cicione; (back) Tina Brennan and Barbara Jo Hahn.

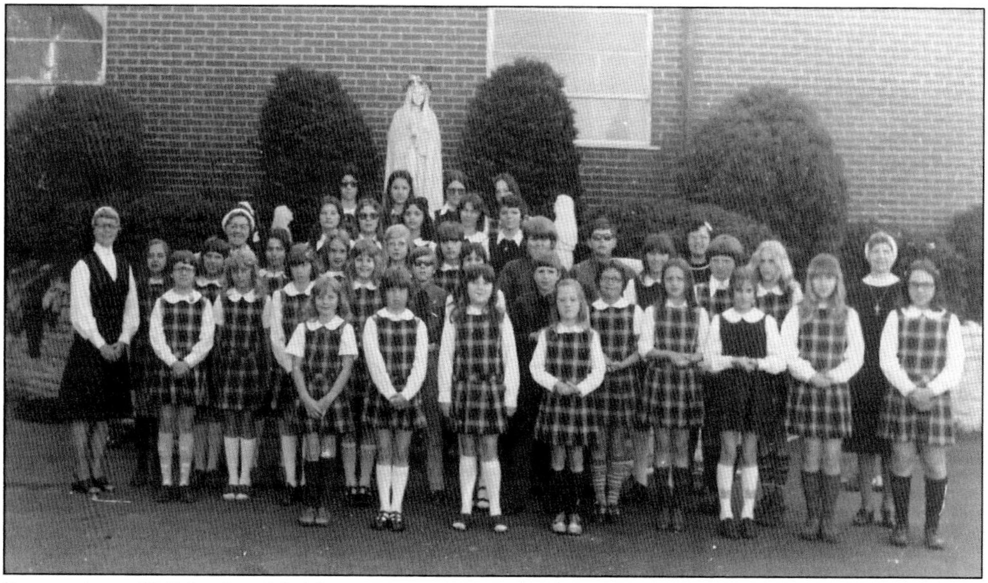

Pictured are BVM schoolchildren in a centennial television show. Some of the children are: (first row) M. O'Boyle, L. Hepler, T. Reiley, and J. Crosby; (second row) A. Kalbach, C. Puka, C. Moran, S. Wascavage, M. Alshon, J. Wallace, G. Haras, A. Pastula, C. Prep, G. Pacenta, J. Jankowsky, K. Berger, and J. Terry, (third row) Sr. Joan of Arc, S. Melefsky, K. Ross, D. Galgay, M. Curry, M. O'Connor, M. Roman, Sr. Concepta; (fourth row) Sr. St. Aloysious, B. Dellock, C. Houser, P. Moran, and J. McKenzey; (back row) C. Post, A. Sippie, and C. Humpf.

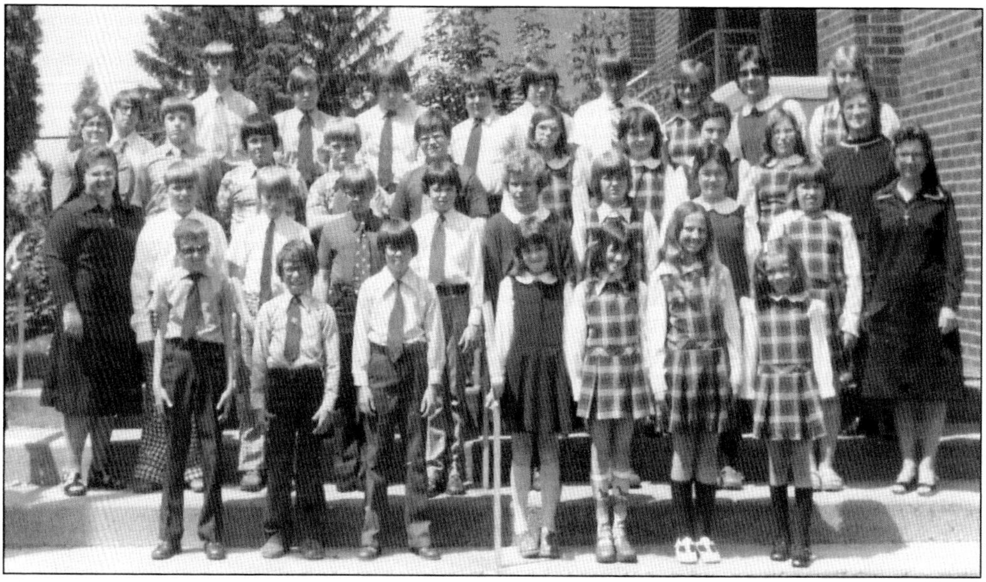

These St. Joseph schoolchildren appeared in a centennial television show. They are, from left to right: (front row) M. Shinkus, J. O'Connell, D. Mulry, A. Kaliher, A. Mastella, H. Setlock, and M. Lizewski; (second row) Sr. Ursula, T. Pacenta, C. Cickavage, D. Rynn, J. Bluge, B. Gownley, M. Mescunas, M. Crane, C. Horan, and Sr. Victoria; (third row) J. Stankavage, C. Jankowski, G. Anthony, C. Wolfgang, A. Cickavage, M. McCafley, C. Wallace, D. Petrovich, H. Galgay, M. Cickavage, and Sr. Sebastian; (back row) E. Karas, T. Solinsky, D. Renhert, D. Humpf, R. Slotcavage, J. Pulaski, P. Sankus, T. Mastella, C. Anthony, and R. Yurkonis.

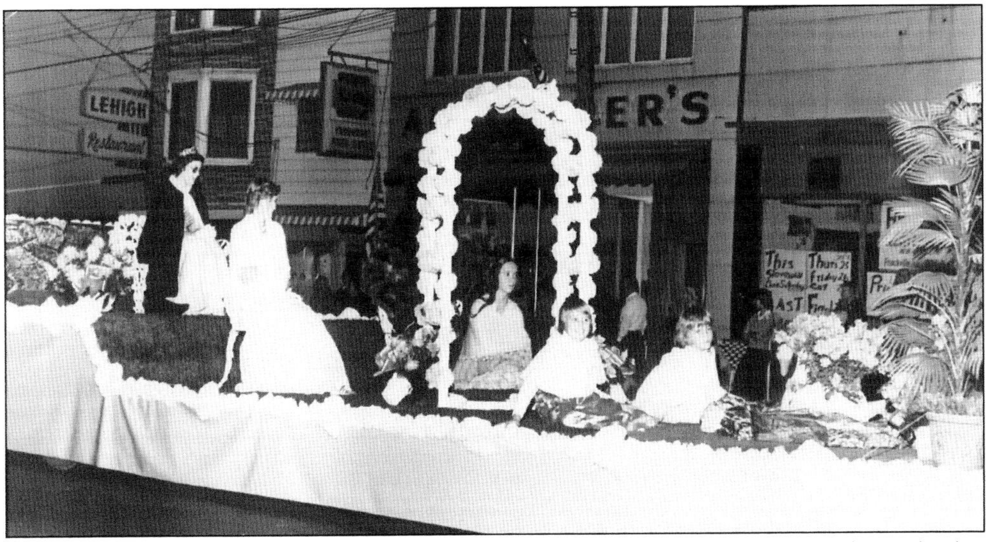

Pictured riding on the Princess Float are, from left to right, Dorothy Humpf, Helen Solinsky, Angela Sippie, Debbie Guziewich, and Patti Swartz.

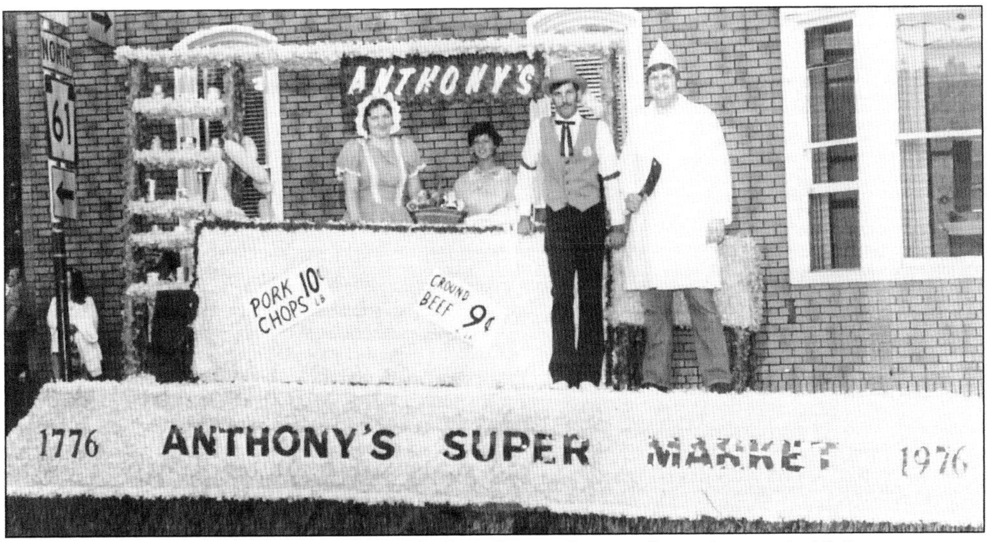

The Anthony's Supermarket Centennial Float featured prices from the good old days.

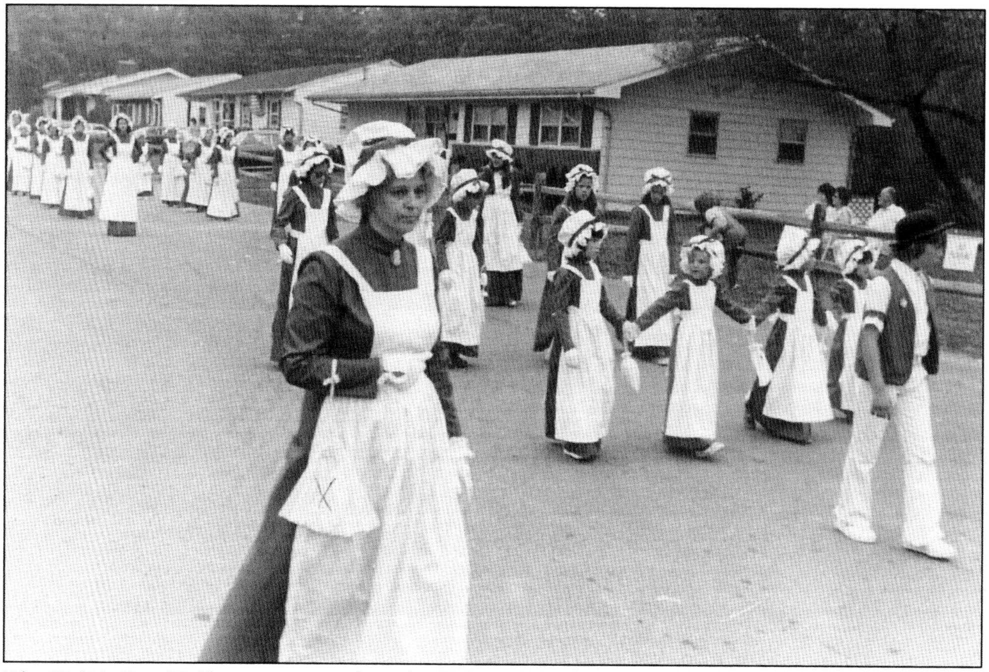

The Polish Star Belles are pictured on Arch Street, waiting to fall into their place in line.

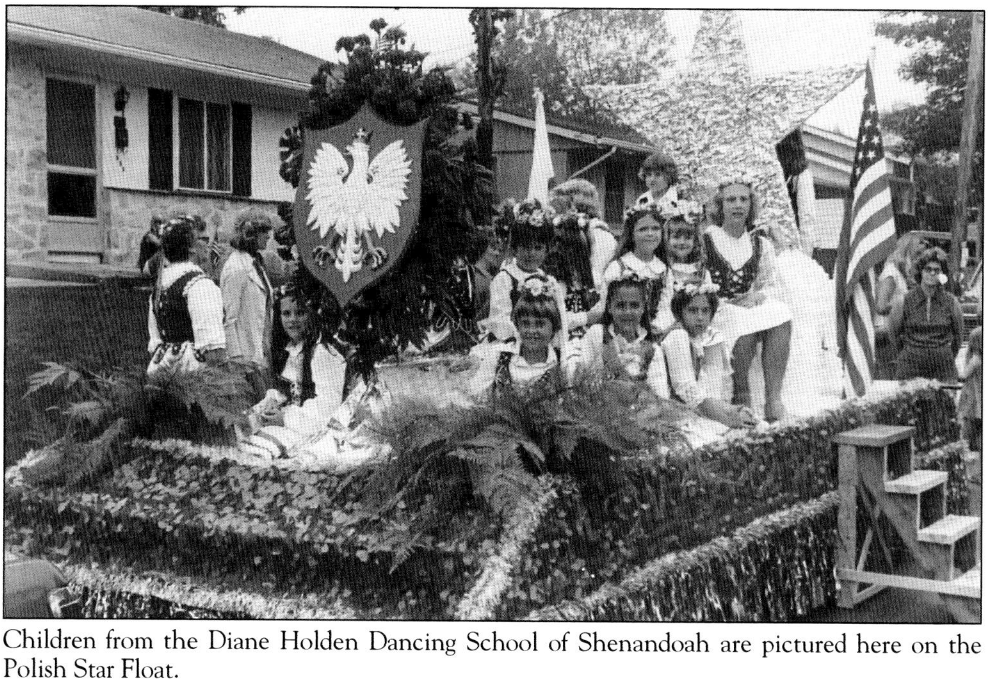

Children from the Diane Holden Dancing School of Shenandoah are pictured here on the Polish Star Float.

Centennial ladies representing the Zion Belles are, from left to right: (sitting) Bonnie Cunningham and Jean Rhoades; (standing) Bernie Hinkle and Janet Dean.

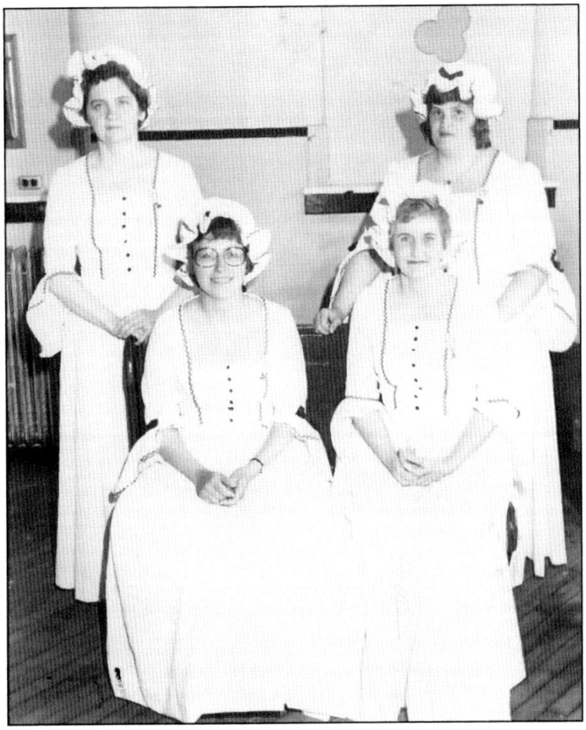

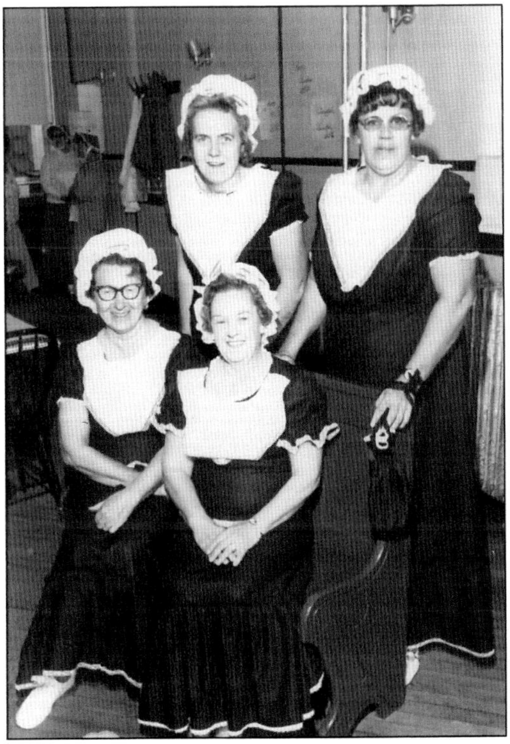

Centennial ladies representing the Goodwill Belles are from left to right as follows: (sitting) Nellie Borzak and Ann Seitzinger; (standing) Shirley Woodring and Jean Lipshaw.

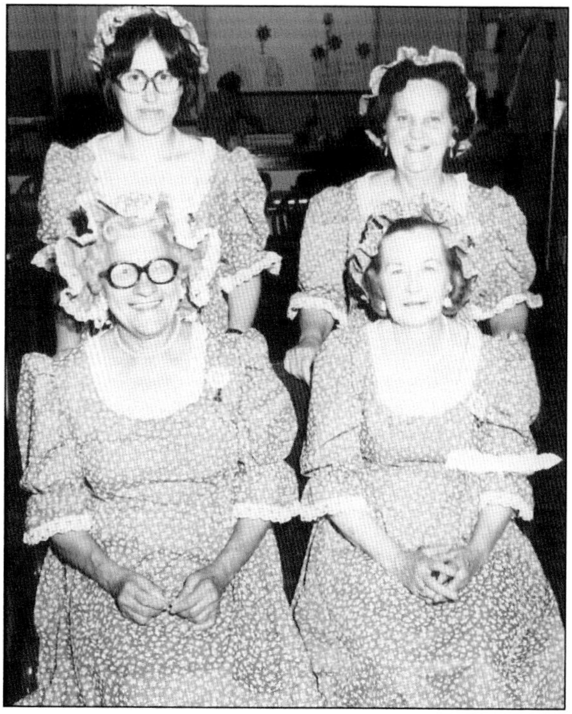

Centennial ladies representing the American Legion Belles are from left to right as follows: (sitting) Margaret Zelonis and Helen Aponick; (standing) Janet Metchock and Mamie Skiptunas.

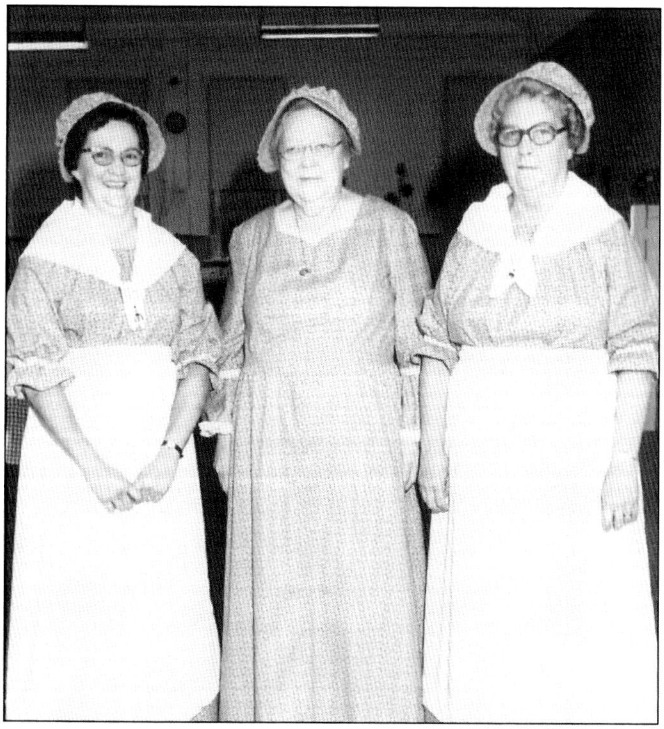

Centennial ladies representing St. Peter's Belles are, from left to right, Ada Filer, Roberta Parfitt, and Ada Montgomery.

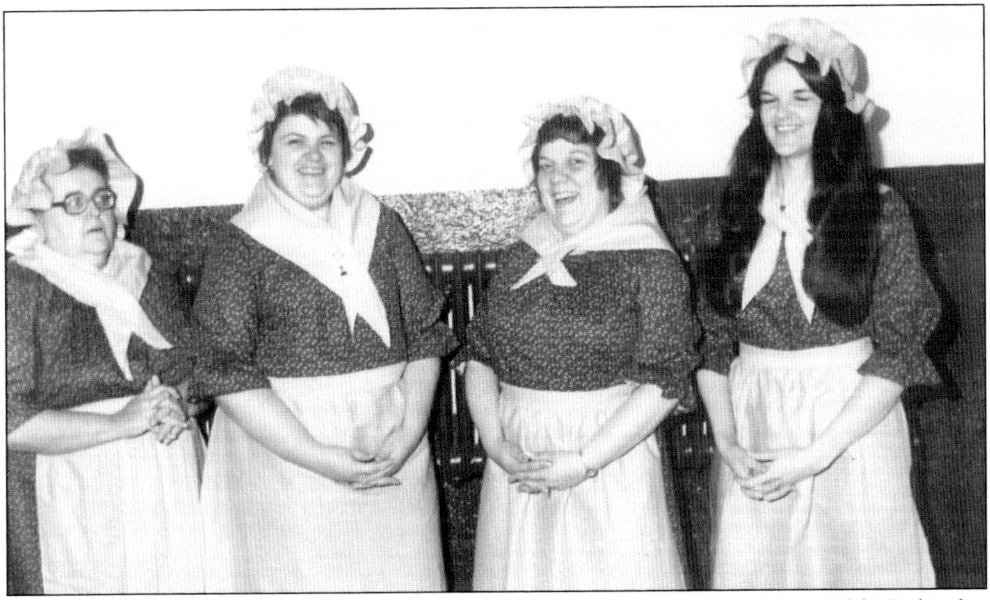

Centennial ladies representing the Carrousel Belles are, from left to right, Nelda Rubright, Donna Finneran, Linda Frey, and Donna Heine.

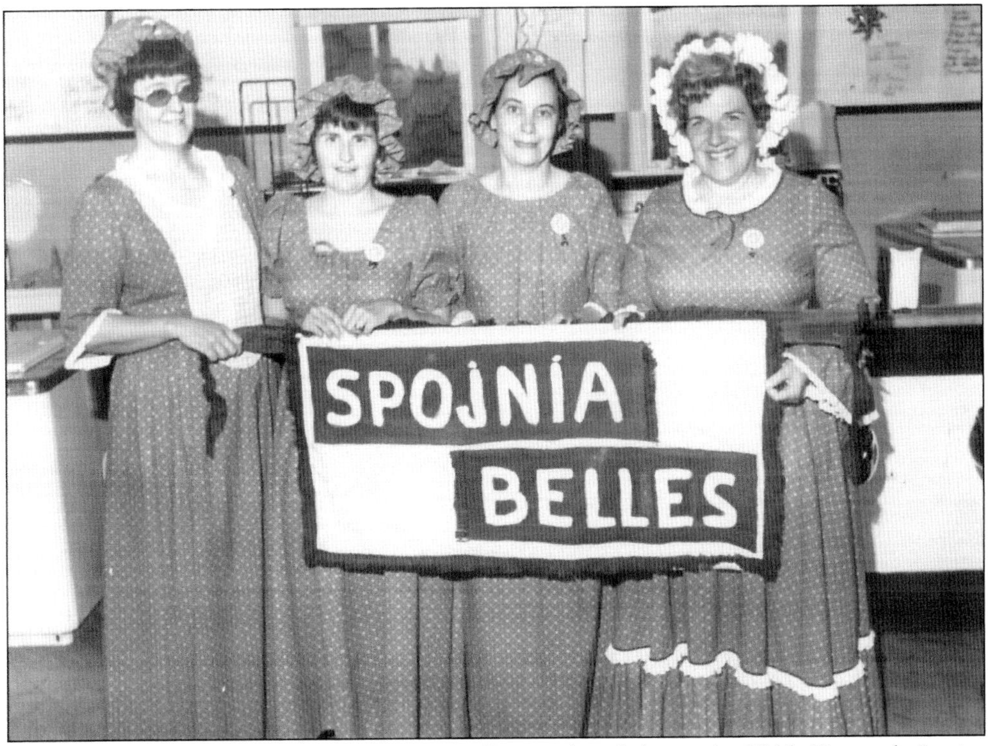

Centennial ladies representing the Spojnia Belles are, from left to right, Hilda Tomczyk, Louise Gursky, Jean Keim, and Flo Bulcavage.

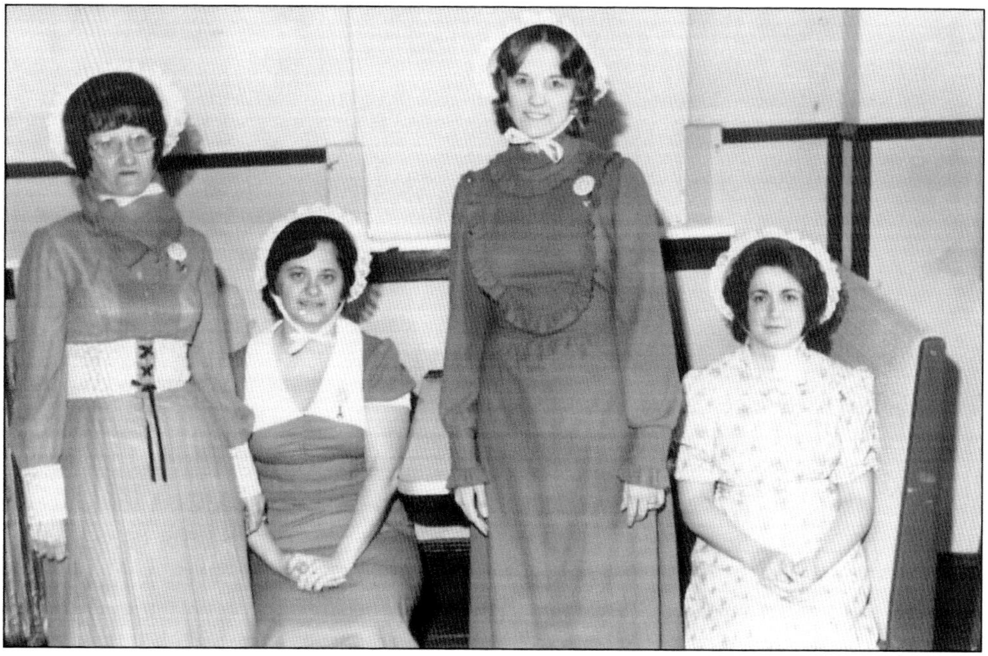

Centennial ladies representing the Trinity Belles are, from left to right, Leah Robbins, Marie Robbins, Diane Moore, and Genevieve Manbeck.

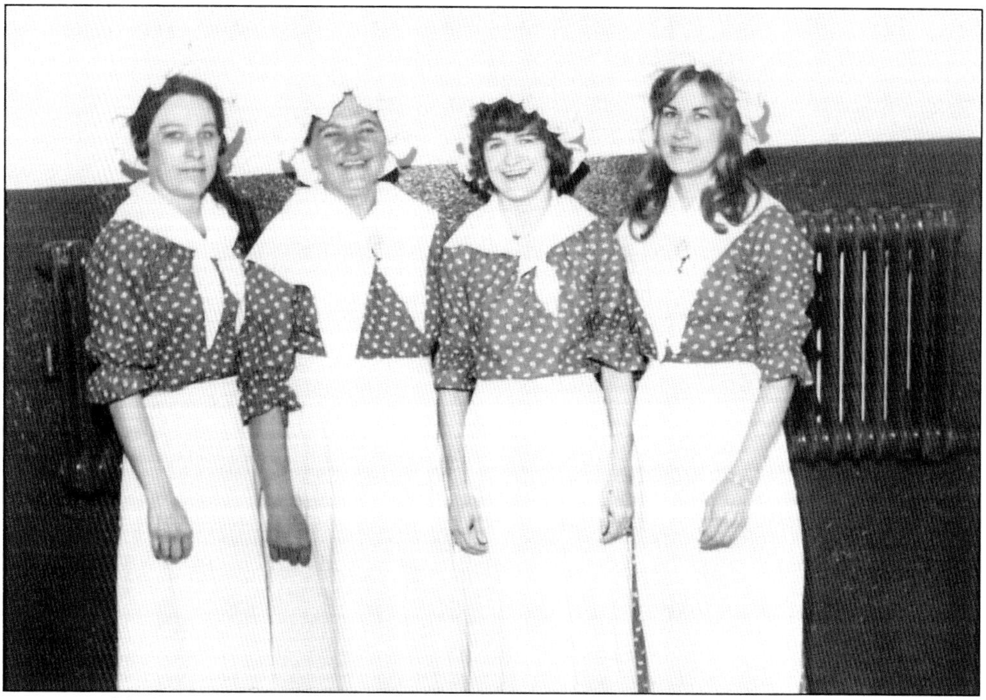

Centennial ladies representing the Hummell Belles are, from left to right, Florence Moser, Peg Manbeck, Dawn Kreitzer, and Mae Steward.

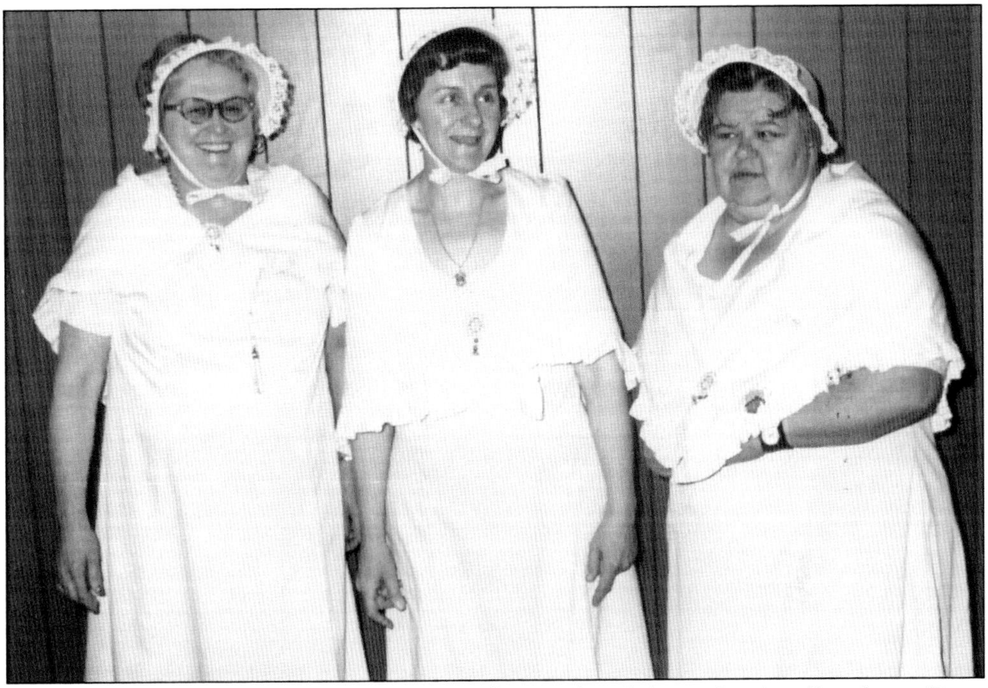

Centennial ladies representing the Catholic Belles are, from left to right, Ann Dougherty, Betty Luciano, and Gus Pulaski.

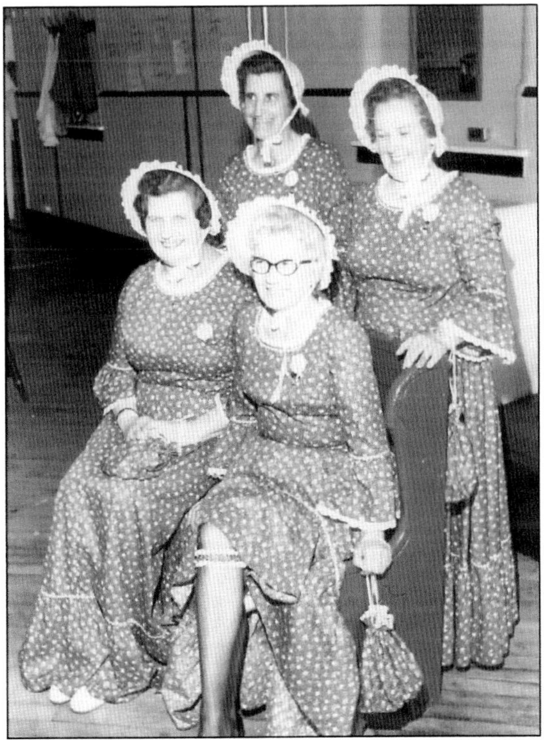

Centennial ladies representing the Martin Belles are from left to right as follows: (sitting) Ann Yatcilla and Julia Viates; (standing) Virginia Mervine and Ann Seitzinger.

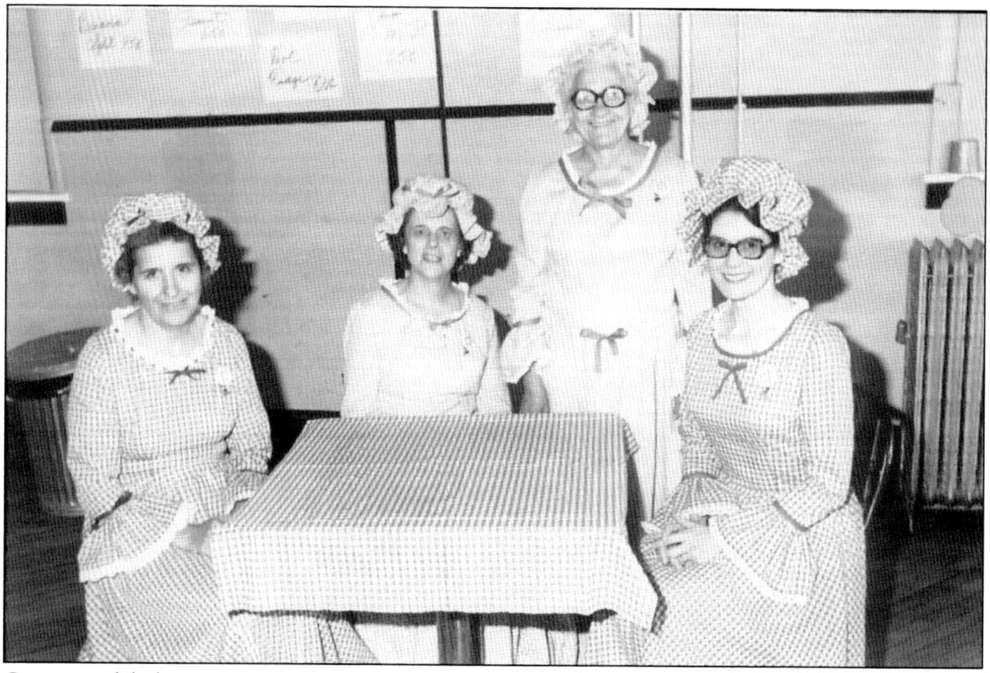

Centennial ladies representing the Model Belles are, from left to right, Ann Yeager, Martha Krull, Margaret Zelonis, and Charlotte Budwash.

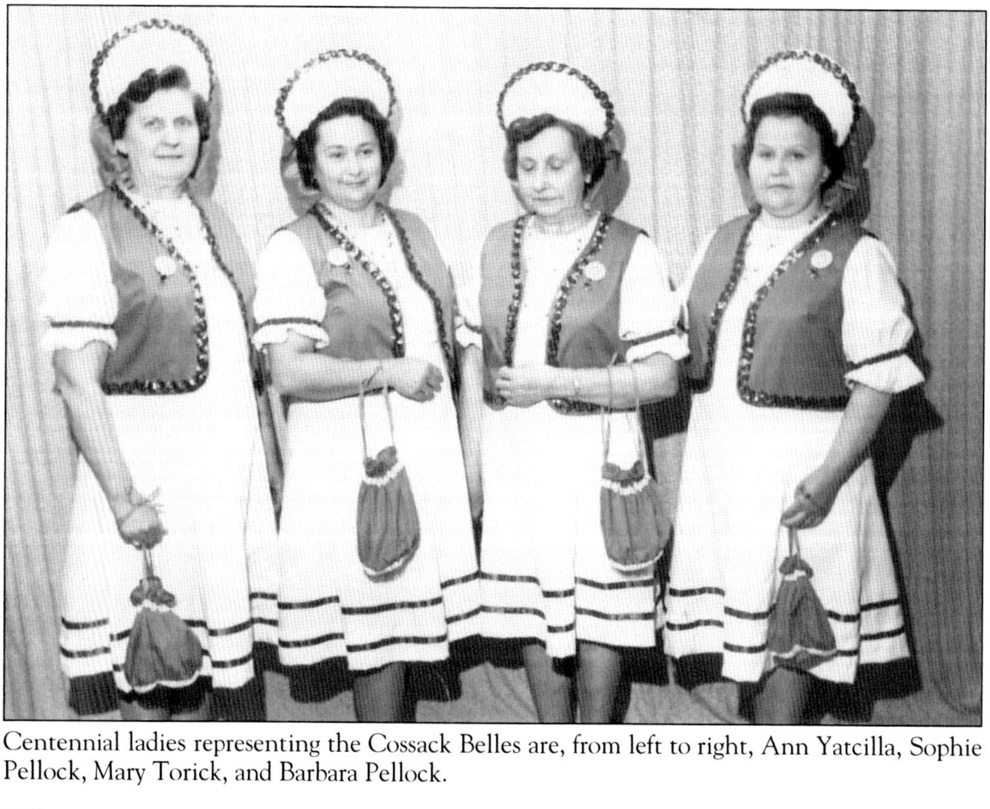

Centennial ladies representing the Cossack Belles are, from left to right, Ann Yatcilla, Sophie Pellock, Mary Torick, and Barbara Pellock.